C. S. LEWIS
SPINNER OF TALES

C. S. LEWIS
SPINNER OF TALES
A GUIDE TO HIS FICTION
by EVAN K. GIBSON

CHRISTIAN
UNIVERSITY
PRESS

A Subsidiary of Christian College Consortium
and Wm. B. Eerdmans Publishing Company

Copyright © 1980 by Christian College Consortium
1776 Massachusetts Ave., N.W., Washington, D.C. 20036
All rights reserved
Printed in the United States of America

Available from Wm. B. Eerdmans Publishing Co.
255 Jefferson Ave. S.E., Grand Rapids, Mich. 49503

Library of Congress Cataloging in Publication Data

Gibson, Evan K.   1909–
    C. S. Lewis, spinner of tales.

    Bibliography: p. 273.
    1. Lewis, Clive Staples, 1898–1963—Criticism
and interpretation.   I.   Title.
PR6023.E926Z654   828'.91209   80-10754
ISBN 0-8028-1826-9

CONTENTS

PREFACE

THIS BOOK is for the common reader. If those who teach Lewis at the high school or college level find insights in these pages which assist them in the classroom, I shall be pleased. But the person I have tried to hold steadily in my vision while writing is the ordinary reader who feels an enthusiasm for Lewis's tales and would like to understand more clearly their ethical and theological implications. For this reason each person will probably feel at some point that I am belaboring the obvious. If there are portions of the book which, in the opinion of all readers, are obvious, these, perhaps, should have been omitted. But my experience in discussing the stories with students suggests that the obvious is something like an *eldil*, who can be seen only by certain eyes and under certain conditions.

I hope that each reader will find pleasure in the reading of even that which he already knows. Lewis agreed with Samuel Johnson's observation that people need to be reminded more than they need to be informed. And although he was speaking of religious instruction, the statement also has a bearing upon the discussion of literature. So if I remind you of pleasures enjoyed, perhaps you will forgive me for telling you of ideas already understood.

Because an understanding of the literary techniques which an author employs enriches the reader's appreciation of the work, each chapter gives some space to Lewis's craftsmanship as a storyteller. In fact, it is often essential to be aware of the writer's techniques in order to understand the themes of the story. I have also included, wherever possible, statements or summaries from his other books, essays, and letters when these reinforce the thought of the fiction, in order to show that we are dealing with recurrent ideas.

This book is not a critical analysis of the merits and defects of C. S. Lewis. The plague of literary criticism has always been those writers who are eager to teach the reader what he ought to dislike. I have tried to avoid being classified under Swift's definition of a critic as "a discoverer and collector of writers' faults." So, I have restricted myself to explanation and have assumed that anyone interested in reading this book will be already convinced that Lewis has something to say to our present age. How long his popularity will last or what his niche will be in a history of twentieth-century literature we can leave to the judgment of Prince Posterity.

In making acknowledgments it is difficult to know where to draw the line. Victor Borge concluded one of his entertainments by thanking his father and mother "without whom this program would not have been possible." But beginning that far back would mean writing my own *Surprised by Joy.* And so, like a good dramatist I will leap into the middle of things and say that every student, colleague, and friend who has shared my enjoyment of Lewis has contributed to the pattern of this book. But a few thank you's must be specific. To Dr. Murray Marshall and his staff at the First Presbyterian Church in Seattle, whose invitation to lecture on Lewis was the inception of this volume, I am grateful for the pressure of a weekly audience. Several friends have read all or parts of the typescript with varying degrees of encouragement, but I am especially in debt to my colleague, Dr. Janet Knedlik of Seattle Pacific University, who served as a literary midwife, reading each chapter as it was completed, and making suggestions and criticisms which contributed materially to the present state of the work. I am also deeply indebted to Mary, my wife, who endured stoically the months in which I was incommunicado and who also typed without complaint each page of this book at least twice.

—Evan K. Gibson

THE INNER LANDSCAPE

CHAPTER 1

JACK LEWIS:

SCHOLAR, APOLOGIST, STORYTELLER

I.

THE "C. S." of C. S. Lewis stands for Clive Staples, but to a boy of four the given names apparently sounded sissified or ugly. At least, one day he suddenly announced, pointing to himself, "He is Jacksie."[1] Within the family he refused to respond to any other name. So Jacksie he became, later shortened to Jacks, and finally to Jack. Not only in the family, but also to his friends in later life, he was Jack Lewis. When his correspondence published as *Letters to an American Lady* reached the stage of first names, he wrote, ". . . my friends all call me Jack," and thereafter signed his letters "Jack" or "Jack Lewis."[2] What fears or hates stirred the mind of the four-year-old boy will never be known, but years later he commented that a certain twelfth-century abbess named Joan Jack "must have been a comfortable, easy-going kind of person." At least, it seems fitting that a man with so common a touch that he could talk theology in the language of the man in the street and spin tales of talking animals to delight the child should have chosen a name which in some contexts means one who is representative of the common people.

In some ways Jack Lewis was most unrepresentative of the common man. His profession could have walled him away from ordinary people. The Oxford don or fellow moves in a world which needs very little from the average "jacks" on the outside but groceries, pipe tobacco, and clothing. As such a fellow of Magdalen College, Oxford, from 1925 to 1954, Lewis lectured on English literature, tutored students in his rooms, participated in the business of the university as a member of the corporation, and moved easily in the world of ideas which such a society enjoyed.

But to a certain taxi driver who knew him well, "He was never an intellectual snob, and he was willing to talk to anyone on any subject." The statement comes from Clifford Morris, who in Lewis's last years frequently drove him to Cambridge, where in 1954 he had been elected Professor of Medieval and Renaissance English. Morris admits that he overheard conversation with other professors which he was unable to understand, but he also tells of rough truck drivers at a truck-stop cafe who were enthralled with Lewis's wit and conversation. One of them approached Morris and asked who "the guv'nor" was. When he learned, he said, "Blimey, he's a toff, he is! A real nice bloke!"[3]

Lewis was "a real nice bloke" to most people who met him, not only because of his quips and entertaining stories, but also because he always showed a genuine interest in the concerns of the other person. "Bright, loud, and jovial," as one friend described his conversation, he often probed a new acquaintance to find what his interests and attitudes were in order to build a bridge between them. Visitors who called on him at "The Kilns" where he lived or at his rooms in the university frequently testified to his warmth, his frankness, and his outgoing courtesy, which quickly made them feel at home.

But as a writer of scholarly books and articles in his special field, he should have been cut off from communication with the common reader. It is true that *The Discarded Image* (on medieval literature), *English Literature in the Sixteenth Cen-*

4

tury, *A Preface to Paradise Lost,* and similar works, while very readable to the person with the proper background, require a vocabulary at least equal to that of the Oxford student. They do not explain the more than 700,000 copies of *Mere Christianity,* the over one and a half million copies of *The Screwtape Letters,* and the total of fourteen million copies of Lewis's books that one publisher alone has printed in this country. In fact, it has been estimated that throughout the world fifty million copies of his works have been published. As we will note later, Lewis wrote much of his fiction from pictures in his imagination. He probably also had a picture of the audience he was writing to. His style seldom falters in speaking to the needs of that image. The simple and oral-sounding sentences, the crystal clear illustrations and analogies, the eye-level meeting with the reader—whether child or adult—indicate a writer with a style for all seasons. The common touch was, indeed, at his fingertips.

II.

EVEN HIS appearance seemed to suggest an affinity with the ordinary. His students reported that when he walked into a classroom, he looked to the uninitiated more like a butcher or other tradesman than like an intellectual. Broad of face and ruddy of complexion, his large head gave an impression of plumpness, although full-length pictures show, rather, a sturdy and compact build. He was simply big—large of fist and broad of frame. Lecturing on the medieval belief in planetary influences, he would often say with a twinkle, "the jovial character is cheerful, festive; those born under Jupiter are apt to be loud-voiced and red-faced—it is obvious under which planet I was born."[4]

I do not know what heavenly influence can be blamed for his carelessness in dress. He chafed under the necessary routines of life, such as shopping and getting a haircut. His brother reported that he had a talent for making a new suit look shabby the second time he wore it. And in an amusing letter Lewis himself tells of starting out to town one day and discovering that he had on shoes that did not match. One was clean and the other was dirty. Having no time to return home and finding the dirty shoe impossible to clean, he decided to make the clean shoe dirty. But, he says, "Would you have believed that this is an impossible operation? You can get some mud on it—but it remains obviously a clean shoe that has had an accident."[5] He cites this as another instance of the malignity of the Little People—that is, of Irish elves.

Lewis may have been loud-voiced, but many have testified to the richness and resonance of his speech. Here we do not need to depend upon witnesses. Although the early broadcast talks which eventually were published as *Mere Christianity* were, apparently, not recorded, his discussions dealing with the ideas published later as *The Four Loves* were put on tape in 1958 and were broadcast in America. They have since been made available to the public in four cassettes. They reveal a baritone voice of pleasing quality, skillfully controlled, varying in pitch and tempo, and employing the pause effectively for dramatic impact. As one reviewer said of the first broadcast talks, "Mr. Lewis is that rare being—a born broadcaster."

No discussion of the man would be adequate which does not mention his humor. The comic muse in Lewis was never asleep, whether he was trading puns at a dinner party, correcting a correspondent's misunderstanding of a lecture, or talking about guinea pigs in a letter to a child. One of the most often quoted examples of his verbal humor is his remark at a dinner which included haggis, the dish of Scotland containing the internal organs of the sheep boiled in its stomach. A Portuguese dignitary beside him, responding to the miscellaneous character of the dish, observed that he felt like a "gastronomic Columbus." Lewis pointed out that he could better sail with his own countryman. "Why not a vascular da Gama?" he asked.[6]

To an American letter writer with whom he was on easy terms he wrote concerning a lecture, "You've got it nearly right; the only error being that instead of saying the Great Divide came between the Middle Ages and the Renaissance, I said at great length and emphatically that it *didn't*. But of course 'not' is a very small word and one can't get every fine shade just right!"[7] And to a child who evidently had written him that she was studying German and that her guinea pig did not pay much attention to her, he observed that most guinea pigs don't take any notice of humans but "they take plenty of one another" and that they go well with studying German because if they talked "that is the language they would speak."[8] Although his friends testify to his dexterity with word juggling, this sort of humor does not appear much in his writing. But the good-natured irony and the playfulness of the other examples are displayed in many pages of *The Screwtape Letters* and *The Chronicles of Narnia*.

III.

ONLY THE briefest sketch of his life will be necessary in this introduction. For the reader who wishes to know Lewis well, there are three indispensable biographical works. *Surprised by Joy* is Lewis's own account of the events in his history which contributed to his reconversion to Christianity. The two others are, in a sense, also primary sources—his brother's "Memoir of C. S. Lewis," which introduces the volume of *Letters*, and *C. S. Lewis, a Biography* by Roger Lancelyn Green and Walter Hooper. The latter, in addition to being well researched, contains many firsthand accounts by the authors. Roger Lancelyn Green was a former student of Lewis and a close friend, and Walter Hooper was his secretary during the last months of his life. They both contribute important personal anecdotes. But, of course, the first requirement for acquaintance is to read that which reveals the inner landscape—Lewis's own writings.

Conveniently for our memory, the man was born just a little more than a year before the beginning of the nineteen hundreds (November 29, 1898), so that the addition of one year to any date up to the time of his death (November 22, 1963) will indicate his age. His ancestry of Welsh farmers and

Irish aristocrats suggests that the green and rose highlands seen on Malacandra and the prose-poetry heard on Perelandra were gifts of his Celtic blood. A native of Belfast, he often drew upon his childhood memory and later vacation trips to the Emerald Isle for the mountains and vistas, the mists and sunlight of Narnia and Archenland.

After some distressing experiences at one British public school (which contributed to the unfavorable pictures of schooling in the Narnian tales), and some very good training at others, Lewis was sent to his father's old schoolmaster, William Kirkpatrick, to prepare him for entrance into Oxford. "The Great Knock," as the retired teacher had been called by his students, was a rigorous logician and insisted that his students build their mental mansions with the same solid bricks. Lewis's first casual remark to his new tutor expressing his opinion of the green and hilly countryside of Surrey provoked a vigorous cross-examination and the conclusion: "Do you not see, then, that you had no right to have any opinion whatever on the subject?"[9]

The right to an opinion was not easily granted by the Great Knock. Lewis's ability to build the case for Christianity with such convincing logic may be traced in large part to the ruthless insistence of his teacher that belief must be based upon evidence, and that unexamined opinions can lead to ridiculous conclusions when held up to the bright light of logical analysis. However, it is ironical that Lewis was armed for battle by a man who was an atheist. In addition, the young student whom he armed had sloughed off with great relief the Christianity he had been taught in childhood. While at public school Lewis, through influences which he describes in *Surprised by Joy*, had also become an atheist.

And so, it was as a more thoroughly convinced young atheist that he left Kirkpatrick to make a brilliant record at Oxford. But his college career was interrupted by World War I. He was sent to France as a young commissioned officer, and after spending some time in the trenches, was wounded by an exploding shell in April, 1918. The wound was not serious, but it ended his military career. He did carry a bit of the metal from the shell in his body for a number of years.

But, as he says in a letter to a friend, it lay there quietly "like an unrepented sin" and then began to give him trouble and had to be removed.

His years as an Oxford student convinced him that a life among books and ideas was what he wanted, and after some frustrating delays he was finally elected to the position of fellow at Magdalen College. But Lewis found that, although he could defend his intellectual position in the jousts and skirmishes with his colleagues at the university, he could not maintain his atheism and be honest with himself. As he tells it in *Surprised by Joy*, he slowly came to believe in the existence of a divine being. But shifting from one conclusion to another he seemed to discover everywhere a conspiracy against his unbelief. The friends on campus who were most intelligent and seemed to have most in common with him turned out to be Christians. The poets and prose writers whom he admired most in literature also seemed to take sides against him—they had the same quirk as his friends—they were Christians. But he continued to fight a rear-guard action, only giving up what ground was absolutely impossible to defend.

Finally, concluding that there must be a universal Spirit—an absolute Spirit, as he called it—he persuaded himself temporarily that such a concept was different from the God of religion. But he found that it would not work. He had opened the door a crack and the divine foot was in it. The ex-atheist found that he was confronted by a Person, that belief must no longer be a matter of playing with theories. Suddenly he was the hunted, the prey of the Hound of Heaven. As he says, "Amiable agnostics will talk cheerfully about 'man's search for God.' To me, as I then was, they might as well have talked about the mouse's search for the cat." In such a condition an honest mind is no defense against the truth. He finally capitulated. "In the Trinity Term of 1929 I gave in, and admitted that God was God, and knelt and prayed: perhaps, that night, the most dejected and reluctant convert in all England."[10] After a period of adjusting his new faith to orthodox theology, he became a member of the Church of England, where he remained for the rest of his life.

The weapons of Christian warfare sometimes come from strange arsenals. Lewis's effectiveness as an apologist or defender of the faith can, in part, be traced to his years as an atheist. Knowing the attitudes, the feelings, the arguments of the skeptic from the inside, he was able to illustrate from his own spiritual history the logical steps which must lead one to conclude that the Gospels are not cunningly devised fables, but the truth of God.

Although there are close to twenty of Lewis's books (including collections of articles) which would be classed as apologetics, that is, direct explanation and defense of Christian doctrine, his religious ideas can be found in his imaginative writing as well—the books we will be discussing in this volume. In fact, most that he wrote was an expression, in story or in exposition, of the convictions by which he lived. One who reads his books reads his life.

IV.

THE STORY of Lewis after his conversion to Christianity is largely the story of paper and ink—his books and articles.[11] As we have noted, his professional life can be divided into the years as a fellow at Oxford and the years as a professor at Cambridge. A part of this life was his contribution to learning in his chosen field—the dozens of volumes, essays, prefaces, and reviews which he wrote as a specialist in English literature. As a scholar and critic he brought honor to the universities which he represented.

But, of course, it is the books dealing with religious questions that gave him a world reputation. People who have no notion that Lewis was a famous scholar have read *The Problem of Pain*, *Mere Christianity*, *Miracles*, *Reflections on the Psalms*, and others. His first attempt to make a statement about his new-found faith was in a form which he never attempted again. *The Pilgrim's Regress* is, as the title suggests, patterned after Bunyan's famous allegory, *Pilgrim's Progress*. Lewis attempts, as it were, to draw a map of the bypaths into tropical jungles of sensuality and the rocky roads into cold deserts of skepticism into which one like himself can wander when he leaves the high road to the City of God. In a sense, it is a record of his own search for meaning and spiritual satisfaction which eventually led him back to the Christianity he had abandoned. But it is a difficult book. He was not aware, at that time, of his talent for speaking the language of the common reader. Written in 1932, the book is addressed to the intellectual who was aware of the currents of philosophical and religious thought of that period. Writing to a friend in 1953 he comments, "It was my first religious book and I didn't then know how to make things easy. I was not even trying to much, because in those days I never dreamed I would become a 'popular' author and hoped for no reader outside a small 'highbrow' circle. Don't waste your time over it any more."[12] The book did not sell very well, and he turned his attention for the next few years to scholarly writing.

In 1935 he completed the book which established his reputation as an authority in his field. *The Allegory of Love,* a study of the medieval tradition in love poetry, had taken eight years of writing and research. It is still regarded as an essential tool to an understanding of the period. Half a dozen scholarly articles and a number of poems and book reviews were also written before 1938. This is a year to remember because it marks the beginning of Lewis's career as a popular writer and a writer of fiction. He had always been interested in science fiction, and in 1938 published his first creative effort in this field, *Out of the Silent Planet,* which is the subject of the next chapter of this volume.

The Problem of Pain, which appeared in 1940, is the first of his volumes of nonfiction aimed at the general reader. It deals with the vexing paradox of suffering humanity and a benevolent Creator. In the same year he wrote an even more popular book, *The Screwtape Letters,* which we will discuss in a later chapter. It is still one of his best-selling volumes. *The Problem of Pain* was instrumental in producing another work whose influence has been very far-reaching. Impressed with the book on pain, James Welch, director of religious broadcasting for the B.B.C., invited Lewis in 1941 to give a series of broadcast talks. The first series on "Right and Wrong as a Clue to the Meaning of the Universe" was an immediate success. His desk was almost buried under a mountain of letters. So between 1942 and 1944 he gave three more. The four groups of talks were eventually revised and enlarged and in 1952 published as *Mere Christianity.* The clear and persuasive chapters of this book continue to change the lives of readers today.

In 1941 his second major contribution to scholarship was completed. It was published in the next year and titled *A Preface to "Paradise Lost."* His discussion of the lightning-scarred lord of Milton's Hell indicates that he had thought seriously about the amputating power of evil upon the spirit of any creature. So it is not surprising that his next book, *Perelandra,* written in 1942, contains the powerful figure of the Un-man, the incarnate demon who tempts the Venusian Eve. This second story of the space trilogy is the subject of chapter three of this book.

In 1943 appeared *The Abolition of Man,* a discussion of the frightening prospect of man's attempts to manipulate his own race by genetic change. The book is closely related to the third of the space trilogy, *That Hideous Strength,* and will be discussed further with that story, which was written in 1944. In that same year he wrote *The Great Divorce,* another subject of this volume, and in 1945 *Miracles,* perhaps his most systematic treatment of theology. During this period (1938–1945) he also published about fifty articles, sermons, lectures, and prefaces—some for the specialist, but many for the general reader. One of the latter group, a sermon preached in Oxford in 1941 and titled "The Weight of Glory," has been called "the most sublime piece of prose to come from his pen."

Such a "sounding cataract" of ideas would have "written out" most other writers. But, although no more books appeared after *Miracles* until 1949, he produced seventeen articles and a number of poems and reviews in this three-year period. But 1949 revealed another hidden talent. That a bachelor in his fifties, with no nephews and nieces and no earlier evidence of such a talent, could create a delightful world with its own genesis and last judgment, its sin and redemption, its quests and rescues, for the enthusiastic enjoyment of children and adults alike is perhaps the most unexpected aspect of Lewis's career. Many feel that after his scholarly and theological books and his science fiction have been superseded by the writings of others, his reputation will still be sustained by *The Chronicles of Narnia.*

The seven Narnian tales were written from 1949 to 1953, during which time he was also working on his longest scholarly book, *English Literature in the Sixteenth Century.* Finished in 1953, it is Volume III of the *Oxford History of English Literature.* In 1955 he completed *Surprised by Joy,* his one autobiographical volume, upon which he had been working for several years. As the book is the biography of his conversion—a sort of *Pilgrim's Regress* in the flesh—it does not record all the events of his life that we would like to know. *Till We Have Faces,* the last of his fiction, appeared in the next year (1956). It is the story of the devouring love of Queen Orual, who was also surprised by joy. During this period (1949–1956) in which he published ten books, he also wrote twenty-three articles and prefaces and numerous poems and reviews.

The last seven years of his life, in which he was in ill health, saw the appearance of seven books. Of a religious nature are *Reflections on the Psalms* (1957), *The Four Loves* (1959), *A Grief Observed* (1961), and *Letters to Malcolm, Chiefly on Prayer* (1963). His scholarly contributions were *Studies in Words* (1960), *An Experiment in Criticism* (1961), and *The Discarded Image* (1963). As elsewhere, I have given the date of completion rather than publication, which is often a year or so later. In this same period he also wrote thirty prose pieces,

A Grief Observed requires for explanation the description of another unexpected event in Lewis's life. After fifty-seven years as a bachelor, Lewis married Joy Davidman, a woman dying of cancer. As he wrote to a friend before the wedding, "I am likely very shortly to be both a bridegroom and a widower. . . ." The details of this tragic-happy period of his life are given in the Green and Hooper biography and do not concern us here. But Joy Davidman, an American writer with whom he found much in common, did not die as expected. There was a remission of the cancer, and they had four very happy years together, even making a trip to Greece. However, the cancer returned, and when she died in 1960, Lewis

13

was overwhelmed. He recorded the story of his devastation in what his brother called "this harrowing book," *A Grief Observed.* It was first published under the pseudonym N. W. Clerk. After his death Lewis's executors confirmed that the book was by him and allowed it to be reissued under his name.

Lewis's final illness did not develop suddenly. He knew he was dying some weeks before the end. Yet he continued to work—if that is the word for the writing of a man who delighted to share his faith. His last article, "We Have No 'Right to Happiness'," was written for the *Saturday Evening Post,* and seven days before his death he was reading the proofs and putting a call through to New York to insist that some changes they had made would cause him to cancel the article if the original passages were not restored.

Perhaps his own words, only intended as a personal comment, pronounce the final accolade upon his literary achievement. Shortly before his death he told his brother, "I have done all I wanted to do, and I'm ready to go."[13] The "Bibliography of the Writings of C. S. Lewis," compiled by Walter Hooper, contains over three hundred items, including books, articles, poems, reviews, and letters written for publication. Looking at such an output one might wonder if the man was driven by some inner agony to produce. But the evidence of friends and colleagues is that much that he wrote was what he "wanted to do." The scholarly books and articles were a part of his expected service to the universities, but even these were not without pleasure. And the religious writings, fiction and nonfiction, were, as he said, his leisure-time activity. His penetrating intellect was alive with ideas and his imagination with pictures. Much that he wrote was written easily and with enjoyment. His bibliography is large because he filled his time with what he "wanted to do."

V.

THE PRECEDING pages, perhaps the biography of a bibliography, have emphasized the output of the man but not the content of his writings. The techniques and ideas of his fiction are the subjects of the remaining chapters of this book. But it might be useful to list here some of the recurrent ideas which by their repetition testify to their importance in the author's mind. First of all, Lewis was a thoroughgoing supernaturalist. He had no time for what he called Christianity-and-water. Any attempt to dilute the gospel by denying the miracles or reducing Christ's teaching to ethical platitudes was an attack, he felt, upon the very heart of the faith. That Christ was just a great human teacher he called "patronizing nonsense." Considering the claims He made for Himself, He was either a lunatic—"on a level with the man who says he is a poached egg"—or a devil, or what He claimed to be, the Son of God.[14]

Lewis did not think of the supernatural as a floating world of ghosts and disembodied spirits who occasionally laid aside their cloak of invisibility in order to put on a show. It is our universe, he believed, which is ghostly and which will someday be rolled up like a garment. The permanent and the solid is in the Land of the Trinity and in those who have accepted the gift of permanence called eternal life. "We shall live," he says, "to remember the galaxies as an old tale."[15] He often uses images which suggest that reality is beyond the universe which we know. The incarnation is an "invasion" of our world by the divine. God as creator of our universe is like a novelist who has created the world of his novel. One approaching the borders of Heaven would feel that he had gotten so completely "outside" that the solar system would seem like an indoor affair.

But Lewis did not confine his idea of a place outside our universe to a belief in Heaven. He suggests that God may have created other "natures," other realities in no way related to the reality which we call the universe. If He has, these other natures "would have no spatial or temporal relation to ours." They would be other "novels" by the same Author. It is just such a discontinuity, a world beyond our universe, to which Lewis introduces us through the talking beavers, the prophetic centaurs, the merry dwarfs and fauns of Narnia.

That the two worlds are discontinuous does not mean, however, that they never touch. Angelic and demonic influences as recorded in Scripture testify to the reality of these contacts, and he deals imaginatively with such possibilities in the devilish espionage and sabotage of *The Screwtape Letters* and in the *eldils* and *macrobes* of the space trilogy. But, as he says, "the grand miracle" is the invasion of our world from the Land of the Trinity by the Second Person of the Godhead. The incarnation is the miracle of miracles. Such a staggering and inconceivable descent might be dimly grasped if we could imagine descending into the life of a slug or a crab.

Lewis believed that such a unique event made Christianity unique. It is the one true religion. But it does not follow that all others are completely false. He believed that there are hints and foreshadowings of the incarnation in earlier religions, that God sent what he calls "good dreams" of what was to come in the "corn-kings" who personify the death and rebirth theme of many pagan beliefs. For this reason *Till We Have Faces* is a serious treatment of an ancient pagan myth—what might be called a Christian treatment of pre-Christian material.

In addition to the "good dreams," Lewis says that in each of us there is a longing for that which is beyond the universe. Like homing pigeons we flutter against the bars of this life. However, as wounded birds, we often do not even know why we are fluttering. In *Surprised by Joy* he tells of the stab of pleasure-longing which he calls "joy"—the memory of a pleasure which, if he could go back to it, would itself turn out to be a memory, or rather, a reminder of a longing. As he says in "The Weight of Glory," the beauty and delight which we remember are not what we really desire. They are images or shadows of it. ". . . they are only the scent of a flower we have not found, the echo of a tune we have not heard, news from a country we have never yet visited."[16]

This longing for a far country, he says, is God's signpost, His pointer to the land beyond the stars, to our true home, which we are searching for without knowing it. In *The Pilgrim's Regress* it is the brief glimpses of the beautiful island which draw John ever onward and which are not blotted out when he enters the bypaths to sensuality or asceticism. In *Surprised by Joy* Lewis admits that he made the longing for remembered beauty a goal in itself until he became a Christian and learned what the longing was sent for. But, he says, "To tell you the truth, the subject has lost nearly all interest for me since I became a Christian." This statement has been misunderstood by some readers to mean that he no longer thought the experience important. But in its context the sentence clearly means that he no longer values the longing which he calls "joy" as something to be sought for in itself. The old stab comes just as often as before, he says, but, when one is on the right road, he does not stop at every signpost "though their pillars are of silver and their lettering of gold. 'We would be at Jerusalem.'"[17]

But the longing does tell us something about the goal we are seeking. In "The Weight of Glory" he points out that we want so much more than merely to see beauty; we want to become part of it. But we are outsiders; we are on "the wrong side of the door." The beauty and purity of a morning do not make us beautiful or pure. We are spectators of a pageant in which we have no part. "But," he says, "all the leaves of the New Testament are rustling with the rumour that it will not always be so. Some day, God willing, we shall get in." He adds that he is not talking about being absorbed into the beauty of nature. Nature is temporary. She reflects but faintly the glory with which God will clothe His own. Only by such images, however, as putting on the splendor of the sun or receiving the gift of the morning star can we approach an understanding of the inconceivable weight of glory that God has prepared for those who love Him.

VI.

BUT NOT only is there a longing for home in man. Lewis believed that within him there is also a sense of right and wrong, what he calls a law of decent behavior. It is not a law which he habitually obeys, but its existence is evidenced by his constant application of it to others. Man judges his neighbor on the basis of a standard of moral behavior and

17

even excuses his own failure to come up to that standard, not by rejecting it, but by arguing that under the circumstances the law does not apply. He still recognizes the law as admirable. And, Lewis says, contrary to popular notion, this standard is to be found wherever human society is to be found. There is no use claiming that all values are relative, that some societies have accepted as virtues what others regard as vices, for the law of decent human behavior is to be found in all cultures. He points out in *The Abolition of Man* that the literature of widely separated ancient civilizations shows that basically the standards are the same. In fact, it is really impossible to imagine a society in which these standards do not exist. As he says in *Mere Christianity*, "Think of a country where people were admired for running away in battle, or where a man felt proud of double-crossing all the people who had been kindest to him."[18]

The law is ingrained in our nature because it is a manual of operation, a guide to our greatest happiness. He believed that rules for decent behavior are directions for the smooth running of the human machine. We often think of a moral code—say, the Ten Commandments—as a standard which God requires of us because it is a pattern which He happens to like. Not at all, says Lewis. God through His law is telling us in love how we are made—how human beings are meant to operate. Just as I cannot put the car in reverse while going fifty miles an hour without doing great damage to the machine, so I cannot ignore God's instructions for human behavior without experiencing disastrous consequences within. To quote from *Mere Christianity* again: "Every moral rule is there to prevent a breakdown, or a strain, or a friction, in the running of that machine."[19]

But man's relation to the moral law is different from his relation to physical law. If he jumps out of a window, his body obeys the law of gravitation whether he wants it to or not. In the realm of moral law, however, he is free to obey or disobey. And that freedom, says Lewis, is essential for a moral universe. Puppets are neither saints nor sinners. As God wanted creatures who could freely love Him, He has relinquished some of His freedom to man. "The happiness which God designs for His higher creatures is the happiness of being freely, voluntarily united to Him and to each other in an ecstasy of love and delight compared with which the most rapturous love between a man and a woman on this earth is mere milk and water. And for that they must be free."[20]

Lewis says much about freedom in both his fiction and his nonfiction. It led him into a head-on conflict with those popular philosophies of the twentieth century which can be lumped together under the general term *naturalism*. The word includes all those schools of thought which explain man as nothing but the product of the irrational forces of this universe. Like the Marxists they may explain him as shaped by the economic forces of society, or like the Freudians by sexual drives and repressions, but all such explanations deny that there is any supernatural part of man which can resist or control the natural inheritance which he receives from the world into which he is born.

Lewis's discussion in *Miracles* of what he calls the "fatal flaw" of naturalism reminds us that he was trained in philosophy before he turned to literature. In fact, he originally regarded his future as being in that discipline and first taught at Oxford on a temporary fellowship in philosophy. So it was not as an amateur that he pointed out that any view of man which regards him as simply a child of the blind forces of the universe does not leave room for the reasoning powers which constructed such a view. Thoughts which are nothing but flashes of electric energy and movements of irrational atoms in the brain are not the materials for building even a house of cards. And so he concludes, "Every theory of the universe which makes the human mind a result of irrational causes is inadmissible, for it would be a proof that there are no such things as proofs. Which is nonsense."[21] And because he did not believe that man was the puppet of a blind universe, he insisted that he is free. It also follows that one cannot talk about freedom of choice in man without admitting that there is an ingredient in him which is beyond nature—which is supernatural.

But the supernatural in man lives in a natural body which lives in a natural universe. And Lewis regarded this as delightful. There is no contempt of the flesh or the senses in his writings. He condemns the wrong use of the flesh or the senses and, of course, recognizes the havoc which sin has made in God's creation. But it is still God's creation, and he believed that God rejoices in it. When "all the sons of God shouted for joy" on the day of creation, they were responding to the joy of the Creator. For, Lewis says, "God likes matter. He invented it."[22]

So, the sensuous delight the floating islands produce in *Perelandra*, or the feasts, the dances, the rollicking merriment, which we associate with Narnia are a part of Lewis's theology. The principle of joy, which is too often absent in our fallen world, he displays as a part of God's original purpose for all of His creation. And, when man shows love for all the creatures of God's world which he was intended to rule, he will be approaching the peaceable kingdom which is a part of that purpose.

The mention of such a future brings us to a concluding comment about Lewis and animals. There were usually pets about the house at The Kilns. When he married Joy Davidman, she brought to the household a cat, which he referred to thereafter as his step-cat. Earlier, there had been a dog of miscellaneous ancestry called "Mr. Papworth," who in his old age developed some oddities of behavior, among which was his refusal to eat if anyone was watching him. Lewis sometimes amused visitors by walking down the street throwing food over his shoulder which Mr. Papworth would gobble up. But, if Lewis turned to observe him, the dog would give him a glassy stare and refuse to touch the food.

In a number of his writings Lewis indicates his belief that animals have suffered from the fall and would participate in some way in man's final redemption. As he says in *The Problem of Pain*, "Man, even now, can do wonders to animals: my cat and dog live together in my house and seem to like it."[23] But one of Lewis's delights since boyhood was to project upon animals imaginary human personalities. The "Animal Land" which he invented as a boy, although very different from Narnia, was a country in which animals entered politics and undertook other honorable and disreputable tasks of the human species. But in Narnia, in spite of the witches and wicked uncles, the general picture we get is of an almost ideal kingdom in which talking mice, dogs, and beavers live in harmony with each other and with the other fabulous creatures of the land.

The space trilogy shows animals not as fantastic creatures, but as potential persons (if I may use the word *person* to mean any being with reason and speech). In *That Hideous Strength* Ransom not only harmonizes his strange household menagerie, but lifts Mr. Bultitude, the bear, to unimagined heights of semi-self-consciousness. In *Perelandra* Tinidril, the Queen, displays a paradisaical relationship with the animals, which she makes "older" every day. But perhaps *Out of the Silent Planet* records the apex of possibilities. On Malacandra three species have risen to the level of rationality and in their composite abilities show a superiority to the race of man in intellect, skill, and morality. But this leads us to the next chapter and the ancient civilization of the *séroni, hrossa,* and *pfifltriggi.*

THE SOLAR LANDSCAPE

CHAPTER 2
OUT OF THE SILENT PLANET

I.

"Out of the Silent Planet is to me the most beautiful of all cosmic voyages and in some ways the most moving. . . . Mr. Lewis has created *myth* itself, myth woven of desires and aspirations deep-seated in some, at least, of the human race."[1] So wrote Marjorie Nicolson in her study of cosmic journeys titled *Voyages to the Moon.* Sir Hugh Walpole described the story as "a kind of poem." Many other readers have been impressed with the mythical and poetic in the account of the trip to Malacandra. As we remember the golden flowers of Meldilorn, "huge as summer cloud," that bloom on their gigantic stocks hundreds of feet above the island, or the deep-chested music of the *hrossa* on those aromatic mornings when the elderly set out on their solemn journey to Maleldil, it is hard to classify the book as science fiction. The mythical and poetic are in the grain; the "science" but a superficial covering.

As Lewis points out in his essay "On Science Fiction,"[2] space travel in some books is simply a device or "machine"

25

for getting beyond our drab world to those unexamined regions where the marvelous can unfold convincingly. As our own world becomes well explored, stories of the strange and wonderful must come to us out of the sky. So we do not read this book for its engineering ingenuity, but for what might be called its "otherness"—its introduction of places and creatures which our imagination can revel in: the purple trees, the blue water, the translucent *eldils* of a faraway planet. He comments in the essay that "good novels are comments on life," and that this other sort of fiction—tales of wonder, which he would perhaps label "romances"—are "additions to life." Good stories of this type give us "sensations we never had before, and enlarge our conception of the range of possible experience." Some readers, he admits, refuse to be lifted out of the rut which they call "real life." Such stories are not for them. But for those who are born to strange sights, tales of other worlds can give a solemn and lasting pleasure. They represent "a mode of imagination which does something to us at a deep level."

And so, Lewis places his story in the pastel canyons of the planet Mars. However, verisimilitude, or the appearance of truth, is a virtue in any fiction. In order to create such an appearance, the author, wherever possible, must invent details which are consistent with beliefs current when the story is written. A high probability factor makes it easier for the reader's imagination to soar with the writer to worlds of moon maids or one-eyed monsters. *Out of the Silent Planet* was published in 1938. Because of earlier speculations of astronomers, it was popularly thought that there were lines on Mars, which were called canals because they seemed to form geometric patterns and to suggest that they had been artificially constructed. It was also known that Mars had a smaller mass than Earth and therefore a weaker gravitational pull.

These, then, were the givens which Lewis had to take into account, which, together with a consistency of action, character portrayal, and setting, would create verisimilitude in the story. Thus, we have a spaceship built by a great scientist. We have a network of *handramits* (which would appear from Earth as canals) artificially cut into the surface of the planet to conserve its meager atmosphere and tap its internal heat. And we have a weaker gravity expressed in the theme of perpendicularity which Ransom notices almost immediately upon arrival. The mountains are higher and sharper, the vegetation reaches farther into the sky, the *sorns* are walking stilts, and even the furry *hrossa* seem abnormally slender for their six or seven feet of height. The reader can easily suppose that a planet with a smaller mass would have a different geological and biological appearance.

But astronomers today believe that the canals of Mars were an illusion. The automated landings on the red planet have found no *handramits,* nor, indeed, the slightest evidence that it has ever had any sort of life during the long eons of its existence. What does this do to the verisimilitude of Lewis's narrative? If the book were written today, no doubt it would be ridiculed as the product of a scientific ignoramus. But we make historical allowance for a work which was consistent with the knowledge of its own time. Just as Brobdingnag still lives in our imagination even though there is no place now for the peninsula which Gulliver discovered in the North Pacific, so we accept Malacandra as imaginatively probable even though its science is out-of-date.

Its imaginative probability is assisted by the last chapter and the postscript. Here Lewis pretends that he knows Ransom personally and that his story is true but must be presented as fiction because of public skepticism. He tells how he became involved with Ransom and in the postscript offers an excerpt from one of his friend's letters. This sort of device is in a long and respectable tradition of storytelling. If a tale has verisimilitude, we will, while reading it, believe that it happened—what Coleridge called "a willing suspension of disbelief." And so, writers will often help our imaginations by pretending that what they are telling is not fiction but history, and will concoct witnesses (Cousin Sympson, who testifies to Gulliver's veracity) or produce other evidence to buttress their claims.

So Lewis ends his story with the assertion that he and Ransom agreed that the true story would not be believed by the reading public, and that it should, therefore, be presented as fiction, and then adds a postscript in which Ransom says that he knew enough about the *pfifltriggi* that he could have faked a visit to their territory, but that he didn't think "we ought to introduce any mere fiction" into the story. Sometimes such tricks have amusing results with literal-minded people. Lewis had to assure more than one inquirer that, in spite of the projection of himself into the story, the whole thing was fictitious.

II.

Out of the Silent Planet is the account of the coming of age of Elwin Ransom, philologist and Cambridge don, a man of about forty years, whom one of Steinbeck's characters might have had in mind when she said "I have known boys forty years old because there was no need of a man."[3] It is true that he was a recognized scholar in his field, whose name immediately called to mind for many people his best-known publication, *Dialect and Semantics*. But when Ransom, along with Whin and Hyoi, had successfully met and slain the snapping, shark-toothed *hnakra*, he had, we are told, "grown up."

In fact, a recognition of the movement from fear to fortitude in Ransom is important to an understanding of both his character and the structure of the plot. As Lewis says in *Mere Christianity*, fortitude is courage both to face danger and to endure pain—what in modern English would be called "guts." When Ransom first discovers that he is in a spaceship, thousands of miles from Earth, fear so possesses him that he wishes he would lose consciousness. When he learns that he will be handed over to *sorns*, whatever they are, he is in an agony of terror of unknown bogies, and determines, in spite of his Christian beliefs, to commit suicide, if necessary, to avoid these extraterrestrial horrors. After his escape from his captors on Malacandra, his flight through the planet's vegetable forest is driven by an almost mindless fear which at times seems to unbalance his thinking.

But the meeting with Hyoi and the introduction to the culture of his species make a great difference in Ransom's acceptance of danger. The *hrossa,* with a confident belief in a hereafter, regard death as the best drink of all, for it is the way to Maleldil. Hyoi calls that dangerous beast, the *hnakra,* "our enemy, but he is also our beloved." It is danger which gives a zest to life, making its colors more vivid and its song more melodic.

And so in almost the exact center of the book we have the turning point in Ransom's fight with fear. The *hrossa* take it for granted that he will want to take part in the *hnakra* hunt. When Hyoi and Whin give him a place in the bow of the boat—the post of greatest honor and greatest danger—he resolves to play the man. The influence of his sojourn among the *hrossa* is apparent. The narrator comments that his determination would have been impossible just a few weeks earlier "when he had lain pitying himself in the forest by night."

And when Ransom has come through with flying colors and is a *hnakrapunt* (*hnakra*-slayer), the movement of the story changes. Up to this point he has been the drugged captive, the intended sacrifice, the fugitive—the terrified recipient of action. From now on he determines his own actions, faces danger and suffering by his own choice, and masters his fears as they beset him. He is his own executive. The action changes from flight to quest as he moves through the forest and pushes up the steep path into the cold and airless *harandra* on his way to Meldilorn and Oyarsa. Fear is not dead, but its paralyzing grip has been broken.

The next chapter leads him to another triumph as his resolution propels him into Augray's cave, and there in the leaping light of the fire he sees the gigantic-chested, stilt-like figure and discovers that *sorns* are not "ogres" but "angels," as kindly in their intellectual way as the *hrossa.* And when the journey ends, and with Weston and Devine he finds himself in the presence of the semi-invisible ruler of the planet, his position is dominant as he translates Weston's speech into the Malacandrian tongue and then narrates for Oyarsa the strange wars of Maleldil against the Bent One. The final evidence of his victory over fear is his free choice to participate in the desperate voyage and almost certain death of the return trip.

The influence of Hyoi upon Ransom, no doubt, accounts for much of the change in his character. The *hross* is in some ways representative of his race, but he is also an individual. At his funeral in Meldilorn his brother Hyahi speaks of him as a *hnakra*-slayer and a great poet and says, "The loss of him is heavy." Hyoi is both adventuresome and meditative. When we first meet him, he has been roaming the water alone. Perhaps the most illuminating episode (and he says it is ". . . a day in my life that has shaped me") is the trip which he took as a very young *hross*—not much more than a cub—far to the north and up into the high country to the dangerous and awesome pool of Balki. The journey was his own idea. As he says, ". . . even Oyarsa sent me no word." This pilgrimage to a holy but perilous shrine, where he stood alone with Maleldil and stooped and drank where the *hnakra* lies hidden, gave him a higher heart and a deeper song all his days. "There I drank life," he says, "because death was in the pool."

But Hyoi is also generous and friendly. When his furry, cannonball head first turns and he gazes at the "thick" form of Ransom lying on the ground weed, he is wary but curious. The strangeness of this new creature does not repel him as he offers him food and drink and brings him to the village of the *hrossa*. The friendship which working and playing together creates causes Hyoi not only to give Ransom a place in his boat for the hunt, but with his dying breath to declare their eternal brotherhood as *hnakrapunti*.

The only other characters in the book which stand out as individuals are Devine and Weston. We do not learn enough of the *sorns* to know in what way Augray is unique among his species, and the other creatures in the story are little more than names. Hnohra, the gray-muzzled teacher, and Kanakaberaka, the *pfifltrigg* artist, are interesting, but hardly portrayed with distinguishing characteristics.

The Thin One, as Oyarsa calls Devine, is a far more important figure in *That Hideous Strength*. Here, his words and actions reveal him as a shallow, self-centered, and ruthless person. Ransom remembers him at school as being very clever at mocking the sentimental and idealistic clichés of the day. He apparently has not outgrown this boyish vice. He tells Ransom that he is sure "you'll live up to the old school tie," and at their first meeting observes ironically, "This is where we get a lump in our throats and remember Sunday-evening Chapel in the D.O.P." Oyarsa sums up his character by saying that he is a dead soul whose animal nature is motivated by nothing but greed. He is not bent but broken. His only motive in coming to Malacandra is to obtain sun's blood (gold), which will provide him with ocean-going yachts and expensive women.

Weston is the "great physicist" of science fiction, not of real life. The comic scenes are not, as sometimes charged, an attack upon science but a caricature of the popular image of the scientist who is also a futurist, a figure often portrayed in science fiction. Lewis believed that the attitude which Weston represents is a danger which should be taken seriously. Too frequently in the popular mind, especially at the time when Lewis wrote, the scientist was regarded as a superman who made no mistakes and whose "method" revealed to him all knowledge which was worth preserving.

The limitations of science have since then been rather graphically demonstrated by the problems created by the atomic bomb. But this story was written before the priestly functions of "the man in the white coat" had been tarnished. Lewis is ahead of his time as he shows the fallacy of such faith by creating a man whose genius had lifted him above all his contemporaries in his chosen field, but whose specialization had made him unable to cope with anything beyond his own discipline. At Meldilorn Devine's imperative to Weston to "stop making a buffoon of yourself," aptly describes the great physicist jigging before the spectators and jiggling the glass beads in front of beings whose creations of beauty in song and in sun's blood had existed from before the dawn of human time. It makes clear Lewis's attitude toward those

31

who claim that science is the messiah that will lead human-kind into all truth.

III.

BECAUSE THE reader is kept close to the protagonist, not much needs to be said about the plot which has not already been said about Ransom. The structure of the action is a very old one—a series of journeys. It divides into seven parts: the walking tour and kidnapping, the forced trip through space, the flight from Weston and Devine, and then the central episode—the weeks spent with the *hrossa*. In the second half we follow the quest for Meldilorn, the interlude with Oyarsa, and finally the harrowing journey back to Earth.

Another part of the narrative technique which is closely related to the protagonist is point of view, or angle of narration. In a broad sense there are two points of view possible in a story. The author can tell the tale himself as the creator looking down upon the world he has created, or he can allow one of his characters to tell the story in the first person, reporting, as it were, from the stage of action.

Within these two divisions there are many variations which accomplish for the author the exact voice of authority and flexibility of narration which he requires for his story. Lewis chooses one admirably fitted to a story in which the significant events all happen to the protagonist. With the exception of the last chapter and the postscript, we are never allowed to depart from the presence of Ransom. But he is not the narrator. Lewis tells the story, but limits himself to the thoughts, feelings, and actions of his protagonist, who is, for the reader, the central intelligence.

The author reserves the right, however, to read his character's mind and to back off and comment on his thoughts and actions. As we are always close, imaginatively, to the man experiencing the adventure, the sense of authority for its accuracy is maintained, and, as it is Lewis's voice we hear, the bias and limitation we associate with a man's story of his own adventure is eliminated. Of course these are only literary tricks, but we do not think of that when we are reading, any more than while watching a movie we continually remind ourselves that the characters are only shadows on the screen.

So, through the technique of the central intelligence we experience with Ransom the fear of pursuit during his flight from Weston and Devine and the uncertainty in the supposed hostile environment. And on the quest for Meldilorn we participate with him in the exhausting steepness of the climb, the cold, the lack of oxygen, the fear at Augray's Tower. We identify with the protagonist and imaginatively live his experiences.

The journey as plot structure and the central intelligence as point of view allow Lewis to introduce the descriptive passages as a dynamic part of the story and not as static literary adornment. Ransom travels through space, down the *handramit*, and up into the *harandra*, and views it all with intense interest. So it is natural for Lewis to describe what he sees. The jeweled darkness on one side of the ship and the golden splendor of the Field of Arbol on the other, the cauliflower-shaped, petrified "trees" of Malacandra, rose-colored and big as cathedrals, the eerie voice of Oyarsa "with no blood in it," are all indispensable elements, inextricable from the action. But the strange and wonderful places and creatures also move us deeply because they are beyond our experience— what Lewis calls, "additions to life."

However, the "otherness" of the setting has theological as well as literary significance. Lewis emphasizes the ugly and dismal details of the particular part of England in which the story opens. The rain, the violent yellow sunset, the sky of dark slate, and the desolate countryside devoted mostly to cabbages and turnips seem appropriate for the mood of the characters. Ransom's resentment of the unfriendly hostess of Nadderby, the mother worried at the tardiness of an imbecile son, the hostile reception by Weston at The Rise, and the implications of criminal activity create a setting and situation which is of the earth, earthy. Here, Lewis seems to be saying, are the grim tokens of the fall, the curse under which both man and nature groan.

But soon, contrasting with this dim and colorless scene, are introduced the brilliance of space and then the multi-colored landscape of Malacandra. Our world, under the rule of the Prince of Darkness—the Bent One, as we learn to call him later—cannot be expected to have the color and life to be found in the rest of the universe, where obedience and love are second nature to God's creatures.

And through this loveless and earthy scene moves the Pedestrian. Not until the end of the second paragraph do we learn that his name is Ransom, but in the first paragraph he is referred to three times as "the Pedestrian" with a capital *P*. The ordinariness of this wayfarer coincides with Lewis's statement in "On Science Fiction" that the characters in this sort of story should be rather commonplace. He says, "To tell how odd things struck odd people is to have an oddity too much: he who is to see strange sights must not himself be strange. He ought to be as nearly as possible Everyman or Anyman."

But Lewis has indicated quite specifically that we are not to read his stories as allegories. They are, he says, "sacramental." In *The Allegory of Love* he draws a sharp line between these two approaches to literary material.[4] The allegorical method, he says, copies immaterial things such as ideas and passions by means of invented places and persons. In *Pilgrim's Progress* despair is represented by a giant and death by a river. The sacramental method, on the other hand, copies an invisible world of reality and attempts "to see the archetype in the copy." The literary events and persons stand for something that is more real than themselves. Just as Christ offered real bread and wine "in remembrance of me," so Ransom, the Un-man, and Aslan are fully realized literary creations unhampered by allegorical straitjackets but also reminders of something more real in the supernatural world.

Thus, the protagonist in the opening sentences of the story plods doggedly on his way, buffeted by natural forces, surrounded by both the unfriendly and the needy and not very well-equipped to deal with either one. He is a "case" with whom most readers can identify as representing their own condition. But very soon "the Pedestrian" is individualized to Elwin Ransom, Cambridge don, philologist, bachelor, Christian, who, in fact, possesses a number of characteristics which make him almost the alter ego of his creator. For instance, in addition to the above likenesses, Lewis was about the same age, was a great walker, and even had a war wound.

IV.

IN *The Problem of Pain* Lewis speaks of this world as a pocket of evil in a good universe. And so, as Ransom moves out of the atmosphere ruled by the Bent One, he discovers a universe whose benevolent influences immediately begin to heal both his body and spirit. Even in the first terrified moments aboard the spaceship he feels himself poised between "delirious terror" and "an ecstasy of joy." And as the unfiltered rays of sun and stars rub and scour his body and mind, he finds the universe a delight to contemplate. The modern mythology, which pictures space as black, cold, and dead, is completely inadequate for the present experience. Even the word *space* is a misnomer. The older thinkers were nearer to reality in calling it simply the heavens.

But not only does the ship move through an ocean of "sweet influences." When it settles to rest in Malacandra, Ransom meets the same benevolence in the rational creatures of the planet as he had felt in the heavens beyond. At the first meeting of the denizens of different worlds, there is tension and uncertainty. But then, Hyoi makes that marvelous gesture of friendship. The *hross* of Malacandra offers a drink to the man of Thulcandra, and their fingers touch. Two species, both made by the hand of Maleldil, find that they have more in common than rationality and speech. They have kindness, which ripens into friendship.

And, of course, the benevolence which Ransom meets everywhere, even from the *sorns*, whom he had fled and feared, is a part of one of the major themes of the book. Lewis is saying here as he does elsewhere that if God is the Lord of Hosts, wherever His hosts appear His nature will be expressed—in the unfallen legions of the sky: the *eldila*, and in the devout creatures of the *handra*: the *hrossa*, the *séroni*, and the *pfifltriggi*.

That the rational beings of Malacandra are devout worshipers of Maleldil is without question. Whether we should call them unfallen is not so certain. In the great hymn of praise at the end of *Perelandra* reference is made to the "peoples of the ancient worlds who never sinned," among whom Lewis probably included the peoples of Malacandra. And yet, we have at least a hint of temptation in the early history of the planet when Oyarsa tells of the attempts of the Bent One to create the fear of death in Oyarsa's subjects. "Some I cured," he says, "some I unbodied." So, the time of the cold death was a time of crisis, but a time in which fear was left behind forever. As Maleldil never does the same thing twice, perhaps we should not attempt to compare their spiritual history with that of the creatures of the other planets.

One thing is certain: Lewis intends us to see that Malacandra is very near the end of its long history as the home of rational creatures that breed and breathe. Before anything lived on our Earth, the red planet had been inhabited by advanced life forms. But now, its thousands of millenniums are coming to an end.

This raises the question of Lewis's view of the history of the human race. In *Mere Christianity* he uses the unpredictable changes in biological evolution as an analogy in describing the new men produced by Christ's work of redemption. When he first mentions evolution, he adds the parenthetical qualification: "(though, of course, some educated people disbelieve it)."[5] And in an essay called "Two Lectures"[6] he shows some skepticism for the theory. Also in "The Funeral of a Great Myth"[7] he comments that later biologists may show the evolutionary theory "to be a less satisfactory hypothesis than was hoped fifty years ago." This essay, however, is an attack upon the myth of popular evolution which, he says, is very different from that of science. "In the science, Evolution is a theory about *changes*: in the Myth it is a fact about *improvements.*" The myth, which he admires as an imaginative picture but ridicules as unscientific folklore, is best illustrated by the picture of eternal progress for our race which Weston describes in his confrontation with Oyarsa.

And so Lewis, recognizing this sort of evolutionary belief as a widely accepted myth, may have simply exploited it for his own literary purposes. However, the casual references to some sort of evolution on Malacandra, Earth, and Perelandra and certain statements in his letters suggest that he thought it possible that a gradual change which might be called an evolutionary process may have been the way that God had brought about life as we know it upon Earth. If this assumption is correct, we can be certain that he found no conflict between the theory and his own Christian convictions. If evidence seemed to show that this was the method which God had used to bring about His purposes, Lewis had no quarrel with it.

Thus it is not surprising that on Malacandra there are three species which, through the creative power of Maleldil and under the supervision of Oyarsa, have evolved to rationality. The *sorns*, with their feathery covering, quite certainly were descended from gigantic birds; the *hrossa* from some furry aquatic mammal; and the *pfifltriggi* perhaps from a frog-like reptile. But whatever their ancestry, on this planet where subjection to rule is never questioned, none, to the amazement of Ransom, had ever attempted to dominate or exploit the other races. Each is respected and accepted for its own contribution to the life of the planet.

The *sorns* are the intellectuals, the experts in abstract thought. To the puzzling theological question the answer was, "The *séroni* would know." The *pfifltriggi* are the artists and artisans, the inventors, the engineers. The shaping of matter for both beauty and utility is their special gift. And the *hrossa* are the poets, the singers, the eloquent communicators of the planet. Because of their gifts in language, their tongue had become the universal speech of the planet even though the other species had their local languages. In fact, as we

37

learn in *Perelandra, Hressa-Hlab,* the language of the *hrossa,* is the *lingua franca* of the solar system. It is the "Old Solar" through which the Un-man tempts the Lady and by which the worshipers offer up their praise to Maleldil on the Hill of Life.

V.

AS BOTH Ransom and his creator were men of letters, it is natural that the book gives more space to the culture of the poetic *hrossa* than to that of the other species. It would be a mistake to call the *hrossa* primitive, as Ransom supposes them to be at first. It is true that their life is simple, agrarian, and uncluttered with the artifacts which we associate with civilization. But they are knowledgeable in astronomy, correctly identifying the planet from which Ransom had come, and orthodox in their theology—even to understanding that the Godhead consists of more than one person. But, of course, it is in their poetry and song that their culture demonstrates its sophistication. Here they are technicians whose art is too complex for even the philologist to master in the time he lives among them.

Ransom's knowledge of the *sorns* is more fragmentary. That their life is partially pastoral and that they are cave-dwellers he knows from the sight of their yellow "cattle" in the purple forest and from the visit with Augray. In the caves "work is in progress" as Augray tells him, but of the nature of that work he never learns. The nearest he comes to a view of communal activity is in the visit to the "great scientist" who is surrounded by assistants and students. Their intellectual capacity is clearly demonstrated by their skillful interrogation of Ransom and by his conversations with Augray, but he never is able to understand how this community of scholars employ their talents.

His contact with the *pfifltriggi* is so brief that it is surprising that we know anything about them. But his conversation with stone-chiseling Kanakaberaka, who sculptures his form for posterity, tells us quite a little, and Augray's remarks shed more light on their culture. It probably comes closest to what humankind would call civilization. The *pfifltriggi* live in houses rather than caves or grass huts and express their artistic nature in elaborate murals of Malacandrian life and history. Although a desire for ostentation would be foreign to the nature of any Malacandrian, the beauty of their dwellings, some with a hundred glittering pillars of alternating gold and silver, surely would have been staggering to earthly eyes. How much of their inventiveness is a result of cooperation with the *sorns* is uncertain. Of the oxygen supplier Augray said, "We thought it and the *pfifltriggi* made it." But among other things they know how to refrigerate and how to disintegrate bodies by a process which Devine describes as very similar to splitting the atom.

Augray's response to Ransom's gesture of gratitude in offering him his watch sheds light not only on the *pfifltriggi* but also on the relations between the species. Although Augray says that the watch delights his heart, he gives it back and requests Ransom to give it to a *pfifltrigg* because he would enjoy it more. The selfless interchange among the three so completely different races reminds us of Lewis's statement elsewhere that if the entire world became Christian, it would take very few years to make this earth into a paradise.

In spite of the specialization of talents among the species, there are significant characteristics which they have in common. As they are all under the benevolent rule of Oyarsa, we may assume that the theological beliefs of the *hrossa* are identical with those of the others. Without question they all recognize Maleldil as Creator and Lord.

Lewis's meaning here should be clear, although one writer says that Maleldil is the Trinity and another that He is God the Father. Both assertions are wrong. When Ransom asks where Maleldil lives, the *hrossa* say, "With the Old One"—probably an allusion to the phrase in the Book of Daniel, "the Ancient of Days." But the most certain indication of Lewis's intent is to be found in *Perelandra*. The King, speaking of what he learned in the land of Lur, refers to new things "about Maleldil and about His Father and the Third One." Clearly Maleldil is Christ, the second person of the Trinity, by whom, as the writer of the Letter to the Hebrews says, the worlds were made and who upholds all things by the word of His power. The theology of the space trilogy is in perfect harmony with the Christian orthodoxy which Lewis explains so persuasively in *Mere Christianity*.

The source of the name *Maleldil* is uncertain, but Lewis may have been influenced by biblical names such as Malchishua (king of help), Malchiram (king of exaltation), and Malchiel (God is king). So perhaps Maleldil means king of *eldils*—that is, king of all spirits, or even Lord of Hosts.

VI.

BUT WE should not conclude that the *eldila* are spirits in the sense of bodiless and insubstantial entities. Although it is difficult for earthly eyes to see them, they have bodies, as Augray tells Ransom, which can pass through walls and rocks, because to them these substances are thin and cloud-like. Because they dwell on the border between the speed of light and things too fast for fleshly eyes to receive, they appear as faint glimmers and half-real bodies. But their reality is as positive as the blaze of the sun. Lewis, no doubt, intended us to think of them as a part of the heavenly host, who are often associated in the Bible with fire and shining splendor (as in Hebrews: "his ministers a flame of fire").

The greatest *eldil* on Malacandra is, of course, Oyarsa, whose name also describes his office. On Perelandra he tells Ransom that here he is not Oyarsa. On this planet he is only Malacandra. And when Tor assumes his place as supreme ruler of the young world, he is addressed as Oyarsa. But the deathless tutelary spirit who rules the *hrossa*, *sorns*, and *pfifltriggi* has guided his planet for all of its millions of years of existence. Lewis implies, particularly in *That Hideous*

Strength, that each planet in the solar system has its Oyarsa, and the history of the Bent One indicates that they are free beings with moral choice. In the postscript Ransom indicates that Oyarsa and his *eldils* are probably of a different order of heavenly beings from the angels and archangels which are associated with Christian thought. He suggests (as does Milton) that biblical angels may be members of a military order on guard against the evil devices of Satan.

But on Malacandra, Oyarsa rules. Each species regards him as the viceroy of Maleldil, whom it is their duty and delight to serve. The happy relationship between ruler and subject is indicated by Hyoi's simile in describing the great moment in his life when he stood on the shore of Balki, a day, he says, that comes only once, "like love, or serving Oyarsa in Meldilorn."

The relationship is not only happy; it is fundamental to the proper operation of the universe. Lewis speaks often in his writings of the importance of subjection—that it is man's refusal to obey accredited authority which has created most of the misery in this world. He firmly believed in democratic government, but only because depraved man cannot be trusted to rule his fellows. The virtue of democracy is in the reins and bridles with which it harnesses its rulers. But such an inefficient system is not necessary in a sinless society. Elsewhere he speaks of the appropriateness of certain parts of the Anglican liturgy where the priest stands and the layman kneels. The old *sorn* at the evening interrogation of Ransom speaks for Lewis when he says that "there must be rule," that beasts must be ruled by *hnau* (that is, rational animals) and *hnau* by *eldila* and *eldila* by Maleldil.

Of course, rule does not mean slavery. One writer objected that the creatures of Malacandra have no freedom of choice because Oyarsa allows no evil to grow there. But such logic would lead one to believe that the residents of the New Jerusalem are not free moral agents because there is in that city nothing "that defileth, neither whatsoever worketh abomination, or maketh a lie." Lewis gives us a picture of creatures at the end of a long history, most of which is hidden

41

from us. Whatever their past, they have learned obedience and have found fulfillment in subjection to ordained authority.

The Malacandrians are also agreed in their attitude toward death and toward sex. Assuming, as we must, that the *hrossa* are representative of all, we can conclude that the fear of death does not exist on the planet. For the unexpected death of Hyoi there is mourning and a sense of loss. But for Hyoi himself it is a culmination. He had told Ransom that death is the best drink of all, and now it comes just after he has become a *hnakrapunt,* an accomplishment he had wanted all his life. Like Lewis in his last days, Hyoi had done all he wanted to do and was ready to go. His going carried with it no sense of incompleteness. Oyarsa also expresses a concept which Lewis elaborates elsewhere when he says that under the influence of the Bent One the people of Earth waste their lives flying from what they know will overtake them in the end.

It is also from Hyoi that we learn of the sexual norms and practices on this planet. Lewis was convinced that the sexual drive in man had become abnormal. He believed that man's excessive sexuality is the result of the fall, that our problems of overpopulation were not a part of God's original intention for man. The instinct has been perverted by sin. In *Mere Christianity* he points out that if there were a country in which people gathered together to see a gradual unveiling of a mutton chop, we would conclude that something was wrong with their appetite for food. And so the strip tease act, in which a girl undresses on the stage, is one of the many evidences that the sexual appetite has overflowed the stream bed of its original purpose.[8]

It is probable that Lewis's ideal for the human race is to be found in the restrained sexual drive of the Malacandrians, whose continence and monogamy apparently keep the population stable. Love, says Hyoi, takes one's whole life, from the youthful search for a mate to the meditation and poetry that comes in the later years. The begetting of young is but one link in love's chain.

In a letter to a friend written after the publication of *Out of the Silent Planet,* Lewis reported that of about sixty reviews only two appeared to recognize in the Bent One anything more than a creature invented by the author. They failed to see the biblical implications of the fall of the Bent One, the Oyarsa of Thulcandra, once brighter and greater than the Oyarsa of Malacandra, but now bound in the air of his own world after the great war in Heaven. The Bent One, of course, is Satan, the Prince of the Power of the Air, the Prince of Darkness, but once "Lucifer, son of the morning."

As he no longer moves freely in the heavens but is the prisoner of his own realm, he cannot communicate with other *eldila* who guide their planets in the Field of Arbol, and so Thulcandra is the silent planet. Although Oyarsa and his compeers have lost touch with their former colleague, they have heard strange rumors of what Maleldil has done to win the world back to Himself. Twice he tells Ransom that "it is a thing we desire to look into." This statement has a biblical allusion that readers often miss. In the first chapter of the First Epistle of Peter, the apostle is speaking of the prophets who foretold the sufferings of Christ and concludes the twelfth verse with the assertion, "which things the angels desire to look into."

In fact, Oyarsa admits that one of the reasons he was so eager to talk with someone from Thulcandra was because he wanted to hear the story of Earth. And when, after the interruption of Weston and Devine, he repeats his request, we must assume that Ransom tells him of the terrible things dared by Maleldil in wrestling with the Bent One. The heart of the matter must have been the incarnation and its significance, but perhaps he also told of the fall, the flood, the faith of Abraham, the law of Moses, the messianic songs of David and Isaiah; certainly of the babe at Bethlehem, the ministry and miracles, the crucifixion and its meaning, the resurrection and its hope; perhaps also of the Holy Spirit at Pentecost, and through Paul, and in the march of His church across the centuries into the citadels of Satan, in ghetto and jungle, in palace and parliament. We do not know what Ransom said, but when the afternoon conversation is over, Oyarsa says, "You have shown me more wonders than are known in the whole heaven."

VII.

IT REMAINS to say something of the theme as it relates to Weston as futurist. Lewis admitted that Weston represents the anti-Christian attitude which first stimulated his writing of the book. He says in a letter that the story grew out of the discovery that one of his students took the dream of interplanetary colonization seriously, and the realization that he represented thousands of people who regarded the perpetuating and improving of the human race as the complete meaning of the universe. They expected science to defeat death. Elsewhere Lewis also mentions Olaf Stapledon's *Last and First Men* and Haldane's *Possible Worlds* as contributing to his decision to write, because they seemed to regard future space travel as a certainty and to display "the desperately immoral outlook" which is ridiculed in the person of Weston.

The physicist's attitudes throughout the book reveal him to be so obsessed with a hope of the continuance of humankind in the future that he is willing to sacrifice any number of individuals in the present. We learn of this attitude very early. Simple-minded Harry is only an object which should be turned over to a laboratory for experimentation. Even Dr. Ransom can be sacrificed to his purposes because philology is a "useless" field of knowledge. His philosophy and set of values are just the opposite of those of Lewis. When Weston is asked for what purpose he had kidnapped Ransom, his answer is "small claims must give way to great." It is the reply of every tyrant who justifies his butcheries as reasons of state. We will see it reappearing in one form or another in the mouth of several of Lewis's villains.

Lewis did not believe there was any claim higher than that of the individual. He constantly criticizes the constructions of men's minds which are made to appear more significant than each single man. In *The Problem of Pain* he points out that one cannot add up the sum total of pain in the world. Pain is experienced individually and is limited to the individual. And in the great hymn of praise at the end of *Perelandra* he says that when Maleldil "died in the Wounded

World He died not for men, but for each man. If each man had been the only man made, He would have done no less."

Of course, the place where Weston's philosophy and purpose is most clearly stated is at Meldilorn when he stands a captive before Oyarsa. Here he declares his goal—the immortality and supremacy of the human race throughout the universe. Lewis makes it sound ridiculous by translating the high sounding phrases into literal and concrete words, but a careful examination of the speech shows it to express a death-dealing philosophy which says that might makes right and that man, as nature's greatest accomplishment, must annihilate all other creatures which are barriers to his conquest of the stars. The speech also represents those whose desperate hope is that man will somehow through science be able to defeat the inevitable, the end of the human race in this physical universe. Such a "scientific" hope, Lewis says elsewhere, is a real rival of Christianity.

But Lewis satirizes Weston's speech by having Ransom turn such vague words as *life* into real entities like *living creatures*. Sometimes this semantic technique reveals the ruthlessness of the words, and sometimes it shows the statements to be nonsense—even untranslatable nonsense, such as Weston's, "Life is greater than any system of morality." Ransom makes a noble attempt but finally gives up. "I cannot say what he says, Oyarsa, in your language."

But the greed, the hatred, the deification of material progress, which Weston and Devine represent are, as Lewis says, but the characteristics of an evil pocket in a good universe. Beyond the dark bastions of the Silent Planet the Field of Arbol is bathed in joy and love. All creatures know that it is not Maleldil's way to make a world last forever. But this is not a cause for grief or fear. Beyond death lies the joy of a better and brighter life. In words from the elegy sung for the dead *hrossa*:

> This is the second life, the other beginning. Open, oh coloured world, without weight, without shore. You are second and better; this was first and feeble. . . . First were the darker, then the brighter. First was the worlds' blood, then the suns' brood.

CHAPTER 3

PERELANDRA

I.

OF LEWIS'S narrative volumes *Perelandra* was his favorite, although he believed that *Till We Have Faces* was his best. His friend, Roger Green, reports that walking with him one evening at Oxford when Venus was the brightest star in the sky, Lewis, gazing at the planet, cried out, "Perelandra!" with the sort of enchantment of a man who had been there.[1]

And for many readers the golden sky, the rainbow-colored storms, the paradisaical floating islands are a reality which no amount of scientific evidence that Venus is too hot to be habitable will destroy. Peter Beagle said of Middle Earth, the location of *The Lord of the Rings,* that Tolkien did not invent it; he discovered it.[2] And that is the way we feel about Perelandra. The vivid sights and smells and sounds with which Lewis has baptized the senses of our imagination surely must have a real existence somewhere.

Although the second story of the space trilogy shows

clearly its relationship to *Out of the Silent Planet*, it creates in the reader a more intense sense of otherness, of far countries and strange airs. It is more obviously theological than the trip to Malacandra and, in fact, contains more of Lewis's basic Christian beliefs than are to be found in any of his other works of fiction. Also, the characters are more clearly defined and the plot more tightly structured.

Perhaps the most obvious difference between the two stories is in the arrangement of the action. In *Perelandra*, although there are journeys as in the preceding tale, most of them are not exploited for purposes of the plot. Ransom's trip to Perelandra and back gives us no feeling of suspense or even of movement as did those to Malacandra and back. The reader can only identify with him at the beginning and end of each trip. And after arrival on the planet his first actions are those of exploration and discovery, rather than movement toward any goal. In fact, the only journey which is used in the plot to bring about its development is that which takes place after the turning point of the story. The pursuit of the Unman, the climb up through the bowels of the mountain, and the further climb to the Hill of Life is a journey which comprises an important part of the plot. But other than that, the action consists of confrontation of persons and intellectual or moral decisions.

The best way to demonstrate the symmetry of the story is to begin in the middle and note how each half is balanced against the other. The heart of the narrative is the temptation of the Lady. There are three temptations (which we will discuss later) recorded in chapters eight, nine, and ten—the exact center of the seventeen chapters of the book. The chapter prior to this action (seven) contains Ransom's debate with Weston regarding spirits and ends with Weston's possession. Chapter eleven, which follows the central action, relates Ransom's debate with God regarding responsibility and ends with Ransom's submission. The four chapters prior to Weston's appearance (three to six) are chapters of exploration and discovery of the land and the Lady. The four chapters following Ransom's submission (twelve to fifteen) include the

47

struggle, pursuit, and destruction of the Un-man and the exploration and discovery of more of the planet. This leaves us with two chapters of introduction and two of conclusion. The former begins with an attack on Lewis by the evil *eldila* of our planet, and the latter ends with a hymn in which *eldil* and man join their voices in praise of Maleldil. Structural balance is one of the striking characteristics of the plot.

The first significant action of the book is the demonic attempt to frighten Lewis, the narrator, away from a meeting with Ransom. As the machinations of Satan and his followers are an important theme of the story, this early skirmish prepares the reader for what follows. Ransom is too sophisticated in such matters by this time to be susceptible to such an attack, and so Lewis makes it fall upon himself. It gives a sense of cosmic struggle to the action and makes the reader aware of more than human participants. The fact that the attack suddenly ceases after Lewis fights his way through into the cottage where the mighty *eldil* of Malacandra waits shows that the supernatural is represented on both sides of the struggle.

The four chapters of exploration and discovery would be a serious defect in the action if the setting were almost anywhere on this earth. Few writers could retain our interest for that long without the introduction of some element of conflict. But Lewis so successfully confronts Ransom with surprising red dragons, yellow wallabies, watery steeds, and a very puzzling green lady, that he creates in the reader the same wonder which the protagonist feels.

But the first serious conflict on the planet takes place after the appearance of Weston. The shock of danger is immediately felt when Ransom is forced at the point of a revolver to remain with the physicist. But soon it is apparent that the conflict is to be one of minds and wills rather than of bodies. In fact, this is the essence of the struggle for the next five chapters as Ransom is confronted by Weston's new philosophy, the Lady is tempted to break the law of Maleldil, and Ransom shrinks from the divine commission to destroy the Un-man.

Not much need be said about the point of view of the story, because it is almost identical with that of *Out of the Silent Planet*. Ransom is the central intelligence, and the story is told in the third person. Perhaps the only significant difference is that here the focus shifts more sharply to other characters. The events are still filtered through the same senses and consciousness, but Ransom is not always our chief concern. At times the Lady and the Un-man hold our attention, although Ransom is still the vehicle by which we are aware of them.

Another difference from the narration of the trip to Malacandra is that Lewis uses the first person technique at the beginning rather than at the end and continues in chapter two to tell the story of Ransom's return from Perelandra. So, we have first the beginning, then the end, and last the middle. The author may have felt that the last chapter and the postscript in *Out of the Silent Planet* were an anticlimax and so placed Ransom's return to earth ahead of the main story in *Perelandra*. Certainly it would be difficult to improve on the final chapter with its soaring paean of praise to God and the moving farewell of Tor and Tinidril to Ransom.

The otherness, the strangeness of its quality of life, which Lewis believed to be an essential ingredient of this type of fiction, is well illustrated in the descriptions. If we could say that the strangeness of Malacandra is in its austere perpendicularity, the otherness of Perelandra is in its sensuous intensity. Ransom's first sensations on the planet demonstrate that intensity. When drinking from its ocean waters, he almost feels that he has met Pleasure for the first time. When his eyes adjust to his surroundings, he catches first the muted, golden iridescence of the sky, the emerald green of the wave shading to a bottle green and then deepening to a blue at the bottom of the wave. The blue-to-violet lightning flash, the enormous purple clouds—all are a part of a visual intensity which is dazzling. In his first five minutes on the planet and on the first five pages describing his experience there are colors and flashes, rainbows and multicolored steam, gleaming water and flaming transparencies which

49

employ more than thirty-five colorful nouns and adjectives to project their vividness on the screen of the reader's imagination.

Ransom's first taste of food has the same sensuous intensity. The yellow gourds create a gustatory sensation of delight beyond description. It is a pleasure so ecstatic that on earth wars would have been fought and kingdoms sold for it. And what can be more intense an experience for the olfactory nerves than the bubble trees whose shower of mist so fills the nostrils and stimulates the consciousness that the surroundings take on new richness and brilliance? And for the ear even the thunder laughs rather than roars. Later the singing beasts with their cello-like voices make their contribution to that intensity and sense of otherness.

But the experience of pleasure so intense as to be unearthly is not to be traced only to individual and separate senses. Ransom feels an exuberance, a prodigality of pleasure, which seems to be communicated through all the senses at once. The garden-planet pours forth its wealth with Edenic guiltlessness and the very air breathes delight. Although in no sense sinful, Venus is a sensuous lady.

Not only in the appeal to the senses, however, are we aware of the unearthly. The supernatural is introduced early, in the attack of the dark *eldila* upon Lewis and in the ghostly emanation by which he is conscious of the presence of the tutelary spirit of Malacandra in the darkness of the cottage. On Perelandra itself, Ransom's intuitive impressions of something restraining his action, of echoes giving him reverberations of vast import to certain sayings of the Lady, and of divine promptings which he struggles to avoid and then to which he finally submits increase our sense of a more than natural atmosphere. But perhaps most astonishing of all is the Lady's almost Enoch-like walk with Maleldil, which gives her extrasensory understanding of events and creatures beyond her experience. Her sudden awareness of the furry creatures on Malacandra, her quiet obedience when divinely directed to desist in her efforts to draw blood from her knee— such guidance indicates an awesome level of communion far above the inner promptings of the most saintly of earthborn creatures.

II.

ALTHOUGH THE point of view from which Lewis tells the story limits the delineation of character to traits in Ransom and those which Ransom can observe, the limitation is actually an advantage. We participate with the protagonist in both the puzzlement and the awe as the nature and position of the Lady is unfolded. And the restriction of Ransom's understanding of the Un-man is essential to the impact of this monster. An author-omniscient angle of narration which would allow Lewis to enter and describe the demonic mind would destroy part of its terror, as well as being, perhaps, a literary task beyond the power of man to accomplish.

Of the two Earth-dwelling characters one shows a happy improvement in virtues displayed in the preceding story, and the other reveals a tragic dedication to vices hardly noticeable before. As we have noted, *Out of the Silent Planet* records Ransom's triumph over paralyzing fear and the acquisition of a respectable degree of fortitude. On Perelandra he demonstrates that this virtue has become a permanent part of his nature. Although fear touches him at times, it never turns him from his purpose. His head remains clear when he is confronted with Weston's revolver; once he determines to fight the Un-man, he goes to the task without flinching; and when facing almost certain destruction in the thundering death of the breakers against the cliff, he displays an exhilarating courage which could have strengthened almost anyone but the pseudo-Weston whimpering at his side.

He also resists the three attacks which the Un-man makes on his mind. These attempts to reduce Ransom to a doubting coward suggest that Lewis believed that man's spiritual, emotional, and physical state can make him vulnerable to the world of evil. The first attack shows how one's

51

own spirit can open the door. He rebels at being placed in this contest with a supernatural being, and immediately doubt sweeps over him like a huge wave, and the arguments of the Un-man seem the deepest truth. The second attack, showing the place of emotion, occurs at the end of the pursuit over the sea when Ransom is already depressed by the immense solitude of the watery wastes of this part of the planet. The third invasion of his mind is felt in the chamber of fire when he is physically exhausted by his climb up through the subterranean blackness of the mountain. Although these attacks cause him discomfort, they do not stagger his faith.

The gist of the Un-man's argument is that things are not what they seem. We who are living think that life is the ultimate reality. But this is only appearance. Below the thin rind of life are the decay of the grave and the lightless miles of Earth's lifeless core. That is where reality actually is. In an essay called "Behind the Scenes"[3] Lewis discusses this question. Are the backstage realities of canvas and paint what are important, or is the play, which they make possible, the essence of the theater? A scientific description of hearing would talk about air waves and nerve reactions, but one listening to Beethoven's *Ninth Symphony* would hardly call that the ultimate reality. Here as elsewhere Lewis takes the position that although scientific fact about nature may be a reality, it is not the only reality and may not be the most important.

Ransom's debate with God in chapter eleven presents the necessary justification of the physical struggle which follows. Do the moral issues of a world hang on the outcome of a boxing match? In order to convince the reader that this is *not* what he is saying, Lewis allows us to hear Ransom make the same objection and finally admit that for the Lady the moral issue has been settled. She had stood the test. His job is to remove the personified malice. He is "the way of escape" promised to those who are tempted. It might be added that this chapter increases the suspense of the story as Ransom projects on his own imagination the horrible picture of what he expects the outcome of the fight to be.

Although when we meet Ransom in the third book we discover that his interplanetary travels have worked a considerable change in his character, throughout this narrative he is still the Cambridge don who, as we noted in discussing the previous story, has much in common with the Oxford don who is his creator. He even acts, at times, just as we imagine Lewis would have done in a similar circumstance—such as reciting as much as he could remember of the *Iliad*, the *Odyssey*, and other classics while he waited fruitlessly in the underground cavern for the morning to dawn.

Of Weston our conclusions are somewhat limited because he appears in only one chapter, during which he argues with Ransom concerning things spiritual. After his invasion by the demonic power, his significance in the story becomes almost nonexistent. It is true that he seems to be allowed to reappear on the surface of consciousness two or three times later, but this may be only a Satanic imitation, as it almost certainly is at the end of the pursuit over the sea. But during most of chapter seven Weston is Weston. He shows much of the vulgar bullying in conversation which characterized him from the first word that he uttered when Ransom interrupted the attempt to kidnap simple-minded Harry. But on Perelandra there is an added unpleasantness. Ransom characterizes him as a monomaniac pursuing a fixed idea.

On Malacandra he appears as a complete materialist. He denies the existence of both Maleldil and the Bent One. The only reality which he admits is that of matter. And the only matter which he values is that of some future race which has descended from man. But a transformation takes place before he arrives on Perelandra. The philosophy which he espouses now is pantheism, a belief in a single pervading spirit which inhabits all things.

There are many shades and hues of pantheism. There is the variety which deifies nature, but, as illustrated in the poetry of Wordsworth, concentrates on the beautiful and beneficial aspects of nature and ignores the fact that in the jungle nature is "red in tooth and claw." At the opposite end of the spectrum is the pantheism which insists that the cancer cell is as much an expression of the divine spirit as the violet and that the special value man puts upon himself grows out of a narrow and provincial view. It is this latter conception of a blind spirit of life which produces all things and plays no favorites which seems to be closest to Weston's position. He speaks of it as "a great, inscrutable Force, pouring up into us from the dark bases of being."

In *Miracles* Lewis speaks of life-force worship as the modern, western type of nature-religion. The phrase in Weston's remarks which classifies him is "emergent evolution." It is the belief most clearly stated by the French philosopher, Henri Bergson, that inherent in matter and impelling it is a force or spirit (he called it *elan vital*) which causes all life forms to evolve. And so Weston admits that it would have been wrong for him to have liquidated the Malacandrians. They too are a product of the life-force. His mission now is to work for this spirit, to spread spirituality.

Thus Weston seems to think of himself as a sort of missionary for the life-force. But we know from the tragic ending of his conversation with Ransom that he is a dupe, a victim of the forces not of life but of death. The supernatural guidance of which he boasts, that helped him perfect his knowledge of the language, was simply a part of the satanic plot to make him a vehicle for the invasion of the planet and a puppet for the attack upon the innocence of Tinidril. There are early hints of what has inspired his life-force philosophy. He speaks of "the final vortex of self-thinking, self-originating activity." A vortex sucks everything into itself, and Lewis elsewhere refers to the legions of Hell as life-devouring and life-destroying. In the above statement there may also be a Miltonic touch, for Milton's devils claim to be self-originating and not created by God.

As Weston continues to talk, Ransom begins to suspect the truth and becomes frightened at the supernatural fire with which Weston seems to have been playing. And there are hints that Weston's traffic with the dark powers of Earth has caused a deterioration of his spirit even before the satanic possession takes place. The senile, cackling laugh; the fixed, twisted grin; the howl of protest; the face the color of putty—all point tragically to a person who has been almost used up by the evil power whose last use will destroy him. Weston's employment of words like "surrender" and "commitment" is a signal that the possession is about to take place. His invitation is all that is necessary to complete the disaster. On Malacandra the physicist is, at times, a comic figure. Here his role is only tragic, and Ransom shows nothing but concern and compassion for him.

Lewis's reason for attaching the life-force philosophy to Weston probably grew out of his awareness of the thought currents of his own day. He believed that emergent evolution was one of the dominant religious heresies of the twentieth century, that the old pantheism of ancient nature religions had reappeared in a scientific costume and presented itself as a brand new idea. To say that he thought it his duty to point out both the fallacy of its logic and the pagan origin of its ideas is to describe the motivation of much of Lewis's writing.

III.

THE UN-MAN is another matter. Let me emphasize that he is a completely different person from Weston. Some writers persist in talking about Ransom's fight with Weston. But the Un-man is literally a demon incarnate. Weston's body is simply the machine through which he operates. It seems to be so completely dominated by Satan or one of his powerful followers that it is indeed an Un-man, that is, not a man but a mannequin. The soul of Weston seems to have been driven down into some corner of unconsciousness while his body is operated like a puppet. The voice is not his own, but does the bidding of the mighty spirit whose evil intentions it serves.

That Lewis did not intend us to think of this spirit as an ordinary devil is certain. It is no apprentice Wormwood fresh from the Tempter's Training College for Young Devils. It boasts of having been in the eternal councils of Deep Heaven; it remembers and utters the Aramaic cry of Christ on the cross; and twice Lewis suggests that it is Satan himself. Ransom tells the Lady that this creature once before on Earth stood as he stands now talking to the woman. And, in addition to this Genesis allusion, there is a Miltonic one, for the

Un-man squats down close to the head of the sleeping Lady just as Satan squatted in the form of a toad at the ear of the sleeping Eve in *Paradise Lost*.

Through the Un-man Lewis expresses his ideas of the nature of evil. As the first temptation takes place at night and Ransom arrives in the darkness, he does not see what has become of the body of Weston until the next day. He finds the Un-man at the end of the path of mutilated frogs and realizes that here is not Weston but a walking corpse. The dead stare, the devilish smile, the terrible power of the face, give Ransom his first insight into the character of whole-hearted evil. Lewis presents the dark *eldils* of Earth in all three books of the space trilogy as being life-destroying. The Un-man constantly demonstrates this characteristic when out of sight of the Lady. When no animal is within its tearing clutch, it cuts the rinds of plants with its nails or even pulls up turf. It is also so completely evil that intelligence is an exterior thing which it uses as a tool in tempting the Lady but seems to lay aside when not so employed. Its petty obscenities seem more representative of its essence than its mental faculties.

It might also be observed that the end of the Un-man in the central fires of the planet seems quite appropriate. It was not Lewis's practice to use symbols, and we should not try to make more of it than he intended, but the freeing of Weston's body from the control of its terrible possessor by committing that vehicle to the flames seems particularly fitting. Although made from a recognizable human being, the Un-man contributes materially to the sense of otherness in the story.

In the meeting of the Un-man and the Lady, we have the confrontation of otherworldly monstrosity and otherworldly perfection. For the Lady, or Tinidril, as we later learn to call her, is herself no earth maiden. Although humanoid in form and rational in mind, she is not recognizably human. There is an otherness and an innocence about her of which we know nothing by experience. In a letter to a friend while he was composing *Perelandra* Lewis commented on the difficulty of creating such a person, and, in fact, wondered if what he had in mind was a possible literary creation. For he envisioned her as "in some ways like a Pagan goddess and in other ways like the Blessed Virgin."[4] Whether Lewis was satisfied with his portrait or not, I do not know, but the queenly radiance, the naive joy of life, the devotion to Maleldil, and love of all that Maleldil has made is woven into an integrated person who is very convincing. She seems just right to be the Queen and Lady-mother of a bright and sinless paradise planet.

Her speech is appropriately metaphorical, full of waves and fruits and animals to illustrate and clarify her ideas. And, although the children are "not yet," her maternal instincts seem to express themselves as she makes the beasts "older" every day. In fact, at one point her words seem to echo the words of another mother, as, after saying, "I am the Mother," she praises Maleldil who "will make me to be blessed" as the future rolls toward the present. The passage suggests the Magnificat of Mary, whose motherhood would make her also "blessed."

It is significant that we know very little of her appearance. While visual details of the Un-man and various animals are given, we do not know the color of her hair or eyes, whether she is tall or short, or any other physiological detail except that her skin is green and that she is naked. That last detail probably explains the absence of the others. Lewis shows considerable tact in presenting Tinidril's nakedness to the reader without forcing him to examine it too closely. And to Ransom her personal radiance is so dazzling at times that he cannot look at her. Desire is "a thousand miles away from his experience."

Perhaps of greatest interest is the unfolding maturity of Tinidril. She appears as if fresh from the hand of the creator, her potentials not yet realized, but without any hint of the incompleteness of the child. Even in Ransom's first interview with her she becomes "older" as she discovers that she can explore her own self-consciousness and think about her own thoughts, stepping into the "alongside" as if she were another person. And in the second interview she discovers with a feeling both of delight and terror that she has free choice and walks with Maleldil freely, "not even holding hands." Lewis gives no hint of how long it was since Tor and Tinidril had awakened to rational life, but when we first meet the Lady, the umbilical cord seems to have been not quite cut. It is almost as if before our eyes the separate personhood of Tinidril emerges, perhaps brought to completion, ironically, by the very temptation of the Un-man.

IV.

THAT TEMPTATION, as we have already noted, comes in the exact middle of the book. So here is the very heart of the story. But let us first be reminded of another temptation which ended disastrously.

> Now the serpent was more subtile than any beast of the field which the Lord God had made. And he said unto the woman, Yea, hath God said, Ye shall not eat of every tree of the garden?
> And the woman said unto the serpent, We may eat of the fruit of the trees of the garden:
> But of the fruit of the tree which *is* in the midst of the garden, God hath said, Ye shall not eat of it, neither shall ye touch it, lest ye die.
> And the serpent said unto the woman, Ye shall not surely die:
> For God doth know that in the day ye eat thereof, then your eyes shall be opened, and ye shall be as gods, knowing good and evil.
> And when the woman saw that the tree *was* good for food, and that it *was* pleasant to the eyes, and a tree to be desired to make *one* wise, she took of the fruit thereof, and did eat, and gave also unto her husband with her; and he did eat. (Gen. 3:1-6)

There are several ways to interpret this passage, but if there is a parallel between the Genesis account and the temptation of Tinidril, Lewis probably interpreted it in this way:

1) The tree was good for food—an appeal to reason. If it was not poisonous, as perhaps they had supposed, why shouldn't it be eaten? It is reasonable to eat that which is edible.

2) The fruit was pleasant to the eyes—an appeal to the imagination. A bright image of forbidden delight, if held too long, can be very seductive.

3) It was desirable to make one wise—an appeal to an enhanced self-image. What a great person I would be if I had this knowledge in my possession.

As Lewis is not retelling the Genesis account, we need not expect all the details of the two stories to be similar—in fact, one ends tragically and the other victoriously. But we do find a parallel in the threefold temptations of Eve and of Tinidril, although the order is slightly different. The Un-man first tells the Lady that Maleldil has not forbidden her "to think about dwelling on the Fixed Land." Here is the first temptation—the appeal to the imagination (the second temptation of Eve). Imagine doing what is forbidden. Then he points out that if she and the King lived on the Fixed Land, they would never be parted as they now have been—the forbidden thing is desirable. And again she is reminded that Maleldil has not forbidden them to think about that which is desirable. It might be something out of which a story could be made.

Lewis here, perhaps, has in mind Christ's warnings against the evil imaginings of the heart. A person who hoards lust in his heart and builds pictures out of it is guilty of adultery. A person who hoards hate of his brother and builds pictures out of it is guilty of murder. A meditation upon the desirability of sin leads one dangerously close to the act of sin. So, the Un-man holds up to her a fruit that is pleasing to the eyes, hoping to cause her to disobey by corrupting her imagination. But the Un-man's machinations come to nothing, for Tinidril's purity and innocence turn his description of the greatness of the daughters of Eve, who have surpassed their mother, into a psalm of praise to Maleldil. She rejoices that perhaps her daughters will be greater than she. Her imagination, instead of being corrupted, is delighted at the thought of relinquishing her position as Queen and Lady to descendants who will exceed her as much as she does the beasts. And so her selfless love defeats him, and the first temptation fails.

The second one, in chapter nine, is like the first appeal to Eve—the tree was good for food—the appeal to man's reason. The Un-man argues that the command not to live on the

Fixed Land is not reasonable, and therefore is meant to be disobeyed. But he approaches the temptation in a very subtle manner.

He first emphasizes the importance of being "older," "young" and "old" in this context meaning immature and mature, ignorant and wise. Maleldil, he says, desires that she be "older" and points out that becoming "older" will mean an independence from Maleldil. A refusal of independence and a dependent obeying would be a sort of disobeying. And as Ransom admits to himself, much the Evil One says is true, even though used for malicious ends. If she is to be more than a glove on God's hand, bending, turning, pointing as his fingers move, she must be free to choose—to walk with God or to walk away from Him. Free creatures are separate from their Creator. Ransom realizes that as Tinidril matures she will become more independent and will more freely bestow her love on Maleldil, on the King, on the beasts, and on all creation.

But the Un-man's aim is not really independence, but disobedience, and so his appeal to the Lady is to be independent and disobey the law because it is unreasonable. Maleldil has given an unreasonable command; therefore, he wishes it to be broken so that she will be really separate from Him. Of course, if Tinidril really thought that this was the will of Maleldil, she would not be disobeying in doing it, but merely mistaken. But the subtlety of the attack is in the Un-man's appeal for her to set up her own reason as a god to be her guide. He says that the truth is coming to her through her own reason, that to be fully herself she must stand up in her own reason and courage even against Maleldil. The Fixed Land, he says, is a test. To become an independent creature she must disobey the law which forbids living there.

It is at this point that Ransom makes his first significant contribution to the debate. He argues that the command may have been given, not so that it would be disobeyed, but so that it could be obeyed independently. Maleldil's other commands appear reasonable and so are obeyed not only because they are His will but because they also seem good to her. Only here can she freely obey in love simply because it is His command. Here Lewis expresses in narrative form one of his profound convictions. The person who is committed to God must trust Him in the dark, when he does not see the reason. When there is nothing but the clear command to go, to do, to speak, to be silent, here, he says, is where love can best express itself. Ransom's statement effectively answers the arguments of the second temptation, and Tinidril immediately recognizes it as the best thing said so far. She sees that although she cannot walk out of Maleldil's will, she can walk out of her own will by obeying a command that seems to have no reason.

The third temptation, in chapter ten, is like the appeal to Eve that the fruit was desirable to make one wise—to make one like the gods, as the serpent told her. And it is here, in the inward look, the view of the self, that the Un-man makes his most potent attack. The innumerable stories he tells of heroic queens who had suffered much, had been maligned and persecuted, but had been vindicated by their great self-sacrifice for children or lovers or country are all aimed toward one purpose. The Un-man is attempting to create an image rather than an idea—an image in Tinidril of herself as a noble and self-sacrificing queen who will dare great deeds on her own. By turning her eyes inward to a heroic picture of what she might be, he hopes to draw her into the greatest of all the deadly sins—pride.

The episode of the feathered robes and the mirror is, of course, a part of this third temptation. In the effort to make her wish to be a heroine, the Un-man's appeal to human vanity in exterior appearances is only a device. He displays for Tinidril's admiration the reflection of her loveliness in the mirror with the intent of awakening in her the much more damaging admiration of herself as a great soul. If such a self-centered desire to seize a grand role in the drama of her world can be generated, persuading her that disobedience is a part of that role will not be difficult. As Ransom realizes, the Un-man is trying to create in her mind a theater in which a dramatic image of herself can play the leading part. For this external and phantom self he has already written the script.

The expression of pride by a dramatization of self, Lewis

believed, is a sin which takes many forms, but which can always be traced back to the same source—a desire for superiority over others. He discusses it in a number of his works and illustrates it in several of his fictional characters. We will note some of them when we examine *The Great Divorce*.

But the third temptation of Tinidril goes on and on until Ransom realizes that although the Lady has repelled the Evil One up to this point, the situation is now not a temptation of the will, but a third degree, in which flesh and blood must eventually be worn down. The thought, "This can't go on," in the end leads Ransom to face and finally accept his duty. But that is another chapter.

So, this is the temptation of the Lady of the Morning Star, with some significant parallels to the temptation of the Lady of the Silent Planet. In the last chapter Perelandra is referred to as "The Morning Star which He promised to those who conquer," an allusion to the statement in the second chapter of Revelation. Certainly Tinidril, as an overcomer, receives her rightful place as Queen of that planet.

V.

OF THE testing of Tor, the King, we have only his own brief report. Apparently, in a vision he saw the Queen tempted, but did not see her victorious. The choice which lay before him was to obey his affections and go with Tinidril if she succumbed to the Un-man or to remain faithful to Maleldil and obey his command. In the Genesis account we are not told how the appeal was made to Adam; only that the woman gave the forbidden fruit to him, "and he did eat." It is likely that Lewis was again influenced by Milton in his treatment of Tor. Milton makes Adam completely aware of the enormity of Eve's sin, but because of his infatuation for her, unwilling to give her up:

> ... for with thee
> Certain my resolution is to Die;
> How can I live without thee, how forgo
> Thy sweet Converse and Love so dearly joined, ...

And so Milton comments,

> ... he scrupl'd not to eat
> Against his better knowledge, not deceiv'd,
> But fondly overcome with Female charm.[5]

And Tor also feels as if giving up Tinidril will tear him in half. They are, indeed, "one flesh." In this crucible of decision he learns of moral choice, of its anguish and joy. In the end he decides that if half of a man turned into earth, the other half must still follow Maleldil.

Until the last chapter we know nothing of the King except that he exists. But in the twenty some pages in which he appears, he is an impressive and majestic figure. What did Adam look like before the fall? The Genesis account tells us that God made man in His own image and gave him dominion over all the earth. Lewis seems to conclude that the first man must have been a more impressive person than that which the human race produces now after centuries of sin. But Tor was created after the incarnation, after Maleldil had come to Earth as a man. And so Lewis does not give us a picture of Adamic perfection but of what might be called Christly perfection. We are told that Maleldil never does the same thing twice. A man created in His image after the incarnation would be different from one created before. And so Tor is an image, a copy of Christ—"an echo, a rhyme, an exquisite reverbation of the uncreated music prolonged in a created medium."

Tor is also Oyarsa. He appears on the Hill of Life to receive from the *eldil* who had been Oyarsa of the planet for many millenniums the office of supreme ruler of Perelandra. As such he must learn to steer his world through the heavens, make rain and fair weather, and cause the beasts to awake to a new life through their masters. Such a responsibility is consistent with Lewis's conviction that in unfallen man spirit and matter were in perfect harmony. He speaks in *Miracles* of the spirit being at home with the organism before the fall like a centaur whose human part is at home with the equine part. And in an interesting poem called "The Adam at Night,"[6] he says that before the fall Adam did not sleep at night but lay relaxed upon the earth and melted into its nature. He became aware as a part of his own consciousness of the growth of roots, the filling of wells, even of the deep bloom of gold and gems and the seething of the central fires. At one with his kingdom he guided it through the night, greeting "his planetary peers," Mars and Venus, as he passed between them. The poem was written after *Perelandra,* and it is probably correct to say that Adam is pictured here as Oyarsa, in much the same position as that of Tor on his young world.

And Tor is a prophet. He tells of the length of his own reign upon the planet. He speaks of the great war in the future when the hosts of God descend to do battle with the Bent Lord of Thulcandra and of the plagues and terror on land and sea as the forces of evil show themselves in their true light. He prophesies of the renewal of Earth after it is freed from its dark usurper and takes its rightful place in the heavens, no longer the Silent Planet. Much of this account is quite obviously drawn from the distress of nations described in the Book of Revelation. It is apparent that Lewis intends us to think of Tor as both the political and religious leader of the planet—a priest-king similar to Melchizedek, the ancient ruler whom the writer of Hebrews describes as a type of Christ.

VI.

IN ADDITION to the ideas which are illustrated in the testing of Tor and Tinidril, there are a few others which merit our attention. When Ransom asks the King how he came to know evil, since he had not been confronted by the Evil One, unexpectedly he laughs—a contagious laugh, in which the whole assembly of beasts and humans participate. But it is not one of amusement but of joy, for then he expresses a principle which Lewis believed to be fundamental to the relationship of all God's creatures. "The best fruits are plucked for each by some hand that is not his own." In a sermon called "The Grand Miracle"[7] Lewis points out the necessity of the incarnation to the Christian religion and states that vicariousness is a law of all creation—the natural as well as the spiritual. No one, he says, can exist on his own resources; one person always profits by the earnings of another. The highest form of this principle is in Christ's death for the sins of the world. But it is to be found everywhere. The fabric of indebtedness binds together man and beast and plant. Only God is debt free. As Tor says, "All is gift." He has come to his position of Oyarsa by the gift of Maleldil, but also by that of the *eldil,* by that of Ransom, that of his wife, and even that of the beasts and birds. The gift which he receives has been enriched by the love and labor of many hands. On the Silent Planet, he says, we must have justice for all because our selfish acts fall below justice. But that is not Maleldil's way. His acts are always above justice. His creatures are not rewarded according to their rights but according to His love.

Another idea is illustrated by the sense of restraint which Ransom feels several times during his first days on Perelandra. Experiencing the rapturous taste of the first yellow gourd causes him to reach for another, but something tells him he is neither hungry nor thirsty now and should not try to have again that delight. The same reprimand is felt as he thinks of repeating the exhilaration of the bubble trees and again when he discovers the "red hearts" among the berries which offer the pleasure of plain food. The desire to repeat a pleasure, to have something over again, to order one's own life according to one's own will, rather than letting time roll God's gifts toward us—this, Lewis believed, was a symptom of human waywardness.

This is related to the prohibition (which proves temporary) against living on the Fixed Land. In the early learning period the couple are taught to trust Maleldil for their daily needs by being kept on the unpredictable floating islands. Like the Israelites in the wilderness, who were not to gather more manna than they could use in one day but were to trust that God would provide for the morrow, Tor and Tinidril are forced to learn early that the will of Maleldil, though unknown, is better than the Fixed Land of their own plans for the future. As the Queen explains to Ransom in the last chapter, to wish to live on the Fixed Land would be to wish to control what time should roll toward us, "as if you gathered fruits together today for tomorrow's eating instead of taking what came." The scope and importance of this concept is indicated by the fact that Lewis describes Satan as the *eldil* who clung to the fruit desired and turned from the fruit given. He felt that this attitude was at the heart of all rebellion whether of men or devils. Tinidril speaks for Lewis when she says that "the fruit we are eating is always the best fruit of all." What can be better for the present than the gifts Maleldil sends for the present?

The hymn of praise at the end of the book in which the two *eldila*, Tor, Tinidril, and Ransom all participate gathers together and sums up much of the meaning not only of the book but of what might be called Lewis's cosmic view of reality. He says that each speech was like the parts of music in which all five of them contributed as instruments. So, it can quite properly be called a hymn. And he gives us the impression that it was divinely inspired, "like a wind blowing through five trees that stand together on a hill."

The hymn comes out of Ransom's troubled question to Tor's statement that our Earth was but a failure to begin, a false start. As an answer Tor requests that the *eldila* tell them of the Great Dance. Lewis felt that the word *dance* was a particularly appropriate image of the infinitely intricate movements of God's creation, each entity the center of God's purposes and, at the same time, a subordinate supporter of the rest. In *Miracles* he says, "the partner who bows to Man in one movement of the dance receives Man's reverence in another." And in *The Problem of Pain* he speaks of the eternal dance which "makes heaven drowsy with the harmony."

To Tor's statement that Earth was but a false start Ransom had said that Christians believe that the incarnation is the central happening of all happenings. Where, then, is the center? Are we, as some would tell us, in a remote corner of the universe, circling a small dying star, with vast stretches of empty space around us? Is the universe so inconceivably great that we could not possibly be in the eye of God? To such questions about overwhelming size and numbers, which someone has aptly called "cosmic intimidation," the hymn gives adequate answers.

The composition is made up of twenty short paragraphs each ending with "Blessed be He." Then, as if the composer turns from his pipe organ and begins to play a color organ, we "see" the Great Dance made up of intertwining cords and ribbons of light which finally blend into a simplicity beyond all comprehension. If it is proper to encapsulate such prose-poetry into phrases, we can list the themes of the twenty paragraphs as follows:

1. There is no beginning.
2. All is growth and change.
3. Each has a unique place in Maleldil's order.
4. Number and size are unimportant.
5. Each is related to all.
6. All is made for each.
7. The ancient worlds are at the center.
8. The Earth is at the center.
9. Perelandra is at the center.
10. The uninhabited places are at the center.
11. The dust is at the center.
12. All are at the center.
13. Maleldil is the center and circumference.
14. Each thing is the purpose of creation.
15. The Great Dance interlocks plans without number.
16. All things are infinitely necessary for each.
17. Nothing is necessary, but all is grace and pure bounty.
18. All is from and to Maleldil.
19. All is an infinitely intricate plan.
20. The incomprehensible is an image of the Father.

The specific answer to Ransom's question about cosmic intimidation is to be found in paragraph four. Number and

size are not important. We must not be intimidated by figures. God is the master of dimensions. All of Him is in the
smallest seed, and all of the heavens is within Him who is in
the seed. In a later book we will learn of a stable in which the
inside is bigger than the outside.

The answer to the question, "What is at the center?" is
that each is the central fact of creation. All is at the center
because wherever God is, there is the center, and God is
everywhere. Which stone in an arch is most important if the
removal of any one stone will cause the arch to collapse? Or
imagine a ball of glass with an intricate, geometric, intercon-
nected design covering the entire surface. Where is the center
of the design and where is its outside edge? So in the unfolding of God's creative purposes (the Great Dance), plans without number interlock, and nothing can be said to be there
simply for the use of something else. All is at the center.

But all is not comprehensible. The plans without number, the roads that seem to lead nowhere, the question
beyond the grasp of the mind of the greatest *eldil* are also part
of the plan. Without them "we should have in our minds no
likeness of the Abyss of the Father, into which if a creature
drop down his thoughts for ever he shall hear no echo return
to him. Blessed, blessed, blessed be He!"

CHAPTER 4
THAT HIDEOUS STRENGTH

I.

THE LAST story of the so-called space trilogy has little to do with space. It is earthbound. Its fascination for the reader is not in interplanetary journeys or extraterrestrial colors and tastes. It begins with the boredom of a faculty-meeting widow, portrays the plots and plans of college politicians, the infighting among the staff of a large institute, and, with poetic justice, ends one thread of the narrative with a massacre perpetrated by the animals that had been tortured for experimental purposes. Although Merlin, the wizard, rides out of Arthurian legend and into the story on a stormy night, he is dressed in a khaki coat, baggy trousers, and boots without toes. Even the appearance of the *eldils* from outer space is muted. Not once do we hear that eerie metallic voice "with no blood in it" of the mighty steersmen of the planets. It is true that the subtitle is "A Modern Fairy-Tale for Grown-Ups" and that in the preface Lewis calls the story a fantasy, but the fantastic in the story does not come from faraway planets, but from either Christian legend or the myths and folklore of our western culture.

The story is also different from the two other books of the trilogy in that it is considerably heavier with ideas. Behind it and formulating some of its themes are two important prose pieces—*The Abolition of Man,* a series of lectures which Lewis refers to in the preface, and "The Inner Ring," an address which is important to the understanding of the psychology of Mark Studdock. While Lewis spoke of *Perelandra* as being written primarily for his "co-religionists"—that is, Christians—*That Hideous Strength* is as much concerned with ethics as religion, and seems to be directed at both the university audience to whom Lewis addressed *The Abolition of Man* and those who listened to such radio talks as "Right and Wrong as a Clue to the Meaning of the Universe."

The structure of the story shows the careful organization which we noted in the other books. There are seventeen chapters, each divided into a varying number of sections or episodes. Of the eighty-five episodes in the book, Jane Studdock appears in thirty-three and Mark Studdock in thirty-four. The same balance is to be found in the presentation of the group that had collected around Ransom, which for convenience we will call the Company, and the group in the N.I.C.E. Although the latter is much larger than the Company, the number of characters in each which come into focus is exactly the same—nine, if we do not count Mark and Jane. On each side there is a supernatural possession—Alcasan and Merlin—and a characteristic relationship to animals; in one, ideal, in the other, devilish.

But a recognition of balance and order does not indicate plot movement. As the story opens, the quotation from the marriage ritual and Jane's bitter thoughts about it would suggest that the plot will be built around proper or improper marriage relationships. As a theme it cannot be ignored, for in the second episode we observe Mark moving away from Jane and further into college politics, while in the next-to-the-last episode of the book Mark is moving back to Jane, and in the last one she descends to the lodge and assumes a proper relationship in marriage. But although this is a theme in the story, and their marriage does become a factor in actions of both the N.I.C.E. and the Company, we can hardly say that it is a motivating force in the unfolding of most of the conflicts of the narrative.

Nor can we say that the struggle between the N.I.C.E. and the Company is the central plot. It is true that Ransom and his friends are increasingly aware of both the evil of the Institute and its purposes, but, until the arrival of Merlin, they seem to be merely waiting for orders, and even after his arrival the only one directly involved in the struggle is Merlin himself. Although the N.I.C.E. is aware that such a company exists and would gladly sweep it out of existence, they do not seem to be preparing for a head-on collision.

As we think of the efforts and actions of both Mark and Jane, we will notice that their tensions or conflicts usually grow out of the question of membership. Mark's delight at being received into the inner ring at Bracton, the fluctuations of his success with the inner ring at Belbury, Jane's reluctance to establish a relationship with the Company, and her exclusion from its councils after her desires have been reversed, all show a progression which is woven into the central action of the narrative.

The steps in Jane's story which progress toward resolution come earlier than those in Mark's, which, perhaps, suggests a strength in her character that her husband lacks. Her world is "unmade" when she meets Ransom, an event in the thirtieth episode, some time before the middle of the book. But it is not until the forty-fifth episode that her relationship to the Company is made clear as she puts herself "in the obedience" of Ransom, and, finally, in section sixty-six becomes a member of the body. The turning point in Mark's story is not in his acceptance by the N.I.C.E. but in his rejection of it. This takes place in the forty-eighth section as he faces imminent death and through it gains some self-knowledge and a sudden realization of the true nature of Belbury. The final resolution of this conflict and his escape from that point of no return through which members are committed to the world of evil is to be found in the seventieth section where he refuses to trample on the crucifix and with unconscious irony tells Frost, "It's all bloody nonsense, and I'm damned if I do any such thing."

II.

ANOTHER DIFFERENCE between this book and the previous ones is in its point of view. It would be impossible, of course, to use Ransom as the central intelligence in this story, not only because of his limited activity but also because action often is going on in two different places at the same time. And so the point of view is author-omniscient. As the god of the story (after all, he did create it), Lewis peers into his characters' minds, explains their motives and fears, shifts in a split second from one place to another, goes backward and forward in time, and even places the reader high in the air so that he can observe the movement of both Mark and Jane at the same time.

The number of episodes and characters require that the story be told by an omniscient author. But it is also a device which lends itself admirably to a story of ideas in which conflicting philosophies contribute to the action. The omniscient commentator can explain to the reader what would be awkward or even impossible otherwise.

However, Lewis uses his god-like powers with some restraint. Within each episode he often employs a central intelligence and uses his prerogatives of omniscience to peer into that one mind only. If it is an episode in Jane's story, he looks at the actions through Jane's eyes and does not shift from mind to mind as the episode develops. There are a few exceptions to this rule, but they are rare. Of the eighty-five sections of the book one is in the first person (Lewis's account of his visit to Bragdon Wood), forty-nine are told through the eyes and mind of a single central intelligence, and most of the remaining thirty-five are told objectively without an inner view of anyone. An example of the few exceptions is the confrontation between Cecil Dimble and Mark Studdock just before Mark's arrest. The inner feelings of each are revealed here. It is also significant that of the forty-nine episodes in which a single central intelligence is used, either Mark or Jane is that intelligence in forty-five of them. In one section each, Wither, Ransom, Feverstone, and Frost are so employed. Quite clearly, it is the inner life of Mark and Jane which Lewis is most concerned to present to the reader.

The one episode told in the first person, as in the other books, presents Lewis himself to the reader. But here again, there is a difference. Although Lewis corresponds with Ransom at the end of the first book, and acts as his assistant in the second, this third account in no way ties the author into the story. In fact, there is no hint here or elsewhere in the book that Lewis has ever been involved in the interplanetary activities of Elwin Ransom. The first-person device injects a brief narrative movement into the description of Bragdon Wood as the author walks through the college, into the Wood, and finally stops at Merlin's Well. His activities make an episode out of what would otherwise have been a static description. But the purpose of this passage is to introduce us to Bragdon Wood, to indicate something of its antiquity, and to prepare us for the waking of Merlin from his long sleep beneath the roots of its ancient trees. We need to have a picture of it in our minds because it is the background for several important activities in the story. Bracton College's decision to sell the Wood, the excavations by the N.I.C.E. (purportedly for building purposes but actually as a part of the search for Merlin's underground resting place), the dreams of Jane about Merlin—all are enhanced by the reader's image of the Wood.

The question of why Lewis appears only in this one unattached episode is answered by the point of view. One who can read the minds of all the characters and can reveal to us their secret councils cannot insert himself into the story without destroying our faith in his omniscience. He must be either human or divine; he cannot be both. In the other books, of course, Lewis is not omniscient. Ransom tells his story to Lewis, and Lewis tells it to us. As a flesh and blood storyteller whose sources are known, he can enter the story without creating a problem. But gods cannot take on the limitations of flesh without being bound by the laws of that flesh. As Lewis needs a god-like freedom in order to reveal many secrets to us beyond the ken of ordinary mortals, he has to speak from his literary heaven in order to accomplish these miracles.

III.

THE MATTER of geographical setting does not need to occupy much of our attention. Unlike the other stories the action is mostly indoors. There are some scenes where nature makes a contribution, such as the sunshine which breaks through the fog as Jane travels from the murk and gloom of Edgestow up the hill to the Manor at St. Anne's. The use of darkness and light to suggest the character of the two opposing groups is significant. But we should note that Lewis also uses darkness to suggest the mystery of the past, both in the description of Merlin's subterranean sleeping place and in the search for him through the woods at night. Most of the story, however, takes place in rooms—Jane's bedroom, the faculty room at Bracton College, the Director's room at the Manor, the various offices and quarters at Belbury.

Of greater interest in creating the background for the story is what might be called its atmosphere. The atmosphere of Belbury is one of intrigue, fear, ruthless cruelty, and behind it the dark machinations of what Frost calls the *macrobes*, but which we know as the fallen *eldila* of Earth, the followers of the Bent One. With the exception, however, of the control of the N.I.C.E. by these evil powers through the head of Alcasan and Wither's apparent ability to project the image of his person throughout the corridors and grounds of Belbury, the Institute does not appear to be any more than a particularly obnoxious modern organization bent upon the aggrandizement of power. Of course, the exceptions make all the difference, but the supernatural side of the Institute does not become apparent to the reader until late in the story. Up to this point the ugliness of Belbury seems to be an ordinary ugliness.

But we can hardly say that the Company at St. Anne's

gives us the same impression. The very first scene of the book introduces us to "the seer" and her dream of the heads of Alcasan and Merlin. Her lunch with the Dimbles brings out more comment about Merlin and King Arthur. We soon learn that she is a Tudor, a member of the royal Welsh line which claimed to be related to the legendary Arthur. In a dream she sees the murder of Hingest, who is perhaps descended from ancient Hengist, one of the leaders of the Anglo-Saxon hordes who made war upon Arthur.

From the Denistons we learn that Ransom has been left a fortune with the understanding that he take his sister's name. He is now the rich Mr. Fisher-King. To the reader acquainted with the Arthurian legends, this would have significant associations. The Fisher-King, sometimes called the Rich Fisher and sometimes the Grail King, is an important figure in the story of the Holy Grail, which is interwoven with the story of Arthur and his Round Table. The Fisher-King ruled at Carbonek, the castle where the Holy Grail resided. According to the legend the Grail was the cup which Christ used at the Last Supper and in which Joseph of Arimathea caught some of Christ's blood at the crucifixion. It appears miraculously at various places in the Arthurian stories, sometimes healing, sometimes feeding, sometimes causing dedication to a religious life. It should also be noted that, like Ransom, the Fisher-King has a wound which will not heal. In fact, he is sometimes referred to as the Wounded Fisher-King. And just as Ransom with his fortune feeds and houses the Company, the Holy Grail miraculously feeds a company who sit at the Fisher-King's table in Carbonek.

We are told that Mrs. Fisher-King, Ransom's sister, was from India and was the friend of a native Christian mystic called the Sura, who told of the danger which was impending in England. Lewis's use of India here may be simply to give the story an air of the mysterious, but it is true that in the eastern church (which did reach as far as India) Christ was sometimes referred to as the Fisherman, no doubt because of His call to Peter and his friends to become "fishers of men." It may be that Lewis believed that the figure of the Wounded Fisher-King came from the East. At least, the name associates

Ransom with the Grail King and with the most religious element of the Arthurian story.

But Ransom is also the Pendragon, the political head of Logres, Arthur's ancient kingdom. The Pendragon was both a title and a sign of authority, a golden dragon, used by Arthur and his father Uther before him. In fact , its origin was a comet in the shape of a dragon, which King Uther saw in the sky and which Merlin interpreted as prophetic of the victories of his house. The special character of Logres as Lewis treats it is first hinted at in the comments of Dimble to Jane which we have already referred to. This first mention of Arthur in the story describes Logres as a Christian kingdom surrounded by the dark practices of hostile sorcerers whose power controlled most of Britain. And the Logres which Ransom heads is part of a continuing kingdom within England, but always at war with its paganism. As Dimble says after the last dinner of the Company, "Haven't you noticed that we are two countries? After every Arthur, a Mordred; behind every Milton, a Cromwell: a nation of poets, a nation of shopkeepers."

The most important part of the Arthurian atmosphere, of course, is Merlin, but he is more than decoration and will be discussed later. However, other details from Logres which contribute are the mention of Blaise, who was Merlin's master in magic; reference to the "airish man" or daemon who was supposed to have been Merlin's father (although Merlin calls this a "lying story"); Druidism, the ancient religion of the Celts; a quotation from *Taliessin Through Logres*, Charles Williams' work on Arthur; reference to the "stroke that Balinus struck," the Dolorus Blow that wounded the Fisher-King and laid his land waste. And the list could be extended.

The Arthurian motif contributes an atmosphere of legend and myth which in this narrative takes the place of the *handramits* of Malacandra and the floating islands of Perelandra. The otherness here is not of other worlds, but of ancient heroes and sacred vows, of a time when man could draw power from nature and control it for his own uses. In addition to the Round Table, mention is made of Numinor and the

True West, the Atlantean circle, Nimrod, and the hideous strength of the Tower of Babel. And the atmosphere includes a man named Ransom whose only food is bread and wine, and who has a wounded heel got when battling with the Evil One. The name, the diet, and the wound, each because of their association with Christ, give the man an aura of mystery, as does his power over animals and his influence upon the Company.

Although some of the above details have a bearing upon the action of the story, a number of them—such as Atlantis, Blaise, and Balin—are there simply for their connotative value. They evoke the haunting images of half-understood myths and legends and make us feel that we are listening to "old unhappy far off things and battles long ago."

IV.

OF THE two dozen characters of some importance in the story only two, Ransom and Feverstone, connect these events with those of the other two books. Lord Feverstone we met before he had been elevated to the peerage. As Dick Devine he was Weston's co-conspirator in the kidnapping of Ransom when it was erroneously assumed that the *sorns* of Malacandra wanted a human sacrifice. Feverstone does not appear in *Perelandra*, but here he is the same ruthless and self-centered person whom Oyarsa had characterized as a talking animal with nothing left but greed. Although in his first private conversation with Mark he describes some of the basic assumptions of the N.I.C.E., it is plain that he is interested in the Institute not because of its ideas but because he believes it is "the winning side." If man is going to take charge of man, he wants to be one of those taking charge. As we learn later, Feverstone knows about the *macrobes*, the evil *eldila* of Earth, but is not interested in that route to power. His loyalty is to nothing but his own pleasures and desires. Although it is clear that Lewis believed that Satan is a power to be reckoned with in this world, the character of Feverstone suggests that he also believed that man had within himself enough evil to effect his own damnation without demonic assistance.

It will not be necessary to discuss all of the characters at Belbury whom Lewis selects to place in the spotlight, but two of the most significant are John Wither, the Deputy Director, and Augustus Frost, whose official position is never given. Because we are told that Merlin's contacts with the world of the supernatural had "withered" him, we must assume that the Deputy Director's name describes his own inner condition. As the story gradually unfolds, we learn of the true authorities behind the N.I.C.E. Wither and Frost are the only persons in touch with the satanic powers who give orders through the decapitated head of Alcasan. This contact with a world not made for man had in each produced a different result. The Deputy Director is effusive and wordy. Frost says very little and shows no emotion. Wither has a vague, chaotic face, while Frost's features are almost unnaturally regular. The influence of the *macrobes* upon Frost had been to sharpen him into a hard, bright needle; upon Wither it had been to distend him into a shapeless ruin.

Although it is finally evident that these men are equal in power and in dedication to the evil spirits that they serve, it is Wither who appears more frequently in the story and is the most interesting. He seems to be in contact with reality like a spider in contact with the world through a strand of cobweb. Although colors, tastes, and other sensations invade his physical receptors, they seldom disturb the center of his being. Lewis indicates that he conducts the business of living with only a fraction of his consciousness. This accounts for the vague and chaotic face, the far-away, inattentive look in his eyes. But even though a divided man, he is a formidable personality, who is able to conduct the affairs of the Institute with a brain and outward attitude which is very effective.

His spirit, however, freed from the senses and even from the reason, wanders "through formless and lightless worlds, waste lands and lumber rooms of the universe." And so, when Mark walks into his office unannounced, he at first thinks he is looking into the face of a corpse. When he realizes that Wither is actually alive, he still has the strange feeling that the Deputy Director is not present even though the body is before his eyes. There is a ghostliness about the man which suggests that he is not so much a body and soul as a body haunted by a disembodied spirit. His appearance in the corridors and on the grounds of Belbury is apparently not a physical reality but a wraith or unsubstantial image which at one time Mark thrusts his arm through.

We are given the philosophical history of the man in the episode which includes his death. "He had passed from Hegel into Hume, thence through Pragmatism, and thence through Logical Positivism, and out at last into the complete void." Hegel taught that idea or reason is true and eternal and that matter is derivative and dependent. Hume insisted that we can prove neither the validity of our reason nor the reality of our sense impressions. The philosophy of pragmatism holds that ideas are really only ideas of sense impressions, and logical positivism denies meaning to any statement which cannot be logically analyzed or verified by experience: pronouncements about the supernatural are rejected as meaningless.

Perhaps we could say that Wither had drifted from "a repugnance for realities that were crude and vulgar" into a scepticism concerning the reality of all ideas, then to a denial of the permanence of all values, and finally to "a fixed refusal of everything that was in any degree other than himself." It is this utter negation of all reality but that of his own ego which accounts for his ghostliness. As he has few ties with the actual, his own existence seems lacking in solidity. Lewis says of the Un-man in *Perelandra* that intelligence was a weapon which he used but which he had no interest in when the Lady was out of sight. And Wither also can display considerable subtlety of thought in conversation, but, when he is free to pursue his own life, his spirit is detached "not only from the senses but even from the reason."

In addition to Lewis's beliefs about the nature of evil, his concept of reality sheds light on the Deputy Director. All reality, Lewis believed, centers in God, and the sense world is an important part of that reality. As already noted, he says,

"God likes matter. He invented it." And so, any philosophical denial of the facthood of our senses and the material world they are in touch with is a movement toward dissipation and unreality, and, of course, a movement away from God.

Of the other members of the Institute three need a brief mention. Although Lewis allows us an inner view of Feverstone, Frost, and Wither by the use of each of them as a central intelligence, for Reverend Straik, Miss Hardcastle, and Professor Filostrato we must come to our conclusions largely through their actions and words. Straik is the priest-turned-atheist who still uses the thundering cadences of the prophets but interprets them in a materialistic way. He speaks of Christianity as made up of myths and symbols which predict events the N.I.C.E. are bringing about. The resurrection of Jesus, he says, was a symbol of the resurrection of Francois Alcasan, the one who was killed and is still alive. He tells Mark that he is being offered the glory of being present at the creation of God Almighty. Man himself is about to ascend the throne of God and rule the universe forever. Here is the apostate fanatic still breathing out prophetic warnings and denunciations, but all blasphemously applied to the deification of man. As Wither tells Frost, it was almost too easy to lead such a man into the final and fatal circle—those who worshiped the *macrobes*. In the creation of Straik, Lewis may have had in mind the statement of Paul in his first letter to Timothy that "in the latter times some shall depart from the faith, giving heed to seducing spirits, and doctrines of devils."[1]

Of Miss Hardcastle, "the Fairy," we need only point out that she represents the totalitarian thrust of the N.I.C.E. As she says, "We're an army." The scientific facade which the Institute displays to the public is actually a perversion of science which conceals the plot to bring all England under a dictatorship. And that perversion is paralleled in the person of the Head of the Institutional Police. The Fairy is herself a pervert. Her masculine deportment and her taste for fluffy little girls make it plain that she is a homosexual. In fact, in some usage the word *fairy* is slang for homosexual.

Professor Filostrato, the great physiologist, is the only person of any real scientific ability in the Institute. But, like Weston, he is a dupe of the dark *eldila* of Earth. As Frost tells Mark, Filostrato has accomplished something remarkable in keeping Alcasan's head from decaying, but his assumption that it is Alcasan who speaks is quite mistaken. All that he has done is to create a vehicle through which the *macrobes* can give orders. It functions much as did the Un-man. Filostrato, like Weston before him, demonstrates how science, innocent in itself, can become a tool of evil powers whose only intent is to destroy humankind. Perhaps the fact that the professor is described as a eunuch suggests the sterility of his efforts in the Institute.

V.

ALTHOUGH MARK Studdock's position in the story of the N.I.C.E. is that of protagonist or leading character, we cannot say that he is the protagonist of the entire book; in fact, Jane occupies our attention for almost exactly as many pages as does Mark. But as we have said earlier, the story of Mark is the story of his journey into and then out of the inner ring. It is important to remember that he is young. More than once Lewis makes such a statement about him. He had been at Bracton for five years and was probably in his late twenties, but like Ransom in *Out of the Silent Planet* he had not yet reached maturity. Just before his interview with Dimble his fluctuating decisions and attitudes are illuminated by Lewis's comment, "Thus, skidding violently from one side to the other, his youth approached the moment at which he would begin to be a person." But this moment is well past the middle of the book. Up to this point most of his efforts had been spurred by a desire to become a member of some inner circle. During the first episode in which he appears, he basks in the glow which Curry's use of the word *we* gives him. What had been to him "Curry and his gang" is now "the progressive element in College."

Many of the actions and events in Mark's life are the working out of ideas which Lewis had expressed in his Memorial Oration at King's College, the University of London. Delivered in 1944, the year before *That Hideous Strength* was published, it was titled "The Inner Ring."[2] Lewis points out the prevalence of such rings of influence and exclusion at all levels of society. They are to be found in schools, in business, in clubs, wherever people congregate for work or play. Although there are not formal membership lists or rules, some people are "in" and some are "out." Those who are "in" call the ring by a different name from those who are "out."

Thus, Mark's earlier designation of the power structure at Bracton was derogatory. But now, as a member of it, his words are complimentary. Lewis says that the desire to be inside what he calls an esoteric group, that is, a small and exclusive circle, is one of the dominant drives of man. It is as important in motivating to action as money, sex, or ambition.

When Mark's expectation of hanging for Hingest's murder causes him to look back over his life with eyes opened by the imminence of death, he realizes that his own history had been one of trying to worm his way into some secret circle or other and then finding that this hidden world was nothing but dust and broken bottles. He views with disgust his schoolboy attempts to get into the society called Grip, his delight at Bracton when "the odious little outsider" became an insider and received the trivial confidences of Curry and Busby, his gullible acceptance of the invitation to join the N.I.C.E. when it shouted from the first day of his visit that it was a world of plots and betrayals.

Although Lewis admits that the informal rings of society are not necessarily evil and are sometimes the only way to get work done, he does say that usually the desire to get into one is not commendable. It often leads to the abandonment of friends with whom one has common interests for friends who are important or powerful. And Mark looks with loathing at the way he had thrown away his friendships with Pearson and Denniston because they could not open the door for him to an inner circle. But the evil of the desire to be an insider is perhaps best illustrated by the way in which the ring of the Institute maneuvers Mark into doing something criminal—as Lewis says in his address, "in making a man who is not yet a very bad man do very bad things." One who, like Mark, lives to be accepted, is vulnerable to the requests of the ring to do something wrong. The path to becoming a scoundrel, Lewis says, does not begin by "obviously bad men, obviously threatening or bribing." When Mark is asked to fake the newspaper reports of the riot which the N.I.C.E. planned to foment, he is hardly aware that he has made a decision, even though he knows that his actions would be a crime. "It all slipped past in a chatter of laughter, of that intimate laughter between fellow professionals." The decision to do wrong, when clothed in the approval of the ring, hardly seems like more than an extra vote for an issue that already has a majority.

But to the circles which had fenced in Mark's past and strung barbed wire between him and those who were worthy of his love we must add the appeal of one more—the invitation into the demonic circle of supernatural power. When Frost explains who the real masters are behind the Institute and offers Mark a position as an initiate within the ring which contains the dark plots of the *macrobes* for the control of all humankind, the appeal is like the sucking tide of an undertow. Its force would probably have been irresistible had not Mark begun already to make some resolutions which had a tinge of morality in them.

He had concluded that his death would be lucky for Jane. She belonged to that other world not of secret circles but of relaxed friendships. Then, he had determined to cling to the fact that the leaders at Belbury are evil and his enemies. Fortunately, or probably we should say providentially, the session with Frost is interrupted, and he has time to fortify himself. Even the demonic attack which he experiences while alone in his cell and which makes him cry out for help strengthens his decision that he has taken sides. His side is now Jane's side and all that that includes. Lewis seems to be demonstrating two points by this crisis in Mark's life: one, that any cry for help and moral effort in the right direction will cause Heaven to respond, and, two, that, as the demonic attack actually strengthened Mark, evil is by its very nature self-defeating.

Lewis carefully displays the gestation of the embryonic personhood of Mark Studdock. He holds up to our view what might be called a series of x-ray plates, which show self-knowledge forming as a result of the expectation of death, revulsion developing at the essential evil represented by Professor Frost, fortitude appearing in his determination to oppose the circle and its power, loyalty growing as the idea of the normal becomes a solid reality, and finally, decisiveness crystalizing as he sides with the Man who had been crucified by the Belbury of His own time. The growth does not take place in a day. Mark spends many hours with Frost and many days in the room with the pseudo-Merlin. And, when it is over, his theology still needs both surgery and nutrition. But, as we leave him in the Lodge at St. Anne's, we feel sure that he is on the right path, and that, with Jane at his side, he will make his way into the Celestial City.

VI.

JANE, OUR second protagonist, the principal character in the story of the Company, also learns the meaning of maturity, but in a very different way. Although she may not be any more of a complete person than Mark when the story opens, it is clear that she has no appetite for inner rings and seems more discerning than her husband in judging people. She is not taken in by Curry or Feverstone, and, as Mark realizes, would have made Belbury stand out in its true vulgar light if she had come to live there. The episode in which Wither asks Mark to bring Jane to the N.I.C.E. shows her functioning in Mark's mind almost as a conscience.

But as a very modern young woman of twenty-three her chief problem is almost the opposite of that of her husband. The two narrative threads act as counterpoint to each other. She also faces the question of membership, but a different sort of membership, and she shows a different attitude toward it. The thought which she clings to like a shield against the world is, "You've got your own life to live." She shrinks back from any membership because it might invade the little circle which she imagines to be her own essential self and value. Something like the hard pebble of the brook in Blake's poem, the shell of her own individuality knows nothing of self-giving. If she had continued on this path, she might well have sung with the pebble:

> Love seeketh only Self to please,
> To bind another to Its delight,
> Joys in another's loss of ease,
> And builds a Hell in Heaven's despite.

Whether Lewis had Blake's poem in mind or not, a closer source is another address which Lewis gave and published in the same year as *That Hideous Strength*. It was simply called "Membership."[3] Here, he points out that membership in the Christian sense is not a gathering of identical counters, but a relationship more like that within a family and most like that of the organs of a body. The church as the body of Christ knows nothing of equality. Each member has a unique place in the body and may be as diverse from the others as the hand and the ear. But it is from the life of the body that individuality flourishes. "The sacrifice of selfish privacy which is daily demanded of us is daily repaid a hundredfold in the true growth of personality which the life of the Body encourages."

As the story opens Jane is not a part of any body. She resents the mysterious and unfamiliar that may disrupt the pattern she has drawn for her life. When she is told that she is the seer which the Sura had predicted, her reaction is, "I don't want to be anything so exciting." Arthur Denniston's sympathetic reply, "No. It's rough luck on you," illustrates a point which appears in several of Lewis's stories. We are all the prisoners of our own gifts and positions. A king is the servant of his kingdom and is not free to ride beyond the end of the world. One with second sight is under obligations because of the gift and cannot be an ordinary person. Her only choice is whether to serve the N.I.C.E. or the Company. The

85

steps of each person must follow a path of obedience to the inherited obligations he has received.

But the hard shell of Jane's private self has a crack in it. She is vulnerable to people she admires. And here is another detail in the counterpoint. Mark is vulnerable because he longs for acceptance by the esoteric group which builds a wall between those "in" and those "out." But Jane is vulnerable because her admiration for the Dimbles and the Dennistons demolishes the wall about her private life and lets in the light and warmth of friendship. You remember that Curry's use of the word *we* was music to Mark's ears because it reminded him that he was in the inner ring. That Lewis is contrasting that with Jane's developing relationship with the Company is evident from the use again of the word *we*. Denniston had said, "We want to be private." And Lewis records Jane's mental response that "we" included her and meant "we three." It "established at once a pleasant, business-like unity between them." Here is not a ring of exclusion but a circle of common interest. Lewis had said in his "Inner Ring" address that a person who takes his work seriously and becomes a sound craftsman will find himself inside the only circle that matters—that of common interest with other sound craftsmen. And he adds that, if you spend your spare time with people you like, you will again find yourself in a circle—not of exclusion but simply of friendship.

So the history of Jane's progress is the history of her response to the goodness and beauty she recognizes in others. Again Lewis displays the counterpoint by a word, perhaps we should say by a pun. Her second trip to St. Anne's is almost an automatic response to seeing Frost walk across her path and get into a N.I.C.E. car. Her horror and revulsion at this evil man of her dreams produces a desire for the Company which expresses itself temporarily on the childish level. "She wanted to be with Nice people, away from Nasty people." The obvious irony of the initials of the Institute is here put to use to show the interweaving of the contrasting threads.

Tennyson's famous line from the *Idylls of the King*, "We needs must love the highest when we see it," is well illustrated in the movement from Jane's friendship with the Dimbles, to her ardent admiration for Camilla and Arthur Denniston, and, finally and climactically, to her dizzy and breathless adoration of the Pendragon when she is brought into his presence and her world is unmade. Although Lewis has been called "the apostle to the skeptic," and brilliantly presents the reasonableness of Christian doctrine in such works as *Mere Christianity* and *Miracles,* he does not discount the magnetic attraction of those who reflect the image of Christ in their lives. In fact, he insists that the emotional pull of the gospel should never be underestimated. In a paper read to an assembly of Anglican priests and youth leaders he says that "the direct evangelical appeal of the 'Come to Jesus' type can be as overwhelming today as it was a hundred years ago." He admits that he does not have the gift to do it, but he says that those who have it should employ their gift "with all their might."[4]

And so Jane's neat little world of understandable components is unmade when she stands before the man who had walked on the Planet of Love. Although she is overwhelmed, perhaps the most significant reaction is her response in moral terms. She feels unexpected scruples at making hypocritical replies to the Director, and she recognizes a change in her attitude toward Mark, from one of grievance to one of pity. Lewis illustrates here that the love of the highest that one knows is itself a moral choice. And any such self-forgetful choice will eventually, if continued, lead one to God. Although Jane puts herself "in the obedience" of Ransom as the highest good that she knows, her later confrontation with death as she realizes that the meeting with Merlin may be fatal, and her further talk with Ransom, bring her at the corner of the gooseberry patch to a surrender to the Person who is highest of all.

VII.

THE INTRODUCTION of the Director to the reader through the eyes of a stunned and overwhelmed Jane displays the last stage in the evolution of Elwin Ransom. He is a very different person from the Pedestrian who was refused lodging at Much Nadderby. Trips to two planets, the refining fire of a life-and-death struggle with essential evil, frequent conversations with the great *eldila* of the Field of Arbol— these have not only polished and perfected his character but have also moved him very close to the line which divides the natural from the supernatural. Tor had told him just before he left Perelandra that he would find it hard to die in the Silent Planet after having breathed the immortal air of that new Eden. And Lewis places him in the select company of "translated ones," who are not swallowed by the jaws of death but are carried out of this world like Elijah in a chariot of fire, or like Arthur on a barge that disappears over the horizon. His elevation to the immortals is, no doubt, the only way to bow him out of the story in a decorous manner.

Dorothy Sayers wrote to Lewis that she enjoyed *That Hideous Strength* immensely, but that she didn't like Ransom "quite so well since he took to being golden haired and interesting on a sofa like the Heir of Redclyffe."[5] Probably most readers would agree that the Ransom who fled in terror from the *sorns* and agonized with God before he agreed to fight the Un-man is a more interesting person, but we should remember that he does not make his entrance in this story until almost all of the other characters have walked upon the stage—more than a third of the book has passed—and even then, he only appears in fourteen of the eighty-five sections of the story. He is discussed in several other sections, and, of course, the voluntary submission of the members of the Company to his orders makes him a person of supreme influence. He is, indeed, the Director, but he is almost not an actor in the story. He functions as a catalyst in Jane's spiritual history and as a conductor of current in the descent of the gods upon Merlin, but it is the other characters whose actions hold our attention most of the time.

As we have known Ransom as a Cambridge don and philologist, Lewis takes some pains to prepare us for the change which has made him the Fisher-King, the Pendragon, and the Head of the Company. The Dennistons' brief explanation to Jane about whom they belong to contributes to our understanding that something has been added. But most effective of all is the device by which we see the Director for the first time through the consciousness of Jane. Because she is deeply shaken by the introduction, we are impressed.

And it is Ransom's impact upon others which gives him his stature with the reader. The reverence which he evokes in the Company and the allegiance which he receives from Merlin after the first skirmish at the door tend to portray him as larger than life. But it is his strange power to make the beasts "safe" which is most astonishing. We are told that he had brought back from Perelandra a "shadow of man's lost prerogative to ennoble beasts." Not only does he make Mr. Bultitude "safe," but in his presence the bear almost becomes a person. For the animal such a meeting is a mystical experience; he thinks the unthinkable and is enraptured with gleams beyond the dim world of his own life. Lewis in *The Problem of Pain* suggests that unfallen man may have had a redemptive task to perform for the beasts. "It may have been one of man's functions to restore peace to the animal world."[6] But man joined the enemy, and Belbury with its creatures caged for vivisection again represents the antithesis of the ideal.

However, Ransom's ability to create peace between men and mice, bears and cats, and to lift beasts to a level in the family of man far above that of their "natural" state does not introduce a new order. It is only a temporary glimpse of what ought to be, and will be, when the lion lies down with the lamb. The Pendragon's work is done when the N.I.C.E. collapses. And so it seems appropriate that he is, we assume, safely transported to the third heaven, the land of Abhalljin in Perelandra, to be with Enoch, Moses, Elijah, Arthur, and Melchizedek the king—all worthies of antiquity who did not die or whose death is open to question.

VIII.

OUT OF the earth and out of the past, fresh from a fifteen-hundred-year sleep and fresh from the far-off age of Arthur and Camelot and the Round Table—it is no wonder that Merlin's presence in the story contributes materially to the sense of otherness which we have noted in the preceding books. As a member of the College of Magicians of his own day he shows some knowledge of Deep Heaven, and as a prophet he reveals some glimpses into the future. But his most powerful influence upon the story is through his rapport with nature. It is fitting that he is dug out of the earth. He is described as having about him a sense of mold, gravel, wet leaves, and weedy water. He seems to be in touch with mice and stoats, the thumping of frogs, the fall of hazel nuts, even the growing of grass. When he first appears at the door of St. Anne's with the wind howling at his back, he stands like a rooted tree. His voice seems to come to the ear through roots and clay and gravel. He comes from an age when Earth was more like an animal than a lifeless clod. It had a soul and Merlin was in tune with that soul. He had loved and revered the spiritual qualities in nature and had drawn his magic from them. His face, we are told, has a strange animal appearance—the patient, unarguing sagacity of a beast. There is a special affinity between him and Mr. Bultitude.

You remember that Ransom takes it for granted that, if Merlin is awakened, he will side with Belbury, and Wither indicates to Frost that he expected the wizard to become the Director of the N.I.C.E. These mistaken expectations are caused by Merlin's somewhat ambiguous birth and by the fact that he was known to be a Druid. According to legend Merlin did not have a human father but was sired by a spirit, a daemon of the air. But if he had been only half human, his right to Christian redemption and membership in the Company might be questioned, and so Lewis has him deny the legend and label it as "a lying story."

Merlin's connection with Druidism also causes some difficulty in accepting him in the Christian fold (where Lewis quite definitely places him). The Druids were supposed to be sun-worshipers. But they were also highly skilled in herbal medicine and were reputed to be able to employ the spirits of nature to accomplish magical results. When Merlin urges Ransom to let him use his powers against Belbury, he promises, "I will set a sword in every blade of grass to wound them, and the very clods of earth shall be venom to their feet." And so we must assume that Merlin as a Druid had had commerce with the spirits of air, earth, and water; but as a member of the Christian court of Arthur, he was also a worshiper of the true God and a baptized Christian. Lewis explains this religious cross-breeding by saying that there were things lawful in Merlin's time which are unlawful now. Perhaps he felt that there is support for such a position in the different standards on certain relationships between the Old and New Testament. In fact, Cecil Dimble comments on Abraham's polygamy in this connection. It wasn't wrong for Abraham, but it would be now.

However, all of this is really Lewis's justification for Christianizing Merlin without relinquishing the legend of his wizardry. His druidical powers are not used. The part that he must play, a sort of martyrdom, Ransom explains reluctantly and with agony of spirit, like a doctor who reveals to his wife that she has terminal cancer. As Merlin's mind had once been invaded by supernatural spirits and is therefore open to another invasion, he is to be "possessed" for the destruction of Belbury. Because he is both a Druid and a Christian, he is the only person through whom the Oyérseru can work. But such an "eldilic possession" is more than flesh and blood can stand. For the victory of Logres, he offers himself and is "used up."

As a literary creation he is a masterpiece. His earthiness and yet elegance (even without the knowledge of forks), his loud lament, which shows the primitive Celt beneath the Roman veneer, his language, full of images of antiquity, his obvious intellectual power and wisdom, all are a tribute to the happy fusion of the talents of Lewis the scholar with those of Lewis the poet.

Of the other members of the Company, not much need be said. They each have individualizing characteristics, but their importance in the story is almost invariably related to the progress of Jane into the Company. The chapter in which gowns are selected for the ladies from the "treasures of Logres" and which produces Ivy Maggs, "the dapper elf," Camilla Denniston, "the Valkyrie," and Margaret Dimble, "the matriarch and fertility priestess," demonstrates the skillful use of costume and the opinion of others in the delineation of character. Finally, we might note that it is generally acknowledged that MacPhee is an affectionate and humorous portrait of "the Great Knock," William T. Kirkpatrick, who was Lewis's tutor as he prepared for the Oxford scholarship examinations.

IX.

WE HAVE already mentioned some of the ideas of the book in discussing its characters. But there are more. And herein is one of the difficulties of the story. There is so much compressed into less than five hundred pages that the reader's impression on a first reading may be that the story is confused. It is not, but with two dozen characters, all of whom are important, at least five narrative threads, and a number of themes which Lewis believed to be significant, the book must be read several times before its scope and complexity are grasped.

In the preface Lewis states that behind this story is a serious point which he had discussed in *The Abolition of Man*. This little volume consists of a series of three lectures which he delivered at the University of Durham in February, 1943, and which was published in the following year under the above title. Actually, all three points of the three lectures are illustrated in the story.

The first lecture deals with the attitude shown in the "objectivity" of Professor Frost, who uses that word frequently in the training program through which he conducts Mark. It always has to do with a denial of the significance of human relationships. Everything emotional he regards as a chemical state in the body. Resentment, fear, social relations, friendship, in fact, *all* motives for action, he says, are animal reactions produced by physical conditions. The training in objectivity through which Mark goes in the Objective Room is an attempt to eliminate from his mind all specifically human relations and sentiments.

Lewis says in his first lecture, which he titles "Men without Chests," that this tendency in modern education to debunk emotions will have serious consequences for future generations. If statements of value are only statements about the emotional condition of the speaker, then man has no basis for knowing good and evil. And, if proper emotional responses which have been trained to rule, are corrupted or destroyed, the intellect becomes powerless against the animal appetites. Using the old metaphors of the body, he says, "The head rules the belly through the chest."[7] Without the "spirited element" which cherishes value man becomes an anarchy—he is a man without a chest.

So Frost is the end product of an educational program which denies the validity of a permanent set of values outside the chemistry of man's own body. Lewis insists, however, that certain objects merit certain emotions. A waterfall may merit the word *sublime*. It may be appropriate to call an aged man *venerable* and children *delightful*. Here, he says, we are dealing with the nature of things—the order of the universe—and not with the individual's feelings. In fact, he cites Aristotle as affirming that the purpose of education is to make the student like and dislike what he ought.

Such an "oughtness," of course, implies a permanent morality or law which is a part of the structure of the universe. It leads to Lewis's second lecture, titled "The Way," which is a closely reasoned discussion of the subject of his first series of radio talks. These he had called "Right and Wrong as a Clue to the Meaning of the Universe." They are the first section of *Mere Christianity*.

For our purposes "The Way" has a bearing upon Mark's reaction to the perversity of Frost's instruction and the crookedness of the Objective Room. The training has a result quite contrary to that which is intended. Mark becomes aware as he never had before of qualities opposite to the perverse and the crooked. The normal and the straight become for him a shape as real as a granite mountain, or sunlight, or Jane, or fried eggs. At this point Mark makes a moral decision without realizing it. He sides with the normal and straight, "the way," which Lewis calls the *Tao*. The use of this oriental word emphasizes that Lewis here is not talking about uniquely Christian values. Whether the source is supernatural or not, the *Tao*, he says, must be accepted as having absolute validity. Its ultimate platitudes are based on the nature of things, the way the world is made. And it is therefore "the way" which every man should tread in adjusting himself to all reality. So the *Tao*, with which Mark sides, is the doctrine of a value outside of man by which man can measure himself—a doctrine to be found in Plato, Aristotle, the Stoics, and in the literature of Chinese, Jews, Christians, and many other cultures. It is a part of the wisdom of the race.

Of course the *Tao* can be rejected. And it is the consequence of this rejection which is the subject of the third lecture, whose title, *The Abolition of Man*, eventually became the title of the whole series. Frost speaks of "that preposterous idea of an external standard of value," but it is really the entire N.I.C.E. which is the "preposterous" showcase of the dehumanizing effect of rejecting the *Tao*.

Lewis points out in his lecture that as man increases his power over nature, he may attempt to master human nature, to remake himself into whatever form of mind and body he wishes. But if he is successful, the result will not be a conquest of man over nature, but of some men over other men. Those who know how to change man, the Conditioners, as he calls them, will decide how man should be changed. Quite clearly the leaders at the N.I.C.E. intend to be those Conditioners. As Lord Feverstone tells Mark, "You and I want to be the people who do the taking charge, not the ones who are taken charge of." Filostrato voices much the same sentiment when he explains to Mark that the talk about the power of man over nature is only for the *canaglia* (rabble). "Man's power over nature means the power of some men over other men with nature as the instrument."

Because they have abandoned the *Tao*, Lewis says, these superscientists or Conditioners of the race will have no guide for their decisions but their own desires. What they desire man to be, man will become. Without traditional standards of right and wrong, all that will be left to motivate them will be their own pleasure. And their final products will not be men but artifacts. Man's final conquest will prove to be the abolition of man.

It is clear that this is what Lewis is illustrating in the story. Feverstone speaks of taking "control of our own destiny." Science, he says, can now recondition the human race, "make man a really efficient animal." Such reconditioning would include sterilizing the unfit, getting rid of backward races, selective breeding, and eventually biochemical conditioning and manipulation of the brain—indeed, an abolition of man. The only defense against such racial butchery is the *Tao*. As a basic principle Lewis declares that "a dogmatic belief in objective value is necessary to the very idea of a rule which is not tyranny or an obedience which is not slavery."[8]

X.

ANOTHER IDEA which is integrated into the action throughout the book is that of "cure" of criminals rather than punishment of them. When Ivy's husband has served his term in jail for petty larceny, he is not released. To Ivy's great dismay he is sent to Belbury for "remedial treatment." Although Lewis, of course, approved of the rehabilitation of criminals (in fact, the last words of Ransom to Ivy are, "Go and heal this man"), he was opposed to the concept of "cure" being substituted for that of deserved punishment. In an article titled "The Humanitarian Theory of Punishment"[9] he points out that the idea of cure robs the individual of his right to a just sentence. If he is to be cured rather than punished, his imprisonment, like that of Tom Maggs, may be extended indefinitely. Under such a system he has no rights. But more ominous than that, such a system plays into the hands of unjust rulers. If crime and disease are to be regarded as identical, he says, what is to prevent a tyrant from labeling any state of mind a disease if he disapproves of it? And, if Christianity is declared a neurosis, its compulsory "cure" in a state institution would be regarded as treatment rather than persecution. As we would expect, Fairy Hardcastle regards remedial treatment one of the tools for enlarging the power of the N.I.C.E. She points out to Mark that if cure is humane, so is prevention. Anyone who has ever been in the hands of the police will come under the control of the Institute. And eventually so will every citizen.

Finally, we must examine what Lewis believed to be the place of obedience in the life of the individual. Miss Hardcastle tells Mark, "Your line is to do whatever you're told." And Ransom answers Jane's question by saying that she had lost love because she had "never attempted obedience." And so the idea is explored at both Belbury and St. Anne's. But here again there is a contrast. Obedience at the N.I.C.E. moves one closer to a vortex, a whirlpool which assimilates and destroys individual characteristics. Wither describes the Institute as a very happy family, but his other images betray a picture which suggest the digestive organs of a giant. He speaks of everyone's work as a moment in "the progressive self-definition of an organic whole," and of the N.I.C.E. as "a single personality." Filostrato tells Mark that the Head "will have all of you, and all that is yours—or else nothing." And most revealing of all is the private conversation between Frost and Wither in which the Deputy Director defines the desired unity with Mark as an interpenetration of personalities. "I would open my arms to receive—to absorb—to assimilate this young man." This is the unity of the *macrobes*—the unity of Hell. It is the unity which Screwtape expresses when he signs his letters, "Your affectionate uncle" but which Wormwood discovers in the end means affection for him as a dainty morsel of food.

Over against this life-devouring and life-destroying organism, more like a cancerous growth than a healthy body, is the hierarchy of St. Anne's, where the *eldila*, the Director, the Company, and even Mr. Bultitude and the other beasts of this "peaceable kingdom" are obedient to their appropriate superiors. And through obedience each one, including the animals, grows in uniqueness and personhood. As Lewis says in the address called "Membership," "Obedience is the road to freedom, humility the road to pleasure, unity the road to personality."[10]

But Jane appears in the story with the determination to shape her life according to her own plans. She is repelled by the Dennistons' talk of promises and obedience to an unknown Mr. Fisher-King. She resents the fact that Mark's approval might be needed in any decision she makes. And it is only as she finds her place in the Company that she learns the importance of obedience in the marriage relationship. It should be emphasized here, however, that the theme of obedience as it runs through the fabric of Jane's life should not be regarded as a statement about male superiority. Lewis says that "obedience and rule are more like a dance than a drill—specially between man and woman where the roles are always changing." Elsewhere he observes that because of our fallen state the authority of fathers and husbands has rightly been abolished. We all need the protection of equality before the law.

Lewis's point is that whether one is single or a husband or a wife, we all must learn humility and obedience. Jane's struggle illustrates what everyone must come to accept—that these virtues are essential in each organ of the body, in each pillar in the temple. But this unity is not self-destroying. "As organs in the Body of Christ, as stones and pillars in the temple, we are assured of our eternal self-identity and shall live to remember the galaxies as an old tale."[11]

THE INFERNAL LANDSCAPE

CHAPTER 5
NEWS FROM BELOW:
THE SCREWTAPE LETTERS AND
THE GREAT DIVORCE

I.

IN AN address delivered at the University of London about two years after the publication of *The Screwtape Letters*, Lewis observed that middle-aged moralists like himself usually talked about the world, the flesh, and the devil. But he quickly declared, "The devil, I shall leave strictly alone." The popularity of his Screwtape-Wormwood correspondence had, no doubt, created a good deal of humor at his expense, for he complained ironically that the association between the devil and himself in the public mind had already gone as deep as he wished. "In some quarters," he said, "it has already reached the level of confusion, if not of identification."[1] This comment not only indicates the success of the book, which has since sold over a million and a half copies, but also illustrates something of the quality of its wit.

Lewis wrote his brother in July, 1940, that the idea for a new book occurred to him after attending divine service.[2] He does not indicate that there was anything at church that caused the inspiration, but he describes the format as a series of "letters from an elderly retired devil to a young devil who has just started work on his first 'patient'. The idea would be to give all the psychology of temptation from the other point of view." He tentatively calls it "As One Devil to Another," and suggests that such a book "might be both useful and entertaining."

The completed work pretty well follows this initial idea, except that Screwtape is not a "retired" devil, but a responsible Under Secretary and a supervisor of his nephew, Wormwood, a junior tempter. The *Letters* first appeared in weekly installments in 1941 in the *Guardian,* a newsmagazine, and were published in book form in the following year.

But as witty and popular as it is, one might ask if this work and *The Great Divorce* belong in a volume dedicated to the discussion of Lewis's "tales." The two books, admittedly, are not organized as stories in the sense that his other narratives are. Although there is a slight thread of plot in *Screwtape,* the focus of the letters is on the pitfalls which are dug along the pathway of the Christian life by the enemies of man's soul.

And in *The Great Divorce* the incidents are not woven into a story with a beginning, middle, and end. They seem, rather, like unconnected and sometimes incomplete pages torn out of a larger novel. But the two books are fiction—in fact, fantasy—and illustrate the sort of story in which the ideas overshadow the form.

Lewis was convinced that the disbelief in the supernatural of this materialistic age needed to be attacked and that both Heaven and Hell should be sent into the battle. From the space trilogy Maleldil and the Oyérseru, the Bent One and the *macrobes* have served admirably to illustrate that all existence does not lie within the spectrum of this visible universe. And now in these two fantasies the regions of darkness are laid open "to the staring day" and their inhabitants forced to serve their tour of duty in the war against materialism.

We are reminded in the preface to *The Screwtape Letters* that the devil is a liar and that Screwtape is not always to be trusted to report facts as they are. But the tone and atmosphere are so consistent that the reader is willing to accept what may be a tissue of lies as, at least, a well-woven fabric, and to accord to "his Abysmal Sublimity" the virtue of verisimilitude if not of veracity. If the names we encounter in the book are not actual names of devils, they ought to be.

Screwtape himself has a name which suggests that he is a hybrid offspring of two parasites, the screwworm and the tapeworm. Wormwood, the apprentice devil to whom he writes, has a name which is a legitimate word for extreme bitterness. Old Slubgob, whom Screwtape believed to be a major disaster as head of the Training College for Young Tempters, probably gets part of his name from "to slubber," meaning to work in a slipshod manner.

The names of other devils such as Triptweeze, who reported on the skeptical couple, Toadpipe, Screwtape's secretary, and Scabtree, whose position is not identified, are compounds whose appropriateness resides in the connotation of the words. Glubose, who is in charge of the patient's mother, and Slumtrimpet, of his girl friend, seem to have names concocted out of sound combinations which suggest that which is evil or repulsive.

But much of Lewis's humor is achieved through reversal, in some cases through a mirror-image of Heaven. Satan is "Our Father Below." The howl of famine (at the loss of Wormwood's young man) echoes not up but down to the throne. Opposed to the beatific vision of Heaven and happiness is the "miserific vision" of Hell and suffering. But perhaps Lewis's greatest success of this sort is in his reference to the structure of Hell. *Hier-* is a prefix meaning "sacred." A hierarchy is simply a religious structure of authority, such as a hierarchy of angels. Only as a pun would it have anything to do with height. But as a reverse mirror it seems appropriate that, when Screwtape refers to the great masters of misdirection in Hell, they are "spirits far deeper down in the Lowerarchy than you and I."

The reader is constantly required to readjust his thinking from the devilish view that God is "the Enemy" and "the Oppressor," that those who are "safe in Our Father's House" are in Hell, that hundreds of converts have been "reclaimed" not to God but to Satan, or that under certain conditions the church might have been a "hotbed" of charity and humility. The sad cases among the physicists are those who have become Christians, the terrible habit which the young Christian has contracted is that of obedience, and certain love affairs, "if all goes well," end in murders and suicides.

II.

SIMILAR UPSIDE-down language is used, of course, to tell of the plots against the spiritual health of the young man who is often referred to as "the patient," the human being whom Wormwood must lure into "Our Father's House."

To summarize his story in a straightforward manner, however, he is not a Christian when Screwtape writes his first letter, but soon becomes one, which, of course, is a black mark against Wormwood's record. We also learn that he lives with his mother and that she is a person who gives Screwtape great hope that she will make her son's Christianity a difficult coat to wear in her household. At this point World War II crashes into the patient's life and leaves him on tenterhooks, for his age and profession make it uncertain whether he will be drafted or not.

After the first blush of his Christian experience, the young man goes through a period of dryness of soul. Wormwood reports optimistically that the religious phase seems to be passing away, which brings a rebuke from Screwtape and a lecture on emotional "undulation" in humans. But to the delight of both devils, their patient meets a middle-aged couple of skeptical bent and is introduced to their entire circle of scoffers. However, a period of gradually drifting away from his faith is arrested by a fresh encounter with God and a renewal of his vows.

For this disaster Wormwood is warned that he will suffer the usual consequences. But he is soon forced to report another major defeat. The young man has fallen in love with a fine Christian girl and has been introduced to her family. These, to Screwtape's intense disgust, are "mere Christians." That is, their common bond is in essential Christianity, not in some crusade or cause which bears the label of Christian and which can be used as a lever to pry them away from the center of their faith. Although such a wall of friends makes the young Christian a difficult target for Wormwood, Screwtape assures him that there is still hope of corrupting the faith of his charge and producing that masterpiece of hellish art, the Pharisee.

But as the war intensifies, the young man becomes involved in civil defense. During his first experience in an air raid he is badly frightened and thinks of himself as a spineless coward. But actually he had done his duty in spite of his fear. To Screwtape's great annoyance Wormwood can produce no significant evidence that the trial by fire had weakened the patient's faith or created a vice worth mentioning.

But then in a second raid all the infernal strategy is brought to nothing, for the young man is suddenly killed by a bomb. Screwtape describes in an agony of rage how the human soul at the moment past death recognized Wormwood for what he was and then stepped into the new life as if he had been born to it—at home with Christ and the hosts of Heaven.

This, then, is the story of "the patient." But it is not quite all of the story. Between Screwtape and Wormwood there is by-play of various sorts as each jockeys for a position of advantage over the other. Wormwood is blamed for every attitude and event which goes wrong, and is rebuked frequently for inadequate reports filled with non-essentials.

The young tempter, in turn, complains of "singularly unfortunate" results from some of the advice his supervisor had given him, asks embarrassing theological questions which cause Screwtape to reverse himself, and even tries to get his uncle in trouble with "the Secret Police" by showing them certain passages in the letters. Although these creatures are united in a common cause, Lewis makes it clear that they are not united in love. As Screwtape explains, each individual

105

is in competition with every other person. The foundation of the philosophy of Hell is that one self is not another self. What one gains another loses.

Lewis probably intends Screwtape to be representative of the mental limitations of Hell, where no one can imagine the possibility of any other philosophy than the self-centered one. The notion that "the Enemy" and, in fact, all of Heaven operates on the principle of disinterested love, he tosses off as a "cock and bull story." Whether Screwtape is representative or not, he comes through as a recognizable person. He has served his turn as a junior tempter and because of his success has risen to his present office as Under Secretary. His position seems to have made him somewhat arrogant. He shows no patience with Wormwood's immaturity and speaks scornfully of the junior devil's "amateurish suggestions," "ignorance," and "infantile rhapsodies."

But Screwtape is knowledgeable. As an old hand, he knows many tricks, and as a person of authority he understands the policies that have been promulgated by the satanic council of strategy. He speaks with admiration of the accomplishments of their "Philological Arm" whose work with words has shaped the attitudes of whole cultures: that blessed word *adolescent*, the solid triumph in the value given today to the word *puritanism*, the effectiveness of the word *complacency*, the subtle change created by substituting *unselfishness* for *charity*.

However, Screwtape is, perhaps, most interesting when he is frustrated by defeat or by the enigma of "the Enemy." His expressions of hate and scorn for humanity, which are to be found in almost every letter, rise to a crescendo of vituperation in letter twenty-two when he learns what sort of girl the young man has fallen in love with. She is a "filthy insipid little prude," but she has a satirical wit and, rages Screwtape, would "find ME funny!" The reader is given a double vision of the Under Secretary spitting out venom and, at the same time, of a very attractive young woman.

To increase Screwtape's rage it is at this point that Wormwood has attempted to sabotage his supervisor's authority by making trouble for him with the Secret Police. The illustrated booklet on the House of Correction for Incompetent Tempters enclosed with Screwtape's letter, no doubt, had a sobering effect upon the young devil. But while breathing out threats and invective the uncle finds his pen brought to a sudden halt. He is temporarily changed into a large centipede.

Here is, probably, a Miltonic borrowing. In *Paradise Lost* the devils suddenly take the form of serpents while they listen to their chief's boasting description of his triumph over Adam and Eve. And so the letter is concluded in a different hand as Screwtape dictates to Toadpipe, his secretary, and expresses his desire to unite himself with his nephew in an indissoluble embrace.

In no other letter does the old master allow himself to be so swept away with vindictiveness as to feel again the punishing hand of Heaven. (Of course, he denies that it is anything more than a periodic manifestation of the life-force.) But he does become greatly exercised as he talks of the utter failure of Hell to find out what "the Enemy" is up to. If, according to the philosophy of Hell, all selves are in competition, then the idea of love as a motivating force must be utterly rejected. And so the all-consuming question is: what does "the Enemy" stand to gain by "the despicable little bipeds?" Almost the last words that Screwtape writes are a lament that, so far, all their research has failed. "Alas, alas, that knowledge, in itself so hateful and mawkish a thing, should yet be necessary for power." But he is certain that the realism of Hell will win in the end.

III.

IT WOULD be a mistake, however, to assume that Lewis only intended to entertain the reader. The somber picture of delight in anguish and of devouring desire to feed on the will and freedom of another is not presented for the fun of it. As a series of sketches of the nature of evil and of the strategy of "the rulers of the darkness of this world," the letters are perfectly serious accounts.

Lewis believed that Hell is a house of mirrors, a reflection of the nature of its occupants. And so when Screwtape says, "We want to suck in . . . we are empty and would be filled . . . our war aim is a world in which Our Father Below has drawn all other beings into himself," he is expressing Lewis's belief in the egocentric and life-destroying nature of sin.

The double vision (which is the essence of irony) is especially clear as Screwtape discusses the nature and purposes of "the Enemy." More than once he describes God as a hedonist at heart. This derogatory word, which usually means one who spends his life seeking and enjoying pleasure, is used ironically to express a great truth about the divine nature. The love which is at the center of the Trinity, of course, produces pleasure—pleasure for all creatures who are in harmony with God.

Lewis even has Screwtape quote from Psalm 16. "At His right hand are 'pleasures for evermore.'" And although the old demon responds with "Ugh!" and speaks of the high and austere mystery of the miserific vision, his scornful statements give a new and blameless meaning to the word *hedonist*. He admits that "the Enemy" invented pleasures, and that all the researches of Hell have not been able to produce a single joy. God has filled His world with hot baths, cool drinks, fragrant mornings, and breathtaking sunsets and, to the disgust and misery of Hell, delights in seeing His creatures enjoying themselves.

Some people have found the *Letters* very distasteful because of the devilish advice, the reference to God as "the Enemy," and the delight which both fiends show in the damnation of humanity. Lewis would sympathize with such a view, for he says that he wrote the book with little enjoyment. "The strain produced a sort of spiritual cramp. The world into which I had to project myself while I spoke through Screwtape was all dust, grit, thirst, and itch."[3] However, the book's popularity indicates that most readers are not repelled by being given the opportunity to spy on a council of war in the enemy camp.

But perhaps its chief value resides in its insights and warnings concerning the booby traps and mine fields which are set by the enemies of man's soul. The strategy of Hell as Screwtape presents it can be divided into four categories: 1) devices to draw one away from the center of Christianity, 2) direct psychological attack upon the individual, 3) endeavors to shape whole societies and cultures to its purposes, and 4) warnings of the dangers to Hell in the work of "the Enemy."

Among the first is the attempt to make the young Christian equate the church with the oddities of its individual members; the recommendation of "party churches"—those divided over minor issues; and the promotion of the "historical Jesus," an imaginary figure who obscures the real purposes of the incarnation.

The second category, the attack upon the individual, is illustrated by the use of humility to create spiritual pride—pride in one's humility; the exploitation of the gluttony of delicacy—the "all I want" state of mind; and the weakening of the believer's faith in petitionary prayer by the "heads I win, tails you lose" argument—if it doesn't happen, prayer doesn't work; if it does, it would have happened anyway.

The wider attacks to shape the attitudes of nations include the encouragement of the notion in society that "being in love" is a necessary emotion throughout married life; the production of a sense of ownership of time by man, who owns nothing; and the successful creation of a horror of the Same Old Thing—the inordinate demand for novelty in fashion, in art, in philosophy.

In Screwtape's discussion of the dangers to Hell in the strategy and goals of "the Enemy" the volume probably reaches its ironical peak. For as he explains the purposes of God to Wormwood so that the young tempter can be prepared to oppose them, the old fiend reveals to the reader some very perceptive and helpful descriptions of God's plans for His children.

Examples of this are: his analysis of true humility, in

which one is so free of self-love that he can "recognize all creatures (even himself) as glorious and excellent things"; his explanation that God does not tempt to virtue as Hell does to vice because He wants man to be free and to walk with Him in love; and his observation that "the Enemy" has created a dangerous world because courage is not simply one of the virtues but the testing point of all the virtues.

And so, as we have seen, although the emphasis in this book is upon its themes or ideas rather than upon the story, there is a plot, there are characters, there is point of view, and there is form—the epistolary form which has been used successfully in a number of novels. Without the framework of fiction the book's popularity would have been greatly diminished.

IV.

IF THE *Screwtape Letters* present the strategy of Hell, then *The Great Divorce* presents the reason for Hell. And that reason is in the choices made by its inhabitants. As George MacDonald tells the narrator, "All that are in Hell, choose it." But it would be a mistake to say that the book is about Hell. Lewis makes it clear in the preface that it is about decision—that all roads do not lead to the New Jerusalem. Wrong roads lead to disaster, and no amount of wishful thinking can make them lead to happiness.

The book does begin, however, in Hell or, at least, in the city of the damned. As it is quite different from the Hell envisioned from the passing remarks of Under Secretary Screwtape, we are reminded that, like the other picture, it is a fantasy. Lewis is very specific about this in the preface. He wants no one to think of the story as, in any sense, a serious speculation about the fumes of Hell or the fruits of Heaven. And so, this Hell has no devils (although they are hinted at, once); it has no hell-fire; it even has no darkness (although, again, it is hinted that the dusk of the gray city will eventually turn to darkness).

In fact, both Hell and Heaven have borrowed something from the inventions of science fiction (as Lewis freely admits). The trip from the mists and murk of the gray city to the light-drenched outskirts of Heaven is by expansion as well as locomotion, for the denizens of Hell come from a world so tiny it would be lost among the grains of soil on Heaven's floor. Also, the land of light to which they come is so real and solid that the inflated and tenuous phantoms find it impossible to live there unless they endure a thickening-up process.

The story, in addition, has borrowed something from the church fathers. The basis for the whole idea of a holiday from Hell comes from the concept of a *refrigerium* or temporary remission of the pains of Hell—an idea which can be found as early as the fourth century in the writings of Prudentius Aurelius Clemens. But he speaks of the shadowy nation as being "free from fire" and the rivers ceasing "to burn with their usual sulphur," hardly a description of the gray city. It is clear that Lewis has simply taken the germ of the idea and developed it to suit his own purposes.

As we have come to expect from the other books we have discussed, the structure shows a careful balance of both characters and actions. The most important person in the story is George MacDonald, who serves as mentor and guide to Lewis. He first appears in the central chapter of the book. Forty-seven pages precede it and forty-six pages follow this chapter. Also in this suburb of Paradise we are given a close look at five ghosts from the gray city before the central chapter and five after it.

But, although the episodes show conscious organization, we cannot say that the story has a plot in the ordinary sense of that word. The structure is haphazard and fragmentary like a dream. This, of course, is Lewis's intent. The title is *The Great Divorce, a Dream*. The narrative begins, "I seemed to be standing in a bus queue"; there are several reminders within the story that it is a dream; and the author awakes at the end as he falls out of his chair.

The dream consists mainly of a series of episodes connected only by the setting and by Lewis, the observer. We have a temporary interest in each of the phantoms who flaunt their ghostly opinions and arguments in the face of the heavenly people, but these incidents do not lead to a climax and final weaving together of the various strands of the plot. In fact, of several of the interviews our sight is shut off before the final decision is made, and we are left in doubt of the outcome.

In regard to such doubts, let me correct a misstatement about this book which appears in several works on Lewis. It is not true that all but one of the inhabitants of the gray city return to Hell after the holiday. The only one whom we see leave for the Celestial City is the man whose red lizard is killed. But there are several other lost souls for whom George MacDonald gives us hope—the lady frightened by the unicorns, the possessive mother, the grumbler, and even some of the ghosts who seem to have come only to vent their envy and spite on Heaven. Lewis's guide assures him that he has seen cases like these rescued. Of course, we are only given a sampling of the interviews. We are to imagine, no doubt, that there were many others which we do not listen in on. So, the crowd in the bus on the return trip may have been considerably smaller.

The point of view, of course, is that of first-person narrator, as was *The Screwtape Letters.* Perhaps the most striking characteristic of this angle of narration is its limitation. When one of the ghosts totters out of sight of Lewis as narrator, its story comes to an end. If events are inexplicable to him, they are puzzling to us as well.

Such a device serves the purpose of the story very well, for the snapshot scenes illustrate the nature of choice, and it is not necessary for the reader to see the outcome of an interview in order to understand what the ghost must choose between or why his decision has been fixed by former choices. And then, the limitations of first-person narrator are somewhat enlarged by the introduction of George MacDonald, whose wisdom and knowledge greatly supplement the understanding of the storyteller. Without the old Scotsman the point of view would defeat much of the purpose of the book.

V.

AS WE would expect from the author of *Out of the Silent Planet* and *Perelandra*, the setting of *The Great Divorce* contributes much to the otherworldly atmosphere which permeates the story. Although not the traditional picture of Hell, the gray city with its mean streets, its rain, its undiminishing twilight, its vast and dreary extent stretching for millions of miles creates an unearthly air of stagnation and ugliness.

As the man in the bowler hat tells Lewis, the inhabitants are so quarrelsome that they cannot live near each other, and constantly move farther and farther from the center of the city, so that the earlier arrivals now reside at astronomical distances from it. MacDonald says that, although Heaven is reality itself, Hell is a state of mind. Every shutting up of the person within the prison of his own mind will in the end become Hell.

Such self-imprisonment perhaps accounts for the vast chronology of Hell as well. Although Napoleon died in 1821 of Earth time and so would have been dead about one hundred and twenty-five years when this book was published, the two travelers who went to see him in Hell took fifteen thousand years of infernal time to make the round trip. In that desolate city of the mind minutes are stretched into years and days into centuries.

But, of course, we are given only a quick and partial glance at this dismal scene. The otherworldly quality of the book is largely created by the landscape of the regions of light—what MacDonald calls "the Valley of the Shadow of Life." Here, we find ourselves in a science-fiction world not simply beyond the orbit of Earth but outside the bounds of the universe—an outside which, as he says, makes "the Solar System itself seem an indoor affair." The location is not surprising if one remembers that Lewis maintained that God is outside the universe in the same sense that an author is outside his novel.

So, we are led into another dimension, into a world of

113

utter reality. The diamond-hardness of the grass, the unyielding stream that Lewis walks on, the apples which take more than human (or ghostly) strength to lift, all suggest that we are being given a representation of ideal reality. Here, we probably have an extension of Plato's famous allegory of the cave, in which he describes the world that we know through our senses as only the flickering reality of shadows on a wall cast by that ultimate and infinite reality which exists out of our sight on a supernatural plane of being. The Valley of the Shadow of Life is, perhaps, the beginning of that world of ultimate and infinite reality.

Whether or not the Valley shows the influence of Plato (for whom Lewis had great respect), it does show the influence of Isaiah and the peaceable kingdom of the future which he describes. It is a world of romping lions and purring panthers, of deer and unicorns, of dogs and cats and horses and choirs of singing birds. But in Isaiah's kingdom, where "the leopard shall lie down with the kid" and the child safely put his hand into the nest of the asp, there will be a ruler who will judge with righteousness and faithfulness.

And in the next-to-the-last interview, we can see who Lewis believes will be the ruler of nature. After the triumphant transfiguration of ghost into man and lizard into stallion, nature sings a coronation song to man which begins, "The Master says to our master, Come up. Share my rest and splendour till all natures that were your enemies become slaves to dance before you and backs for you to ride, and firmness for your feet to rest on." The song (which is the author's adaptation of the first four verses of Psalm 110) ends with the statement: "Master, your Master has appointed you for ever: to be our King of Justice and our high Priest." The statement parallels the fourth verse of the psalm: "The Lord hath sworn, and will not repent, Thou art a priest for ever after the order of Melchizedek."

The New Testament writers read these verses as prophetic of the royal priesthood of Christ, with which Lewis would, no doubt, agree. But in this song he seems to imply that there is a sense in which man will also act as a priest-king. Adam was commanded to "replenish the earth and subdue it, and have dominion," but he abdicated his responsibility, and Earth still waits for its king.

But the time will come when redeemed man will serve as both the ruler of nature and its mediator with God. Because Christ is the second Adam and has become one with us, man's position in nature is also to be after the order of Melchizedek. Lewis here expresses his conviction that nature will be redeemed in the consummation of man's redemption, basing his conclusion, no doubt, upon Paul's statement in Romans that all creation is to be delivered from its bondage to corruption and is to share the glorious liberty of the children of God.

VI.

SO, SOME of the themes of the story are served by a setting which is more than a background for the action of the narrative. But of even greater importance in illustrating the themes are the characters—not what they do, but what they are. Of the uncertain number of ghosts who come on the bus, there are about a dozen who hold our attention for any length of time. And of the multitude of solid saints who come to meet them, there are only seven about whose earthly life we are given any information. There are also two angels who speak—the "burning one" who kills the red lizard, and the angel of the waterfall, who speaks to the ghost trying to steal one of the golden apples.

Of these twenty-one or so characters, the most useful person to the author is the bearded Scotch saint who acts as Lewis's interpreter. George MacDonald is the only person in the book, aside from Lewis himself, who is not fictitious. It is not surprising that he appears as the narrator's mentor, for Lewis claimed that in actual life this nineteenth-century Scotch minister, novelist, and writer of devotional material was his master, influencing him in probably every book which he had written.

In fact, this story appeared at about the same time as

another work titled *George MacDonald, an Anthology* by C. S. Lewis. Both books were published in 1946. *The Anthology* is a collection of cuttings which Lewis had made from the writings of this man. In the preface he introduces MacDonald to the reader by giving us some facts about his life and his influence upon Lewis himself, and then by describing his supreme talent as a myth-maker. But the collection in the *Anthology* offers us examples of MacDonald as a Christian teacher rather than as a creator of myth. Most of the extracts were taken from the three volumes of his *Unspoken Sermons*. The reference in *The Great Divorce* to Lewis's discovery of *Phantastes*, one of MacDonald's novels, is factual and is told in greater detail in *Surprised by Joy*.

Most of the ideas of our story will be found in the conversations or confrontations that take place between the joyous solid saints and the human vapors who limp painfully across the diamond-hard lawns of Heaven. The first five of these illustrate the desires which turn inward and like a hidden cancer weaken or destroy the power of making a self-forgetful decision. Then follows the central chapter in which, in addition to MacDonald, we are introduced to brief glimpses of the grumbling ghost, the flirting ghost, and the various forensic ghosts, who lecture, preach, exhort, and harangue the heavenly people. And then we look at five more. These balance the first five in number but show a differing posture. The choices which have shaped their destinies have turned outward. Like a spider at the center of his web these have manipulated their lines of power to feed on the attitudes and activities of others for their own pleasure.

Of the first five, the Big Man, or more properly, the Big Ghost, had already displayed his violent nature in the queue and on the bus. His self-centered attitude takes the form of demanding his rights, with over sixty uses of the pronoun *I*. He represents the domineering person who is very hard to live with or work with, who is ready to settle with his fists and loud voice any imagined affront to his own self-image. His insistence upon his rights draws the comment from his former employee that it is not as bad as that. Demanding one's rights, he implies, means demanding justice when our only hope is for mercy.

Here is another facet of the truth expressed in *Perelandra* by the King. God is above justice. All is gift. A love relationship is not concerned with rights. One of the best lines in this book is the answer to the Big Ghost's statement, "I only want my rights. I'm not asking for anybody's bleeding charity."

"Then do," says his companion, "At once. Ask for the Bleeding Charity." The word *charity*, of course, once meant *love*. The shocking contrast between the Big Ghost's scornful "bleeding charity" and the solid person's capitalized use of the same term plus the reader's sudden realization of the vast appropriateness of calling Christ the Bleeding Charity make this passage one of great power.

It is ironic that the Big Ghost had knocked a man down in the bus queue who thought he was too good for the others there, and yet when he is offered the bliss of Heaven, turns it down because he would have to go in the company of a redeemed murderer. He hardly ever seems to hear what his heavenly guide tells him. He is interested in demanding his own rights, but not in receiving truth. Like the hardened footpath in the parable, no seed of truth could penetrate the thick crust of his own self-importance. He probably got what he asked for when he returned on the bus, for his rights were to be found not in the mountains of light but in the city of darkness.

VII.

THE SECOND conversation is between one of the bright people and the apostate bishop who had told the narrator on the bus that educated opinion no longer believes that the twilight of the town will finally turn into night. "What we now see in this subdued and delicate half-light is the promise of the dawn." This sort of unfounded and empty optimism is characteristic of much that he says to the heavenly being who meets him. The bishop has spiritualized fact and reality away, until he now finds it impossible to believe in anything. Vital questions of eternal life and eternal death are for him only the means of producing interesting discussions. He has avoided coming to grips with truth for so long that he is no longer interested in finding answers.

In the apostate bishop we have the tragic picture of the end product of the sins of the intellect—the disastrous other side of Christ's statement that if any man will do the Father's will, he shall know of the doctrine. The bishop had not come to his religious opinions because of his love of truth. His views were shaped to conform to the spirit of the age. He was a teacher having itching ears, eager to hear the praise of men.

As his heavenly guide points out to him, his public rejection of the doctrine of the resurrection was not the heroic act which he claimed it to be. Coinciding with the temper of the times, it resulted in popularity, sale of his books, and a bishopric. His guide reminds him that as young men together they had not wanted to accept a crude salvationism. They were afraid of ridicule if they broke with popular opinion. To the bishop's insistence that his opinions were honestly held, his companion makes the perceptive comment that a man may be sincere at the moment about an opinion which is the result of wrong moral choices in the past. Such sincerity does not make him guiltless.

But the old habit of avoiding issues which deal with reality continues to operate even when Heaven lies before him for the taking. To every question of his friend, he has a vague and evasive answer.

"Will you repent and believe?"
"I'm not sure that I've got the exact point you are trying to make."

"Will you believe in me?"
"In what sense?"

"Do you not even believe that he [God] exists?"
"What does existence mean?"

"Can you, at least, still desire happiness?"
"Happiness, as you will come to see when you are older, lies in the path of duty."

118

All the trippers from Hell are referred to as ghosts because of their insubstantial appearance, but the bishop displays also a ghostly mind. He had perverted his reasoning powers for so long that they are hardly more than a few wisps of smoke. His thirst for truth had been satisfied by a fog of evasion, and with it had died his freedom of choice.

The next ghost is the one in the bowler hat who had told Lewis on the bus that he did not intend to stay in Heaven but hoped to start an import business by bringing some heavenly goods back with him to set up a shop which would deal in a little reality. His desperate attempt to carry the smallest apple back to the bus illustrates the obsession with materialism which completely obliterates all else and destroys one's power of choice. The irony of his struggle with his very small prize is expressed by the angel of the waterfall when he tells him that there is not room in Hell for it. And as we learn later, there would not have been room in Hell for even one seed of the apple. The great divorce is not a separation of equals but the separation of reality from that which hardly exists.

Like the man in the bowler hat the next person is also unaccompanied by a representative from the celestial mountains. He is called the Hard-bitten Ghost. He has been everywhere and seen everything and, according to him, there is nothing to it. His cynical attitude arises from his denial of all value. His whole view of life is based on a conspiracy theory of society. Everything is run by a World Combine. Heaven and Hell, wars, the tourist traps—all are operated by the same ring, who are referred to as "they."

Lewis is, perhaps, illustrating the common tendency to personify the vague forces which move society: of social attitudes and fashions ("they" aren't wearing it that way now), of government policies ("they" won't let you use that as a deduction any more), and of international attitudes ("they" want the U.S.A. to pay all the costs of the United Nations). And if one becomes bitter or skeptical about life, "they" becomes a malicious conspiracy or secret cabal of Jews, or Roman Catholics, or oil companies, or whatever group appears to the speaker to have more power and wealth than they should have.

119

THE INFERNAL LANDSCAPE

The Hard-bitten Ghost has "seen through" everything, and, as Lewis points out in *The Abolition of Man*, to see through everything is to make everything transparent and, therefore, not to see at all.[4] The ghost's cynicism has made him blind to beauty, to truth, to hope. He has chosen to close his mind to any possibility of goodness. Such a decision has fixed his destiny.

The tone of the next chapter is one of fear and shame. The narrator himself had been left in a state of fear by the Hard-bitten Ghost's view of Heaven as a place of sinister mockery in which a drop of dew or an insect might pierce one like a bullet. And the female ghost he meets next is fearful of the eyes which can pierce her like a shaft of sunlight through a smudged windowpane. Her false modesty prevents her from going to the mountains because the solid people can see through her. This seems to her worse than nudity.

But the real problem is one of comparison—her ghostly appearance compared to the bright reality of the solid ones. On the bus with the other shadowy people she, no doubt, had not been ashamed of the way she looked. But she says, "They ought to have warned us. I'd never have come." The other side of pride is shame—the sense of damage to one's own self-image.

In the sudden appearance of the herd of prancing unicorns—each at least twenty-seven hands high (nine feet) Lewis is saying that fear sometimes has a legitimate place in the making of choices. Not that anyone is going to be frightened into Heaven, but that one who is hesitating out of fear or shame can sometimes be moved to a decision by a greater fear. We are not told of the outcome of this confrontation, but later George MacDonald says that it may have worked. If it took her mind off herself for a moment, she may have been saved.

Lewis's use of the unicorns for this task is significant. The swan-white herd with flashing indigo horns and gleaming red eyes and nostrils must have been breathtaking. But, although beasts of great beauty, they thunder into the scene with an impact that no pride of roaring lions or herd of trumpeting elephants could have accomplished. For they are completely alien—from no land where man has walked. Their otherness contributes to the fabric into which is woven the unpluckable apples and unpickable daisies. To the ghostly visitors it is a fabric of both beauty and fear. The seeds of doubt sown in the narrator by the cynic who claims that this is a place where no man can live, seem verified.

Heaven itself will be a fearful place, Lewis suggests, to those who refuse to submit to certain changes within themselves. Even the solid people admit that they were rather ghostly when they first arrived. The fork in the road which separates those who descend to the drizzling twilight town and those who climb the mountains of light is at this point of willingness to adjust. As MacDonald says, "There are only two kinds of people in the end." To those who cling to the self which they have shaped by their own choices, God must finally say, "Thy will be done." Those who yield their ghostly nature for the solidifying process say to God, "Thy will be done." And of the former is this tally of the first five ghosts— the self-mutilated ones with their inflated inner-image, their intellectual dishonesty, their materialism, their cynicism, their false shame.

VIII.

THE SECOND five, following the central chapter, are also mutilated, but more by their desire to control and exploit others than by a turning in upon themselves. The meeting between the two artists perhaps comes closest of all the episodes to Lewis's own field as poet and storyteller. The ghostly painter wants to start painting immediately. One look at the blazing beauty of the scene and he thinks he is ready. To him reality, even the reality of Heaven, is only of value as a springboard, a stimulant for self-expression.

Although at one time he had been interested in telling people what he saw, giving them the glimpses of Heaven that he had caught on Earth, he had in his later works become more interested in the medium than the message—in paint as a thing in itself rather than as a means of communicating reality. As his heavenly companion tells him, that is a danger that all artists must guard against. Without the grace of God the artist may sink down from the love of the thing he tells to the love of the telling and finally to a self-centered love of nothing but his own reputation. But the artist whose labor has been redeemed from self-serving rejoices in his work for its own sake, as if it had been done by someone else, without pride and without modesty. Although the ghost says that he doesn't think he is troubled much with concern for his name, his actions soon belie his words, for he turns his back on Heaven when he learns that his reputation on Earth desperately needs defense.

The temptation of the artist to fall in love with his colors or the sound of his words and think of them as ends in themselves is corrupting, Lewis believed, to both the art and the artist. Whether he himself had ever been tempted to make either the tools of his art or his reputation the ends of his work is not recorded. Once, however, when he was asked how he felt about his worldwide reputation as a writer, he replied that it was a thing which he tried not to think about at all.

The second ghost of this pentad can be summed up by Lewis's statement elsewhere, "She's the sort of woman who lives for others—you can always tell the others by their hunted expression." The ambitious wife, who claims that she is doing it all for her husband, pushes him up the social ladder until he has a nervous breakdown. Like the grumbler she presents a continuous monologue, and her heavenly companion, who is perhaps her husband's sister, is given no opportunity to speak.

But the ghost is more than a wife ambitious for social position. She is a person with a lust for power over others. The gray city is Hell to her because she has no one to manage and change. They won't be altered down there. As she says, "I must have someone to—to do things to." A person who robs another of his freedom by managing his life against his will becomes a slave of that habit. The desire for control is a desire

122

for power, and "power corrupts." Her last remarks, revealing the hatred which lies at the center of her being, illustrates the final result of that corrupting habit.

The next interview displays another person with an obsession, the possessive mother. But the problem here is not one of power but of love. Her love for her son Michael had excluded and dried up her love for all else. For her brother who meets her, her only greeting is one of disappointment that it is not her son. For her husband, her daughter, her mother, she has no kindness. And yet, she calls mother-love the highest and holiest feeling in human nature. Her brother reminds her that it is a natural affection which she shares with the tigress and points out that no natural feelings are good or bad in themselves. They become holy if turned over to God, but if allowed their own freedom, may become demonic false gods.

In *The Four Loves*, which Lewis wrote some years later, he states that natural love such as mother-love if allowed to run without restraint can develop into something quite different and even become a rather complicated hatred. In fact, as MacDonald suggests, such a possessive mother-love as the ghost displays can end by demanding that the child be with it in Hell. Lewis also quotes another writer as saying that "love ceases to be a demon only when he ceases to be a god."[5] That is, natural love tends to claim for itself a divine authority— with demonic results. As Screwtape says of romantic love, it ends, "if all goes well, in murders and suicides."

And so the love of this mother for her son had become a tyrannical god who demanded a life-consuming allegiance. When her son died, she tried to keep his memory alive by embalming the past and attempting to relive it, keeping his room unchanged and commemorating his birthdays. Lewis believed that neither erotic love nor natural affection are sacred. In their original state they are earthbound and limited.

The ghostly love shown here displays its fanatic possessiveness in her demand, "He is mine, do you understand? Mine, mine, mine, for ever and ever." As her brother had told her, it is only when one loves God that he can love his

123

fellow creature fully. We leave before this interview is over, but MacDonald gives us some hope that there is still a spark of something unselfish in her love which possibly can be blown into a flame.

And now we come to the only ghost whose journey to the mountains of light we can be certain of—the one with the lizard of lust. We have discussed the response of nature in song to his triumphant ride but not the event itself. Most of the ghosts are assured that if they agree to go to the mountains, the thickening up process will gradually take place as they are helped by the solid people, who have already gone through the experience. But the mountain track is not the setting of the story, and we see no such transformation take place.

It is perhaps for this reason that Lewis changes his method and allows us to see the solidifying take place quite suddenly. For this work he needs higher heavenly powers than those of the solid saints, and so we are introduced to one of the "burning ones," an angel with authority greater than that of the heavenly guides we have already met. It is significant that Lewis chooses as the barrier to heavenly bliss a vice which most people would place at the lowest level of debasing sins. But he implies that no sin can keep one out of Heaven if he is willing to allow it to be killed. In fact, when the ghost makes his final decision, he says, "It would be better to be dead than to live with this creature."

Although we can understand the transformation of the man when he becomes willing to die, what is the meaning of the transformation of the lizard into the magnificent stallion? Are vices changed into virtues in Heaven? However, the red lizard does not represent the vice of lust, *per se*, but man's animal nature. Although perverted by sin, man's body and his natural appetites are still God-given. Paul says in Romans that the whole creation groans, and we groan within ourselves waiting for the redemption of our body. And prior to that redemption, there must be a death. George MacDonald insists that the narrator must not forget that the lizard was killed. But out of such death comes, not weakness, but surging strength.

IX.

THE LAST and longest interview covers two chapters. Up to this point the emphasis in the conversations has been upon the transparent trippers from the gray city and the conditions and attitudes which influence their choices. The earthly relationship of the solid ones to the ghosts has sometimes been identified, but not much attention has been given to anything but their arguments. Here, however, the spotlight turns on a great and famous saint, Sarah Smith of Golders Green. You may never have heard of her, but, as MacDonald tells us, fame in Heaven is quite different from fame on Earth.

It is true that we also have a very interesting ghost, but his double role does not detract from the paradise of love which surrounds the lady. The procession of joyous angels, humans, and animals who dance and sing before her indicates that her retinue is made up of those who delight to respond to her love.

Sarah Smith is Lewis's picture of one whose abundant love on Earth has been transfigured to radiant heavenly love. In her former life every boy and girl she met became her son or daughter, and every cat and dog found a place in her affections which enriched its selfhood. But now that she has met Love Himself in this place of infinite reality, her dazzling beauty and unconquerable joy display the intensity of her love. Lewis speaks of "the unbearable beauty" of her countenance, of the love which shines not only from her face, but from her limbs as well "as if it were some liquid in which she had just been bathing." Her presence is an invitation to joy, which sings "out of her whole being like a bird's song on an April evening."

Now that she has come to know the meaning of *agape*, or divine love, she speaks of earthly love as primarily need-love. "I loved you for my own sake: because I needed you." But now she says, "What needs could I have, now that I have all?" And so she indicates that only when creatures have no need of each other can they truly love. As the hymn in

125

Perelandra declares: love should not be of need nor of deserving, "but a plain bounty."

The dwarf ghost who had been the husband of the lady is accompanied by his theatrical puppet, who represents the roles he had played on earth to get his own way. The two figures are all that remain of what had once been one person. Lewis has placed this interview last, in the place of greatest emphasis. Perhaps he believed that role playing for the triumph of one's own selfish desires is the household sin which creates more misery than any other.

But the ghost has been a role player so long, using the pity of others as a weapon to get his own way, that his real self finally shrinks to nothing, and his empty theatrical self is all that is left. His attempts to play his melodramas here are without effect. He can make himself wretched, but he cannot infect the lady with his misery. As she says, "I cannot love a lie. . . . I am in Love, and out of it I will not go."

When the interview is over, her company of spirits sing a song describing God's love and protection of the lady. As in the previous interview, the psalmist is called upon for the music. The eleven verses are a free adaptation to the person of the lady of more than half of Psalm 91. The only verse in the song which does not find its parallel in the psalm is the sixth, which refers to her ghostly husband's failure to blackmail her with his role-playing lies. Lewis does some modernizing such as "bullets" for "arrows" and "germs" for "pestilence," but employs in his song verses 1–7, 11–13, and 16 of the psalm.

This interview is placed last also because it reveals the limits of the reach of love. Although Sarah would gladly have gone into Hell on a mission of love, MacDonald reveals to Lewis's astonished gaze the sort of hairline crack in the earth in which all of Hell is to be found. It could not open its mouth wide enough to receive her. The reality of evil is almost nothing as compared to the reality of good.

And so it is choice, says Lewis, which creates the great divorce between Heaven and Hell. But what is choice? His episodes have shown us the alternatives that face some individuals, but he does not pretend to be able to explain the mystery of human decision. The vision in the last chapter of the gigantic forms and the chessmen upon the table raises the unanswerable question: When is decision made? Were the scenes in the book but the outcome of choices made long ago; were they pictures of present choices; or were they anticipations of choices to be made at the end of time? But he implies that as long as man floats on the stream of time, the best antidote to such befuddling problems is a healthy recognition that some questions are beyond our comprehension.

BEYOND THE UNIVERSE

CHAPTER 6

IN THE DAYS OF THE HIGH KING:
THE LION, THE WITCH AND
THE WARDROBE AND
THE HORSE AND HIS BOY

I.

"But do you really mean, Sir," said Peter, "that there could be other worlds—all over the place, just around the corner—like that?"

"Nothing is more probable," said the Professor.

C. S. LEWIS'S mind was a king's highway down which marched not only the strange furry creatures from Mars, the green royalty of Venus, decayed ghosts and solid saints from the regions of darkness and light, but also whole universes whose skies and seas are not to be discovered by following the endless light-years of our own sun and stars. Such worlds are not far away—just around the corner, as Peter says (near the beginning of *The Lion, the Witch and the Wardrobe*)—but they are only entered by magic pictures, gates, or wardrobes. Our clocks and cubic miles of atmosphere in no way overlap or are connected with their time and space. Charn and Narnia are completely "other" than our universe.

But any discussion of their significance must tread softly. *The Chronicles* are lightly told. It would be disastrous to hang

131

weights on their wings. However, that there is significance—ethical and theological—no perceptive adult reader would deny. Perhaps the clearest statement of the author's purpose is to be found in the words of Aslan just before he opens the door in the sky at the end of *The Voyage of the "Dawn Treader."* He tells the children (Lucy, Edmund, and Eustace) that in their world he has another name. "This was the very reason why you were brought to Narnia, that by knowing me here for a little, you may know me better there."

As the other name is clearly that of Christ, one might expect the stories to be thick and cumbersome with theology. That they are not is a tribute to Lewis's skill, but also an illustration of the method by which he wrote. In discussing his stories he insisted that he did not begin with a theme, but with a picture. Narnia was not created as a spoon for feeding Christianity to children in small morsels. It began, he tells us, as an image in his mind of a faun with an umbrella in a snowy wood carrying some parcels under his arm. The picture remained there for many years without ethical or religious meaning. But finally Aslan leaped into the picture along with some other images such as a queen on a sledge, and Lewis decided to see if he could put together a fairy story addressed to children.

So goat-footed Mr. Tumnus with his horns and tail was the first inhabitant of Narnia. As a creature out of Greek mythology he is not a very promising character for a story concerning Christian truth. And that, of course, is the point. Lewis begins with a story, not a theme. From the folklore and fables of many cultures he invites creatures of all sorts—dryads, dragons, giants, and talking animals. And as they enter through the magic portals, the Narnian air works a change in their natures. The Greek centaurs, German dwarfs, British witches, become Narnian through and through. They may be evil or good, but they have the stamp of the new world in which they find themselves.

The unique colors and shapes of this world, however, flow out of the imagination of a man who was a Christian and dedicated to the purpose of making his faith both seen and heard. Inevitably, from such a spring came bubbling the genesis, the gospel, the apocalypse of this new world.

But as you may have noted from the Table of Contents, I have put the genesis and apocalypse of Narnia (*The Magician's Nephew* and *The Last Battle*) together in the chapter called "First and Last Things." The reason for beginning our discussion with *The Lion, the Witch and the Wardrobe* perhaps deserves explaining. Although second in the chronology of Narnia, *The Lion* is the first book written. It is clear from some of the details of the story that Lewis did not at that time have the entire series worked out in his mind. There are some minor inconsistencies.

For instance, Mr. Beaver tells the children that they are the first sons of Adam and daughters of Eve in Narnia, but in *The Magician's Nephew,* recording events centuries before the Pevensie children appear, we are introduced to Frank and Helen, the London cabby and his wife, who become the first rulers of Narnia, and Polly and Digory, the children who brought the Queen of Charn to the new land. Also, Mr. Beaver tells us that Jadis, the White Witch, is the offspring of an affair between a giant and Lilith, Adam's first wife, who was a Jinn. But in *The Magician's Nephew* Jadis comes from a completely different world where she had been a queen and had had an impressive set of royal ancestors. These are minor points and do not dampen our enjoyment of the stories, but they illustrate that the whole of Narnia had not quite emerged from its shell when Lewis removed the back from the wardrobe and introduced Mr. Tumnus to a daughter of Eve. And so here, it seems to me, is where our discussion should begin.

II.

ALTHOUGH, AS Narnia grew from *The Lion, the Witch and the Wardrobe* to *The Last Battle*, it changed slightly and became enriched by the introduction of new histories and the exploration of distant lands and foreign worlds, the voice of the narrator does not change. The style and the point of view are constant throughout the seven tales. The special position of the narrator (different from that in any of his other stories) is in his relationship with the reader.

Perhaps the word *raconteur,* a skilled spinner of tales, describes Lewis's relationship to the story. He is not so much a narrator as a storyteller, if I can make that distinction. It is as if he is here in the room with us, his feet spread out to the fire, his hands gesturing, his face smiling, his eyes twinkling as he makes a humorous point. Notice how often in *The Lion, the Witch and the Wardrobe* he reminds us of his presence: "As I have said," "I agree with them," and of our presence too: "I hope you know what I mean by a voice sounding pale," "ten to one you have never seen a giant with his face beaming." The *I's* and *you's* scattered throughout the book referring to the storyteller and his friend, the reader, establish a common ground which is almost a one-to-one relationship.

Of course, the story is addressed to the young reader. But Lewis did not believe that a person should leave his childhood behind like a train leaving a railway station, but that as he became older his life should be enriched like a train taking on more and more goods. In fact, he says, using the word *poetry* to mean all imaginative literature, that "only those adults who have retained, with whatever additions and enrichments, their first childish response to poetry unimpaired, can be said to have grown up at all."[1]

The reader should learn to enjoy Tolstoy and Shakespeare, he thought, but need not abandon his early taste for fantasy nor apologize for an adult enjoyment of what are called "children's books." He refers a number of times with relish to Kenneth Grahame's *The Wind in the Willows,* and observes that "no book is really worth reading at the age of ten which is not equally (and often far more) worth reading at the age of fifty."[2] And he admits that at ten he read fairy tales secretly and would have been embarrassed at being discovered, but "Now that I am fifty I read them openly." And so if the raconteur of Narnia uses words and images a child would understand, it is to welcome the child into the circle of listeners whose childhood has not been left behind at the railway station.

We can say, then, that the point of view, like that of *That Hideous Strength*, is author-omniscient, although with a "presence" we did not feel in the other book. The story shifts back and forth from Edmund's encounters with the White Witch to the other children's snowy trek with the Beavers and their meeting with Aslan. We know Edmund's inner longings as he stares at the empty box of Turkish Delight and Peter's sickening fear as he charges at Maugrim, the wolf. The thoughts of the children are often revealed to us.

But here omniscience stops. We do not peer into the minds of the other creatures. What we know of the inner life of dwarfs, mice, and marshwiggles is revealed through their words, their actions, or their looks. *The Chronicles* are about human beings whose adventures in Narnia extend from tea with fauns to flights on winged horses, but the stories are always about the human beings. The omniscient author knows which race he belongs to.

III.

THE FAIRY tale, as Lewis says elsewhere, is a severely limited form. It is hostile to analysis, and it excludes, among other things, a detailed portrayal of psychological states.[3] So we should not expect a complex character study of the four youngsters who emerge from the wardrobe into the White Witch's kingdom. Their differences can be summed up briefly.

Peter, the oldest, is a natural leader. As he is to be the High King of Narnia in its Golden Age, he shows, as we would expect, some royal qualities even as a boy. When he thinks of animals in the woods around the professor's house, it is of eagles, stags, and hawks—kingly and heraldic birds and beasts. He acts with courage when Susan is in danger, and does not flinch when Aslan leaves the conduct of the battle in his hands. He rebukes the spiteful tongue of Edmund, is kind to Lucy even when he thinks she is out of her mind, and apologizes to her when he discovers that her story is true. We are not surprised that he grows up to be a tall, deep-chested ruler of Narnia, known as King Peter the Magnificent.

Tender-hearted and peace-loving Susan, next in age, often shows a timidity which does not step eagerly into dangerous waters. More than once in Narnia she wants to go home or wishes they had never come. When she learns that Aslan is a lion, she wants to know if he is safe, and she wonders fearfully if it is safe to bring Rumblebuffin back from stone statue to living giant. When the Stone Table cracks, she is afraid to turn around to see what has happened, and when Aslan comes back to life, she wants to know if he is a ghost.

But her sense of duty is stronger than her timidity. She votes to stay in Narnia to save Mr. Tumnus, and agrees that they should risk the unknown by meeting with the dark and furry stranger who beckons them to come deeper into the woods. Her loving nature shows itself in the tearful all-night vigil with Lucy after Aslan's death, and her love of peace is demonstrated in her rebuke of the quarrel between Edmund and Peter. There is a practical strain in her nature. It is she who thinks of the need of coats and dinner during their adventure. But most apparent is the quietness of her spirit which causes her to be known later in Narnia as Queen Susan the Gentle, whose beauty was desired by many kings and was the source of some of the excitement of *The Horse and His Boy*.

Edmund, the prodigal, is the most important of the children to the theme of redemption in the story, but as to his character we should perhaps say that he is just a small boy whose tendency to selfishness and bullying needs to be checked before it colors his whole life. And this is one reason why he has found his way into Narnia. Most of the visitors from Adam's race are better people for having been there. To soften our censure of Edmund we should remember that he had begun going bad at "that horrid school," so there were outside influences. But it is plain that he is an unlovely sight.

Bad-tempered when tired and a grumbler when it rains, his chief delight is in being spiteful and superior to his younger sister. His selfishness makes him an easy prey to the Witch's lying promises, and causes him to shiver with horror at the name of Aslan.

But all that Edmund needs is a glimpse of what true meanness is like in order to start the process of repentance. The lesson in misery he learns at the hands of the Witch does its proper work. His sympathy for the little animals at the Christmas dinner which the Witch turns to stone in spite of his pleas shows that a change is taking place. That his transformation is complete and permanent is made clear when Aslan knights him on the battlefield. Perhaps his first experiences in Narnia had a sobering effect upon him, for we are told that he grew up to be a graver and quieter man than Peter, noted for his wise counsel. Appropriately, he is known as King Edmund the Just.

Lucy, light-hearted and golden-haired (although the illustrator always makes her hair black), is perhaps the most prominent human being in the entire series. She appears in five of the seven tales, and is used by Lewis frequently as the central intelligence. Aslan seems to find greater rapport with her than with the others, for she is the one to whom he most often reveals himself. Her loving nature displays itself in her kind treatment of the faun after his repentant confession that he had planned to turn her over to the White Witch.

She is given the task of leading the reader into Narnia, for she is the adventuresome one. As she enters the land for the first time, she is somewhat frightened, but also very curious and excited. And her fear does not stop her. She is, no doubt, correct when she tells Father Christmas that she thinks she would be brave enough to enter the battle, although he tells her that she will not take part. It is not surprising that during the Golden Age the princes of all the nearby kingdoms are in love with Queen Lucy the Valiant.

What was said of point of view cannot be said of characterization, however. We view Narnia only through human eyes, but we do not learn only of human character. Although Peter, Susan, Edmund, and Lucy each stand clear as individual persons, the same may be said for many an odd native of Narnia. Horses, mice, badgers, marshwiggles, bears, and unicorns may show something of the nature of their species, but each also displays habits and states of mind which declare the uniqueness of his own personhood.

We could not imagine Mr. Beaver shedding the tears of Mr. Tumnus, nor the faun indulging in the sarcasm of Mr. Beaver during the interview between Aslan and the White Witch. Although Mr. Tumnus is a little more folksy and friendly than a classical faun (almost nobody stands on ceremony in Narnia), he still quite properly talks of dryads and nymphs and of the times before the White Witch when Bacchus visited, and red wine flowed in the stream beds. Mr. Beaver, on the other hand, whose house contains gum boots and oilskins instead of books, is the outspoken, practical person whose shrewd observation can recognize a boy who has eaten of the Witch's Turkish Delight.

IV.

WHEN EDMUND is on his way from the Beaver's house to the Witch's castle, he indulges in some daydreams and determines how many cars he will have when he is king of the land, where the railways will be placed, and what he will have in his private cinema. Each of these strikes a sour note in our minds as we think of it in Narnia. Lewis's own handling of setting skillfully avoids such jarring discords. In a letter to a young writer he says of fantasy that one must be careful "never to break the spell, to do nothing which will wake the reader and bring him back with a bump to the common earth."[4]

And Narnia never touches the common earth of our own life. There is a marked contrast between the modern England from which the children come and the archaic land of Narnia in which they arrive. We must call the country archaic rather than ancient, because it seems to be contemporary with our twentieth century, but its culture and lifestyle (where it is human at all) is one of castles and antique weaponry. When wars must be fought, in addition to giant's clubs and bear's claws and teeth, there are bows and arrows, swords and shields. The curse of cannon and gunpowder, of steam or internal combustion engines is unknown beyond the wardrobe.

But although the setting is archaic, it is not one of dim shadows and indistinct forms. Narnia is a land of sunlit hills for roaming the starlit lawns for dancing, where life is sharply outlined. After reading the description of Mr. Tumnus no one could fail to recognize a faun even if he met him by moonlight, and the sudden rush of spring when the Witch's power is broken and Narnia leaps from January to May in a few hours is a triumph of flowers and birds and running water.

As we have noted, however, in our preceding discussions, Lewis does not introduce setting simply as pictures to decorate the walls of his story. It is always joined to the action or the theme. The melting snow slows down the Witch so that the Beaver party gets to Aslan first. The bird songs and crocuses are evidence that her magic has been overcome by a greater magic. And when a hint will spur the reader to employ his own imagination, Lewis does not drown us with details. Cair Paravel is a wonderful castle and the capital of the whole country, but the Great Hall with its western wall of peacock feathers and roof of ivory is all the author gives us. With such a beginning the reader can serve as architect for the rest.

The contrast between modern England and archaic Narnia is also used to accomplish Lewis's purposes. In most of the stories the English scene (and situation) is very ordinary. In *The Lion, the Witch and the Wardrobe* we are introduced to four children with common names who have been sent out of London into the country during World War II. To those reading the story in 1950 when it was published, nothing would seem more natural. Lewis himself had been host to a group of such "evacuees." And the huge house to which the Pevensie children come, with its halls and stairways, its harps and armor, its galleries and libraries, although not commonplace, is certainly the recognizable "historic mansion" which tourists delight to visit.

So the story begins with people and scenes which the reader can recognize as real and perhaps even as familiar. In fact, the place where Lucy's adventures start is a room empty but for a dead bluebottle fly on the windowsill and an ordinary-appearing wardrobe against the wall. We go from the expected to the surprising, from the natural to the supernatural, from the humdrum to the adventurous.

One reason for the contrasts is just that—contrast. The light is more bright if we drive into it from a long dark tunnel, and the adventure is more exciting if it suddenly erupts on a dull, rainy day. But as we have indicated, there are Christian reverberations in the story. The proximity of Narnia to everyday existence, even though it does not overlap, reminds the reader that the supernatural is not far from the commonplace. Surrounding us are the hosts of Heaven; at our elbow is the Tempter; and God is a very present help in time of trouble. As Francis Thompson has expressed it in a poem called "The Kingdom of God,"

> Yea, in the night, my Soul, my daughter,
> Cry—clinging Heaven by the hems;
> And lo, Christ walking on the water,
> Not of Gennesareth, but Thames!

And so, through a wardrobe lies Narnia.

V.

BEFORE DISCUSSING the themes we should say something about plot. Lewis's first story of *The Chronicles* is quite different from the others. In most of the tales the children and their Narnian companions accomplish deeds of derring-do, sometimes with Aslan's help and sometimes simply by following his instructions. In *The Lion, the Witch and the Wardrobe*, we could almost say that Aslan does it all. It is true that Peter kills the wolf, and that he and Edmund conduct themselves honorably on the battlefield, but the contest with Maugrim is very brief, and we are not present to see the exploits of the brothers in the field.

The essential action of the plot begins with two disasters, the arrest of Mr. Tumnus and the betrayal by Edmund. Then we are assured by Mr. Beaver that both problems must be turned over to Aslan—that any other stratagems would be hopeless. When Edmund is rescued and set right by a quiet talk with Aslan, we learn that he still has a price on his head—a price which only Aslan can pay. And even the minor matter of turning Mr. Tumnus, the stone, into Mr. Tumnus, the faun, is done by the magic breath of the lion. Finally, Aslan arrives at the battle to turn the tide and give the sorceress her just deserts. The book might be called the Acts of Aslan.

The reason for this spotlighting is again in the fact that the story is an introduction. It focuses upon the unifying character of the entire series. Here is more evidence that one should begin his reading with this story. Just as one who reads the Bible for the first time should begin with the Gospels and perhaps the Acts of the Apostles before going back to Genesis, so we begin here and will discuss next the deeds of some of Aslan's disciples before we get to first and last things.

One cannot consider action for very long, however, without talking about theme. The first hint that the story illustrates religious ideas (although perhaps not apparent without further reading) is the statement of Mr. Tumnus that since the White Witch has spread her spells over Narnia, it has been always winter and never Christmas. Lucy says, "How awful!" Perhaps the child reader would feel the impact of such a condition more than the adult.

But a winter without spring is without hope, and a winter without Christmas is without love. The evil power of Jadis had destroyed, or at least driven underground, two of the Christian virtues. And without hope it is difficult to maintain faith. As gentle a person as Mr. Tumnus had intended to turn Lucy over to the usurper. Even some of the trees had gone bad and sided with the horrible creatures who made up her army.

The first indication that, as Mr. Beaver says, "Aslan is on the move," is that Father Christmas can no longer be kept out. Some critics have objected to the introduction of this character, as not belonging to Narnia—"breaking the magic for a moment" as one writer puts it. But I fail to see where the weakness lies. It is true that Father Christmas does not belong to the same genus as the nymphs, dryads, and centaurs of Narnia. But neither do the witches, gnomes, and werewolves. As we have said, Lewis levies tribute from the folklore of more than one culture and stamps it anew as the coin of the realm of Narnia. Father Christmas in England (like Santa Claus in the United States) has been somewhat tarnished with commercialism. But in Narnia he is not a jolly old elf selling television sets or pipe tobacco. Lewis reaches back even beyond the sainthood of Saint Nicholas. Here is the Spirit of Christmas. He makes the children feel very glad and also very solemn. He is the giver of gifts, associated with the day since the time of the wise men. And you remember that the children's gifts were not toys. Like the gifts of the Spirit listed by St. Paul, these were to be used in the service of others.

VI.

THEN, THERE is the religious significance of Aslan. He is the King, we are told, the Lord of the whole wood and the son of the great Emperor-Beyond-the-Sea. Here, of course, is a representation of Christ. Like Christ he is a divider of houses. At the first mention of his name three of the children react with delight, but Edmund's guilty conscience causes him to dread this mysterious person and to turn to the lying blandishments of the Witch. Why did Lewis make him a lion? Probably for two reasons. In Revelation Christ is called the Lion of the Tribe of Judah. But, after all, the lion is the king of beasts. In a land of beasts who talk and make moral decisions what better form could he have? And the more one reads the tales the more he feels that Lewis's choice was exactly right.

The form of Aslan does not account for all of his characteristics, however. To the girls' trembling question: "Is he safe?" Mr. Beaver says, " 'Course he isn't safe. But he's good. He's the King, I tell you." Goodness, wisdom, and majesty may not always be predictable. The lion's acts and orders are sometimes breathtaking. But his righteousness can always be counted on. Lewis refuses to present to children a picture of God as an indulgent old grandfather. His demands draw a sharp line between good and evil.

But Aslan is more than good. He is the son of the Emperor-Beyond-the-Sea. We must not leave him in the Old Testament. When God became a man He demonstrated that He was approachable. The message of the angel at Bethlehem was, "Fear not." And so, although Aslan is majestic, he is not haughty. The children approach him the first time with trembling, but his voice takes the fidgets out of them. They feel glad and quiet. The lowliest subject is always put at ease in Aslan's presence and given evidence of his love.

But of course, Aslan's love is best demonstrated by his death. So we must face the question of his relation to the crucifixion. Is this an allegory of salvation? I have called the lion a representation of Christ and have carefully avoided the word symbol. For as we have already said, Lewis insisted that his stories are not allegories. He does say in a letter that he is convinced that "the wit of man *cannot* devise a story in which the wit of some other man cannot find an allegory."[5] But this only underlines his view that many allegorical interpretations of literature are fabrications which the original author did not dream of. He scornfully calls such scholarly structures "the discovery of the mare's nest by the pursuit of the red herring."[6] So we must not commit the same sin here.

In a letter on *Till We Have Faces,* which we will discuss later, Lewis gives us the words to use. He speaks of "parallels" and "instances," not of "symbols." And this makes a great difference. What we have in *The Lion, the Witch and the Wardrobe* is atonement in Narnia, not an allegory of atonement on Earth. Lewis does not need to write with his eye on Christ's crucifixion. Instead he is free to show how far the love of God will go by telling a story which has some obvious

143

parallels to the Gospel account, but also some differences. As we have explained in the discussion in chapter two, the narrative is "sacramental" rather than allegorical.

One of the differences is that Aslan died for one small boy. To quote again the hymn of praise at the end of *Perelandra,* "When He died in the Wounded World He died not for men, but for each man. If each man had been the only man made, He would have done no less." And so Aslan died for Edmund. The truth of the gospel is there even though the story is different. But there are many echoes of the passion of Christ. There is the Way of Sorrow as Aslan treads the path from the Fords of Beruna to the Stone Table—from the place where his followers slept to the place of sacrifice. On the way, there is even a stumble, perhaps to suggest the fall under the weight of the cross. And the mocking and sneering of the evil creatures as they bind the lion, shave him, and prepare him for the sacrifice is an obvious parallel to the derision and scourging of Jesus by the Roman soldiers. After Aslan is bound and muzzled, the crowd gather around "kicking him, hitting him, spitting on him, jeering at him."

VII.

ASLAN IS sacrificed on the Stone Table, the place where Edmund would have been killed if the Witch had had her way. "That is the proper place," she told the dwarf. "That is where it has always been done before." The reader may at first conclude that the Table represents the law. The Ten Commandments were written on tables of stone, and the Narnian Table is described as a grim slab with figures cut into it as if of an unknown tongue. The Stone Table was broken, however, when Aslan came back to life. And yet Christ said that He had not come to do away with the law but to fulfill it. And Aslan makes it very clear that he would not think of working against the Deep Magic of his father, the Emperor, which is written on the Stone Table, as well as on the Emperor's sceptre. I think it is safe to say that the *writing* on the

Table is the law—that is, the *Tao*, which Lewis describes in *The Abolition of Man* and discusses as the Rule of Right and Wrong in the first chapters of *Mere Christianity*.

Lewis points out in these chapters that God's law of righteousness is frightening, for it is inflexible. It allows no exceptions or excuses; it is as hard as nails. And the Witch tells us what it means for those who transgress it. "Every traitor belongs to me as my lawful prey and... for every treachery I have a right to a kill." (Sin, when it hath conceived, bringeth forth death.) "Unless I have blood as the Law says," declares the Witch, "all Narnia will be overturned and perish in fire and water." (Without the shedding of blood there is no remission of sins.) So these are the demands of the law. And it is these *demands* rather than the law itself which are represented by the Stone Table and which are satisfied by Aslan's sacrifice. The cracking of the Table represents the destruction of the enmity in the law. Never again will it demand death.

But are these concepts for children? No doubt, children from Christian homes will see some of the relationships between Aslan and Christ. But surely here are theological subtleties for them to discover when they reread the stories as adults. Lewis uses as a title for a short article the statement, "Sometimes fairy stories may say best what's to be said."[7] But if "what's to be said" is theology beyond the grasp of the child, then the fairy tale is a form intended for adults as well. The story, the vocabulary, and some of the ideas are at the level of comprehension of the young reader, but other ideas are for the older reader's consideration.

The resurrection of Aslan is also Narnian, but, like his death, echoes the Gospel account. The weeping Lucy sobbing, "Oh, its *too* bad; they might have left the body alone," reminds us of Mary Magdalene in the garden, especially when behind her is heard the great voice of the risen son of the Emperor-Beyond-the-Sea. But what are we to make of the romp which takes place on this Narnian Easter morning between Aslan, Susan, and Lucy? Is this proper for His Majesty the King? Does it damage his position as a metaphor of Christ?

145

If we think so, we need to be reminded that Christ says a great deal about joy—His joy and the joy He gives to His followers—and that only those who become as little children will enter the kingdom of heaven. In spite of some ideas for adults, Narnia is a child's world. The Pevensie children are not allowed to enter it after a certain age. This episode of laughter and leaping arms and legs expresses the joy of Easter in Narnian images. In *Reflections on the Psalms* Lewis speaks with approval of the close association in the child's mind of the festive and the religious and tells of one small boy devoutly murmuring to himself on Easter morning a poem he had written which began "Chocolate eggs and Jesus risen."[8] Aslan's romp expresses that same union of physical delight and spiritual triumph.

There is nothing solemn in the romp because Lewis felt that in his own childhood solemnity had been a problem. Religion had had too much adult reverence. In the short article alluded to above, he states as one of his intentions in the Narnian tales to "steal past the watchful dragons" of stained glass and Sunday school—barriers which had paralyzed his religious feelings as a child. By displaying the nature of God and the sufferings of Christ in an imaginary world stripped of the trappings of ritual and hushed devotion, he thought he could display them to the child in their real potency. The enthusiasm of children around the world for these books would indicate that he was correct.

VIII.

THE ONLY Narnian tale which does not include a magic entrance from Earth takes place during the long reign of the four who came through the wardrobe. In a sense *The Horse and His Boy* can be called a sequel to *The Lion, the Witch and the Wardrobe*, although actually it should be inserted within the last few pages of that story. In point of composition it was written after *Prince Caspian* and *The Voyage of the "Dawn Treader"* but was held back until *The Silver Chair* had been written and published. So all of what I have called the Caspian Triad was available to the public before Lewis took his readers back again to the Golden Age of Narnia and the adventures of the lost prince of Archenland.

More than half of the book is set in Calormen, the vast despotic kingdom to the south of Narnia and separated from it by a desert. Modeled after the Turkish and Persian empires of the Near East it stands out in sharp contrast to the free state where justice is administered by King Peter and his compeers. The contrast allows Lewis to illustrate the mentality of the slave as opposed to that of a freeman. Like *Out of the Silent Planet* the plot is made up largely of journeys, but journeys beset with dangers, barriers, and oppositions. What starts as an escape from slavery turns into a race to carry a warning to an endangered kingdom. But perhaps the most striking aspect of the plot is in the parallel actions of the two young protagonists.

The story begins with a slave who does not know he is a slave. Shasta had always assumed that he was the son of Arsheesh, and only when he hears the fisherman bargaining with Tarkaan Anradin for his sale does he realize that he is a property. A little later we hear of another sort of slavery as Aravis tells her story. The position of women in Calormen is also that of property. The young Tarkeena had been *offered* by her father to be the wife of a rich and powerful lord. And by comparing the stories of Shasta and Aravis we can follow the plot structure of the book as it illustrates one of the themes. It is Bree, the Narnian horse, who saves Shasta from death as a slave to Anradin and persuades him that they run away to Narnia. And it is Hwin, the Narnian mare, who saves Aravis from death by suicide and persuades her that they should escape to Narnia. Then after the two parties are herded together by the rough shepherding of Aslan and make their way to Tashbaan, both the children are "recognized" and both make important "discoveries." Shasta is recognized as a son of King Lune of Archenland by the Narnian lords (although they are mistaken as to which son) and taken to their abode. Aravis is recognized by her friend Lasaraleen and taken to her home. By listening to the plans of the Narnians Shasta learns of the best way across the desert, and by eavesdropping on the Tisroc, Aravis learns of the treacherous plan of Rabadash to cross the desert and attack Anvard. Before the desert crossing Aslan serves as Shasta's protector, and after the crossing as Aravis's teacher. When the race to warn King Lune is done, Aslan reveals himself to Shasta on the road into Narnia and to Aravis at the Hermit's home. And finally, Shasta experiences the warm hospitality of Narnia in the home of the red dwarfs, Duffle, Rogin, and Bricklethumb, and Aravis is welcomed into the warm hospitality of Archenland at the court of King Lune. Although Shasta is a true northern prince and Aravis a Calormene Tarkeena whose blood can be traced back through Tarkaans and Tisrocs to the great god Tash, the balanced handling of their stories illustrates that Lewis does not intend to say that freedom is a matter of geography and race (or sex). It is a state of mind that grows out of fortitude and expresses itself in respect for all other individuals.

IX.

THE STORY of Shasta is the familiar fairy tale of the slave boy who turns out to be a lost prince, but as Lewis handles it, it is more than a plot built on a series of lucky accidents—in fact, luck has nothing to do with it. In addition to the mystery of divine purpose, the character of the boy has a significant influence upon the events which shape the story. Very early we are given evidence that Shasta has a sense of right and wrong. He knows that boys should love their fathers, and he had been uneasy because he could not love Arsheesh. He has a conscience against stealing, and only when Bree explains it as the spoils of war will he use the money of the Tarkaan. He sees the unfairness of Aravis in drugging her slave and then allowing her to be beaten for sleeping late.

In addition to his moral sense he has a characteristic which Lewis prized highly—an imagination. He longs to know what lies beyond the northern horizon, and his mind is aflame at the possibilities of his parentage when he learns that Arsheesh is not his father. But perhaps his most spectacular virtue is the spontaneous courage which reacts to need without counting the cost to himself. His behavior in facing the lion who is attacking Aravis and Hwin not only displays his character to the reader, but also creates in Aravis a new attitude toward him.

Aravis, the little aristocrat, needs some lessons before she is ready for the free society of Narnia, but in spite of her upbringing in a slave state she is at heart a free soul. Having always lived in the country and loved a vigorous life of bows and arrows, dogs, horses, and swimming, she loathes Tashbaan with its crowded streets and smells and piles of rubbish. She is clear-headed in emergencies such as Lasaraleen's recognition of her in the street, and is determined and courageous in her decision to commit suicide rather than marry the abominable Ahoshta Tarkaan.

She also displays the sort of courage which Lewis most often holds up for our admiration—that which acts in spite of a quaking fear at the center of one's bones. Her training told her that the Tombs of the Ancient Kings were haunted by ghouls. But she sticks out her chin and in the face of her fear walks straight toward them. Perhaps her outstanding trait is her loyalty. Lewis tells us that she is "true as steel." Her answer to Lasaraleen's plea that she change her plans is, "I promised."

The companionable horses, Bree and Hwin, are also creatures worth knowing. The gentle and high-bred mare always seems to have the most sensible advice to give in facing problems or troubles. Her motherly rebuke and her descriptions of Narnia direct Aravis into a new path, and her plan for getting through Tashbaan is the one accepted by the others. Her timid nature is easily silenced by the self-confident pronouncements of Bree, but where there is a difference of opinion, she is usually right.

Bree is a good horse whose life among slaves and witless horses has had an unfortunate influence upon his attitudes. But he shows the Narnian love of truth and love of freedom. In spite of his disparaging remarks about Shasta's riding ability, he shows a real fondness for the boy. He has come, however, to have too high an opinion of himself and too great a regard for his appearance and his position in society. The self-knowledge which comes through failure and humiliation begins to do its work before the story is through, and we have hope that Bree's essential virtues will dominate his nature before he has lived long in Narnia.

The gracious qualities of good King Lune can best be seen by setting him beside the Tisroc of Calormen, the Supreme Highness, whose numberless subjects cannot utter his name without wishing him everlasting life. The ruler at Tashbaan is a vast jelly of a man who must heave up "his enormous body" from the sofa after the secret council with his son is over. The ruler at Anvard is also fat, but active. In fact, we first see him with a hunting party. He is described as apple-cheeked and jolly. Typical of the tyrant that he is, the Tisroc regards his subjects with contempt, even referring to his Grand Vizier as a vile person. King Lune, on the other hand, shows respect for everyone including Bree and Hwin without in the least detracting from the authority of his position.

The Calormene potentate is cruel and heartless, ruling even his son and the Vizier by threats. The Archenlander is courteous and sympathetic to Aravis and even merciful to the treacherous Rabadash. And, finally, the Tisroc can think with ruthless and unnatural tranquility of the possible death of his son, while King Lune shows the natural fondness and pride of a father in both of his twins. Here is a part of the mosaic which Lewis creates of a slave state and a free nation. The character of the ruler reflects the character of the country.

The traits of Rabadash the Ridiculous remind us of another characteristic of the story—its humor. There is the gentle fun with Bree, who is torn between his love of rolling and his fear of being improper at his homecoming. And at the other extreme there is the open satire of tyranny. The picture of the secret meeting at which Aravis and her friend are unwilling listeners is a travesty on the majesty of kings. The obese and bejewelled Tisroc sits enthroned on the divan. Before him the Grand Vizier is on his elbows and knees with his face in the dusty carpet (no doubt, because he does not have the right like the father of Aravis "of standing on his feet in his shoes before the face of the Tisroc"). And then to the delight of the juvenile audience the inflammable Rabadash reacts with vigor to the maxims of the poets by administering kicks to the vulnerable parts of the Vizier. The final scenes of this comedy show the Calormene prince fighting the air from a hook in the walls of Anvard and then visibly turning into the ass he had been making of himself by his foolish blustering.

In addition, there is another sort of gentle humor that Lewis is master of—the light touch of comedy that he sometimes gives to things of which he thoroughly approves. The kindly dwarfs who welcome Shasta to breakfast on his first morning in Narnia demonstrate the charm which the author so often throws over the scene. But at the same time we smile at Duffle's muttered self-reproach and at the noisy hushing when it is discovered that their guest has fallen asleep. Although Lewis was a master of the pun and other such verbal juggling, most of the comedy in Narnia, like the above, is dramatic or situational. It appeals to the eye or is demonstrated by attitudes or actions which the entire age-spectrum of his audience can appreciate.

X.

THE CULTURE of the two nations is inextricably woven into one of the themes—a comparison of oppression and liberty and their effects upon the attitudes of citizens and society. It is appropriate that Lewis makes one of the distinctions between Narnia and Calormen a difference in their poetry. The southern nation is practical and unimaginative. Their literature is largely made up of formulated sayings—balanced phrases which the older generation can quote to give embellishment to their conversation or admonition to the young.

The reaction of Rabadash to the maxims of Ahoshta suggest that the younger generation at times chafes under this sort of instruction.

And it is a society riddled with clichés. Not only are the poets quoted tiresomely, but such expressions as "Oh the delight of my eyes," "the sun appeared dark in her eyes," "to hear is to obey," and the ever-present parenthesis for the Tisroc, "may he live forever," indicate the stereotyped thinking that is to be found in this nation of slaves.

Narnia, however, is a place where each individual expresses himself according to his own personality. The free and equal talking hedgehogs, rabbits, and horses speak as we would expect them to, directed by their natures. And the poetry of the northern land is lyrical and romantic. A rocket seems to go up inside the heads of Aravis and Shasta as they hear for the first time, while the fiddlers play and the poet sings, the great old lay of Fair Olvin. And in a later story the reader feels a throb of pleasure as a blind poet comes forward and sings of the adventures of Bree and Hwin and of their human companions Prince Cor and Aravis.

But, of course, the difference between the two kingdoms is more than a literary one. In Calormen life is cheap. Slaves are beaten for mistakes and hanged for idleness. One expects his superiors to be rude and insulting. The great gulf between the rich and the poor is clearly displayed in Tashbaan (the only city described in the entire *Chronicles*). The cooling fountains and lavish gardens of the aristocracy are walled away from the peasants, water-sellers, porters, and beggars who crowd the filthy streets. But in Narnia, where everyone is free-born, where the first word Shasta hears is "Good morning, neighbour," each lives his own life with contentment and allows his fellow to do the same. It is mainly a rural land with a castle for the king and appropriate burrows, caves, nests, and huts for the natives of the country. Each is rich according to his own set of values.

Perhaps the political philosophy of the citizens of each nation can be summed up in the words of two people. After overhearing the treacherous plot of which the Tisroc approved, Lasaraleen says, "It must be right if *he's* going to do it!" There are no moral standards (no *Tao*) in such a system. The Tisroc is the law. In a slave state the despot's whim is the standard of righteousness. But over against this philosophy is the statement of King Lune. "The King's under the law, for it's the law makes him a king." So he tells Cor that, as he is the older of the twins, he has no more right to give his crown to his brother than a sentry has to leave his post. A free kingdom is one in which all are under the law. "The rule of right and wrong" is fundamental to a just society.

XI.

AS WE have said little about Aslan so far, it is certain that we have not completed our discussion of the ideas of the story. Some commentators have stated that *The Horse and His Boy* has fewer Christian references than any of the other *Chronicles*. As it would be difficult to tabulate "Christian references," it would be difficult to refute such a claim, but if the statement means that the book is less Christian in its implications, such a charge can be easily disproved. As with all of Lewis's fiction the doctrine is in the grain.

Most pervasive is the divine providence which over-arches the plot. Shasta is "between the paws of Aslan" from the time he is pushed ashore as a babe to be cared for by the wakeful Arsheesh—or perhaps we should say from the time of his birth, for the centaur's prophecy, we must assume, came from Aslan. Just as the wrath of men is made to praise God, so the evil schemes of Lord Bar make it possible for the kidnapped prince to be living in Calormen at the right time and to carry the warning from Tashbaan to Anvard before Rabadash arrives.

The task is not done, however, without the able assistance of Bree, Hwin, and Aravis. In the divine providence the threads of many lives are woven into a tapestry, but what the pattern will be we do not know, for "no-one is told any story but their own." As Aslan makes this statement to a number of people in various stories, we must assume that Lewis believed in the importance of Christ's statement to Peter. To the question, "Lord, and what shall this man do?" He replied, "What is that to thee? Follow thou me."[9] But for each of the four the divine care is manifested in the leonine appearances which drive and guide and protect and teach. Narnia is not a universe of chance. When Aravis says of her superficial wounds, "I *have* had luck," the Hermit replies, "Daughter, I have now lived a hundred and nine winters in this world and have never yet met any such thing as Luck." And when Shasta sees the path which led him into Narnia in the dark, he says, "What luck that I hit it!" But as he had by now looked into the eyes of Aslan, he corrects himself and says, "It wasn't luck at all really, it was *Him*." There are no loose threads in the tapestry.

A Calormene aristocrat and three Narnians stolen into slavery in their earliest years could have no personal knowledge of Aslan. But as the King above all High Kings in Narnia reveals himself to each, something of the divine nature is illustrated. When Shasta asked, "Who are you?" to the person pacing beside him in the dark, the answer, "Myself," repeated three times, suggests God's answer to Moses, "I Am that I Am." No description of the Self-existent One is more adequate than the statement of His self-existence. And when the darkness fades and the great lion is clearly seen, Shasta's face to face but speechless adoration speaks to the experience of more than one reader. But the little spring that flows from the footprint of Aslan illustrates Lewis's use of the connotative or associative faculties of the reader. From the spring Shasta drinks deeply, then buries his face in it and splashes his head. To allegorize here (or elsewhere) would be to destroy the magic spell that is Narnia, but we remember in passing the One who offers the water of life to all who are thirsty . . . and the washing . . . and even, perhaps, a baptism? The associations must be lightly made, and each reader will select what touches him. Lewis offers only echoes and reverberations.

When Aslan appears in the Hermit's compound, Hwin is the first to come to him. Her response is a self-forgetful surrender to his beauty. Although shaking with fear, she can do nothing but offer herself to the terrible beauty that enthralls her. To Bree the revelation is that Aslan is a true beast. The incarnation is no metaphor of some ghostly theology. Christ is very man of very man. His divinity is forever united with our dust. So Aslan, although glorious in beauty, has the whiskers, the tail, the paws of a very lion. And to Aravis, whom he calls "my daughter," he is the Father who chastens his children that they may partake of the divine likeness. Separated from the poor and the needy in her upbringing, the little Tarkeena needed to learn compassion through suffering.

And so, in the days of the High King, Aslan does much, and much is learned by the creatures whom he oversees. But even though there are some things that the lion alone can do, often the learning process for his subjects requires action and decision, journeys, and battles. There as here, character is achieved by fighting the good fight of faith.

CHAPTER 7
THE CASPIAN TRIAD:
PRINCE CASPIAN, THE VOYAGE
OF THE "DAWN TREADER,"
AND THE SILVER CHAIR

I.

IN *The Chronicles* there are four periods of adventure separated by vast unrecorded stretches of Narnian history. The peaceful years of this pleasant land when happy reign follows happy reign make up the majority of its millenniums. But just as Eden did not have a story until the snake appeared, so Narnia does not need a raconteur until it is entered by witches or attacked by tyrants. *The Magician's Nephew* records events which take place perhaps millenniums before the days of High King Peter and Bree and Shasta. And there are uncounted centuries between that Golden Age and the years of Caspian and the "Dawn Treader" and the Green Witch's silver chair. Then, there are again many generations before the final days of Narnia, when King Tirian fights his last battle.

Of these four recorded periods the longest is that which covers the life span of Caspian, the tenth of that name, called the Seafarer, King of Narnia, and Knight of the Order of the Lion. *Prince Caspian* begins when he is a very small child;

The Voyage of the "Dawn Treader" records one of his major achievements; and *The Silver Chair,* although not primarily about him, ends with his death and then his return to youth and vigor in Aslan's country. So it seems logical to treat these three books as a unit.

When *The Lion, the Witch and the Wardrobe* was completed, a friend asked Lewis what the lantern was doing in the wood where Lucy first stepped into Narnia. He tried to answer the question by writing a tale explaining the events leading up to that adventure. But the story refused to be drawn into the light of day. Perhaps there were no suitable pictures yet in the storehouse of his imagination. So he laid aside this attempt and developed an idea which had come to him for a sequel to *The Lion.*

Many stories tell of magicians who employ powerful spells or other magic devices to draw supernatural beings into this world. Lewis asked himself, How would it feel if it worked the other way? What if humans were at the mercy of magic powers in other worlds which could snatch them from their humdrum pursuits and plunge them into mysteries and dangers more strange than their strangest dreams?

For such a story he had ready at hand an unused bit of magic. While Lucy's gift had healed many after the battle with the White Witch, and Peter's sword had seen yeoman's service, the horn which Father Christmas had given to Susan had not been employed for magical purposes. And so the second story begins as the horn does its work and draws the Pevensie children from an ordinary railway station into a jungle of Narnian mystery. Lewis's interest in this deviation from "normal" magic is indicated by the fact that *Prince Caspian* was first called *Drawn into Narnia* and then *A Horn in Narnia* before the present title was settled on.

II.

BUT THE children are drawn into a Narnia very different from that which they left only a year earlier. As they finally discover, an aeon of time has elapsed, and they are thought of as we do of King Arthur—as legendary figures from a dim and doubtful past. You remember that this matter of time created one of the difficulties which made the other children doubt Lucy's story when she returned through the wardrobe after spending several hours at tea with Mr. Tumnus. She had used up no time from her own world, and that was the only time there was, they thought. But as the professor explained, a completely different world would very likely have its own time, not at all related to ours, so that while you were there you would never use up any of the time of the world you came from. And every book in which there is a trip from world to world illustrates this matter of times which are not parallel.

In fact, there seems to be no relation at all between Narnian time and Earth time. In the first of the Caspian Triad, an unimaginable number of centuries has wasted the ruins of Cair Paravel while the children on Earth are growing but one year older. Yet, in the second story, after one more year in England, Edmund and Lucy find Caspian only three years older. Finally, only a few weeks have elapsed between *The Voyage of the "Dawn Treader"* and *The Silver Chair*, but Eustace finds that many years have passed in Narnia, and his friend Caspian is an old man.

Also, like Lucy on her trip through the wardrobe, the children always return in the instant that they leave, without spending any of Earth time in their adventures. And to make history even more confusing, Polly Plummer and Digory Kirke, who were there on the day that Narnia was created, are also there on the day that it ends. The millenniums of its existence all occur during their lifetimes.

What does it mean? Why does Narnia have a different time-stream from Earth? As a literary device it is admirable, for we have the record of a vast and complete stretch of history—not the history of a nation, but of a world—all unified by the close circle of the friends of Narnia from our world. Their visits in time of need are all related. When the Pevensie children discover the wardrobe, it is in the house of the Professor, who, as a boy, had seen Narnia created. When Eustace falls through the picture, it is with Lucy and Edmund. And when Jill rescues Prince Rilian and later King Tirian, she does it in company with Eustace. The continuity of *The Chronicles* is accomplished through the sons of Adam and daughters of Eve.

But Lewis's purpose in presenting two chronologies is religious as well as literary. Most of us are victims of limited thinking because we are natives of a single time-stream. It does not occur to us that this time-space continuum which we call "the universe" may not be the only "nature" which God has created. As Lewis points out in *Miracles*, there may be other systems of life not related spatially or temporally to our universe—"natures" for whose borders no space-flight could be charted and whose history in no way runs parallel to ours. We do not know that our "reality" is God's only creative act.

Such ideas are not idle speculation. They are a part of Lewis's vigorous and continuing attack upon the anti-supernaturalism of the twentieth century. Narnia with its different space and time reminds both the child and adult of *possibilities* beyond those upon which the materialist bases his atheism.

In *Mere Christianity* there is a chapter called "Time and Beyond Time." Here Lewis points out that God does not exist in our time. "His life is not dribbled out moment by moment like ours."[1] He is a master of our time just as an author is the master of the time in his novel. The writer may pause for hours before writing of an action which takes place a split second after an event he has already described. Lewis's point in this chapter is that God has all the time He needs to hear the millions of prayers that are offered to Him, even if they are all offered at the same time. But the chapter also illustrates Lewis's interest in the concept of time and the relevance of Narnian time to his serious thought.

III.

IN REGARD to characterization in *Prince Caspian* not much needs to be said of the sons and daughters of Adam and Eve. Caspian shows the loyalty, courage, and concern for truth which give good promise that he will be a noble and upright king when he matures. The Pevensie children present us with few surprises. Peter demonstrates his leadership, Edmund his good sense, and Lucy her winsomeness and rapport with Aslan. Only in Susan is there a somber hint of her future. She is the same practical person who thinks of the need for coats and lunches, but her fears seem more sharply outlined than before. When she finally meets Aslan, he breathes on her and tells her to forget her fears. But when he asks, "Are you brave again?" she answers, "A little, Aslan," which is not a very positive response.

This is the last book in which Susan appears, and we are told in *The Last Battle* that she is no longer a friend of Narnia. As we have noted already, Lewis believed that fortitude is a virtue fundamental to all others. Only the soldier or martyr who stands firm in the face of danger or death can claim the virtues of loyalty or faith. Susan's final dereliction illustrates again the sword of division which Christ becomes in families through the choices of free individuals.

Of the natives of Narnia the two dwarfs represent opposing attitudes. Nikabrik is willing to believe in Aslan—or the White Witch; "anyone or anything," as he says, who will give them victory over the tyrant, Miraz. His venture into the supernatural is entirely unprincipled and practical. If Aslan does not help, he is willing to turn to hags and werewolves. His concern is not for matters of righteousness but for victory at all costs. And his loyalty is only the narrow and extremely prejudiced loyalty to the dwarfs.

The first words we hear from him are "Kill it." And when he hears that Caspian is the nephew of the hated Miraz, he tries to take the task upon himself and stab the prisoner then and there. In spite of his willingness to believe the old stories he seems to be largely motivated by hatred. He hates Caspian because he is a Telmarine, and he hates Dr. Cornelius because he is a half-breed. As Caspian says after the dwarf is slain, "He had gone sour inside from long suffering and hating." In Nikabrik Lewis illustrates that an interest or belief in the supernatural is not enough.

Trumpkin, however, is quite a different person. His wry

humor and cheery courage make a colorful contribution to the story. Although a doubting Thomas in regard to supernatural matters (until his confrontation with Aslan), he abounds in virtues. Of vast integrity, his granite-like loyalty is illuminated by his statement to Caspian, "You are my King. I know the difference between giving advice and taking orders." And so, although he does not believe in the horn, he volunteers to make the trip to Cair Paravel. His skepticism suggests that Lewis did not believe that honest doubt about spiritual matters is a very serious problem. Trumpkin discovers the reality of Aslan in a rather breathtaking way as he is tossed into the air, but the lion offers no rebuke for the dwarf's doubts. One who determines to do right will eventually be led right.

Trufflehunter, the badger, is the believer who is on the right side for the right reasons. He is a receptacle for the truths of the past, for as Glenstorm, the centaur, says, the gift of the badger is to remember. In an age when faith has been driven underground and the ancient records are nothing but oral tradition, he does not doubt. He knows that, although Narnia is a land for nonhuman creatures, it is always happiest when ruled by a descendant of Adam. He is the first to give his allegiance to Caspian. His faith in the horn and expectation of help from Aslan never wavers in the long wait for Trumpkin's return from Cair Paravel.

Of the other creatures, most of those who stand out as individuals display personalities consistent with their species. Pattertwig acts with the nervous energy and speaks with the rapid-fire chatter which we would imagine of squirrels if they had intelligence. The Bulgy Bears are true talking bears but a little woolly of voice and brain. Wimbleweather, like most giants, is not very clever.

But the most dashing, heroic, honorable, and courteous knight of them all is Reepicheep, the mouse. As he is a major figure in the next book we will become better acquainted with him later. But it would be safe to say that he is one of Lewis's most successful creations. The psychology of Reepicheep can, no doubt, be traced to his size. In order to be taken seriously, he and his followers must shine. And, although there is a comic element about the High Mouse, he is taken seriously.

He is referred to later as one of the famous heroes of the Battle of Beruna. The humor, of course, is in the incongruity. Reepicheep seems a contradiction in terms. But "timid as a mouse" is not a phrase that is ever heard in Narnia.

IV.

IF THE plot of *The Lion, the Witch and the Wardrobe* is "Aslan does all," the plot of *Prince Caspian* could be called "Aslan does nothing." Both are exaggerations, but they emphasize the difference between the two stories. Although the great lion appears and does some guiding and awakening, his disciples are left largely to their own swords and wits in dealing with the enemy. When Nikabrik is prepared to call up the ghost of the White Witch, Aslan simply tells Peter, Edmund, and Trumpkin to "hasten into the Mound and deal with what you will find there." He does not alert them to the treachery they must face. And while Peter and the Old Narnians are fighting Miraz and his army, the lion is leading a merry party in a gambol through the land.

Aslan's relation to the plot is typical of his position in each story. His actions are always consistent, not only with his divine character, but also with his purpose in the lives of the human sojourners in the land. The tasks which they are sent to do, they must do on their own. Even when he quite appropriately gives guidance to Trumpkin and the children, it is Lucy who must waken the party and convince them that they must follow an invisible leader in the middle of the night.

Aslan creates, redeems, guides, protects, and does such other acts proper to this representation of Christ. But he is never what the ancients called a *deus ex machina,* a contrived means of getting the author out of a hole. He does not solve Lewis's problems of plot as a when-all-else-fails-rescuer. And so, Peter must fight Miraz alone, Shasta must run till he almost drops to carry the warning to King Lune, and later, because they fail to remember the signs, Eustace and Jill must work out their own escape from the Gentle Giants of Har-fang. Lewis's theology is not passive. He believed that there are tasks to be done in the world, and that God works through His children.

The plot is divided into five sections or movements, each of which contributes to the central purpose—the restoration of Narnia to its original state of freedom and happiness. The first section, the discovery of the ruins of Cair Paravel and its time puzzle, illustrates the ruinous condition of Old Narnia. But it also serves as an admirable tie with the preceding book, for the closing pages of *The Lion, the Witch and the Wardrobe* had promised a return to Narnia. So the reader participates with the children in the mystery of a land centuries older while only one year has passed in England.

The first movement of the plot also gives significance to the second. After Susan's unerring archery rescues Trumpkin, he tells the story of Caspian—a flashback to the early child hood of the prince and down to the rising of the remnant of Old Narnia under his leadership. And so the children realize that the horn has drawn them into the middle of the rebellion against the tyranny of Miraz, the usurper. Trumpkin's story makes clear to the kings and queens of the Golden Age that they must join the new king who is fighting to restore the land to its former state.

It is this link with the past which Miraz is determined to destroy. The exile of the old nurse and the uncle's denial that there ever was a time when animals talked indicate that the Telmarine ruler is conducting a siege against the legends of antiquity. And the verification of those legends, as Caspian is introduced at hole of mouse, cave of dwarf, and burrow of badger to living proofs of the ancient stories, is a step toward the lifting of the siege and the overthrow of the enemy.

In the third section of the plot, after the education of Trumpkin concerning the abilities of ancient kings and queens, the long journey to join forces with Caspian sets the stage for the final conflict. The appearance of Aslan on the journey indicates that he will be involved in the action, but as he tells Lucy, "Things never happen the same way twice." The lion's action will be one of liberation. The defeat of the enemies is left to his followers. Lucy's two nocturnal encounters with the trees, first in which they stir but do not wake, and then, when Aslan is present, briefly wake and put on their human forms, is a foreshadowing of the coming restoration in which all nature springs to vibrant life under the influence of its life-giver.

Although some of part four (the conflict) and part five (the restoration) takes place at the same time, we are made to follow the conflict first and only after the victory at Beruna learn what has been accomplished by Aslan and his party of liberation. While he wakens Old Narnia with his roar, Trumpkin and the kings take care of Nikabrik's party and then defeat Miraz and his army with the help of the awakened Dryads and Hamadryads (which in Narnia are both male and female).

Then we are allowed to rejoin the merry parade which, at the direction of the lion, frees the river of its chains (the Bridge of Beruna) and liberates all captive creatures in the town. When the wrongs are all righted and Caspian again greets his old nurse, the prodigality of nature under its Lord is demonstrated by the abundant feast which is miraculously provided.

V.

THERE ARE two themes which motivate the story. One might be called "faith in an age of doubt." When Lewis accepted the professorship at Cambridge in 1954, he spoke in his inaugural address, "De Descriptione Temporum," of the present as a post-Christian age and stated that Christians and pagans had much more in common than either would have with the post-Christian. "The gap between those who worship different gods is not so wide as that between those who worship and those who do not."[2]

It appears that Narnia is in a post-Aslan age at this time. The statement of Miraz, "And there's no such person as Aslan," indicates the atheism which he hopes to implant in the young mind of Prince Caspian. His denial of the existence of dryads and naiads and yet his fear of woods and running water suggest that atheism is sometimes the result of a bad conscience. It is comforting to be skeptical of the existence of beings you have wronged. Other facets of this dark age of doubt are the unprincipled faith of Nikabrik, the honest agnosticism of Trumpkin, and the steady belief of Trufflehunter.

But what should be done with one's private vision in an age of doubt? Or what if other fellow-believers refuse to follow your personal convictions? It is this problem that Lewis illustrates in Lucy's glimpses of Aslan. If one is outvoted by the majority, one should still walk in the light which he sees. Aslan makes it very clear that Lucy should have followed him up the side of the gorge when she knew that that was what he wanted, even though the others determined that they should go down. One cannot even be sure that all other followers of Aslan will see him when you do. To Lucy's objection, "But they won't believe me!" Aslan replies, "It doesn't matter." Following one's own vision may mean a lonely walk, but there is no substitute for obedience.

The second theme might be called, "the rule of man over nature." When Caspian meets Glenstorm, the centaur tells him that the time for war has arrived, for, in addition to signs in the heavens, "a Son of Adam has once more arisen to rule and name the creatures." When Adam was created, he was given dominion over "every living thing" on the earth and given the task of naming each animal. After the fall he was sent out into a hostile nature of thorns and thistles and to the fierce struggle of wresting a living from the soil. The Pevensie children are introduced to the results of nature without its lord when they first arrive in Narnia. The jungle where there once had been a park-like orchard illustrates the planless and self-defeating growth of nature without the guiding hand of man. And the wild bear during the journey who tried to have a little girl for breakfast demonstrates nature "red in tooth and claw."

The rebellion of Old Narnia against Miraz was not an attempt to throw off rule, but a fight to establish a rightful dominion in which man would recognize the names and characteristics of the creatures, directing and controlling all for the good of each. When Aslan roars and the trees throw off their death-like sleep, the victory over the exploiter and destroyer is assured. We are confident that Caspian, the true king, will rule his peaceable kingdom with kindness and wisdom and that Narnia will return to its innocent and merry ways.

That Lewis had no desire to present a pantheistic nature "impelling all thinking things, all objects of all thought" is evident in the sudden and surprising appearance of Bacchus and his Maenads. As we associate Bacchus and his party today with the bacchanalia or drunken orgy, it may seem puzzling to most readers to find him in Narnia. But Lewis did not need to do much cleaning up in order to bring the god of wine into the land. For he was really the god of animals and vegetation, and the vine was simply the symbol of his domain. His wildness and the breathtaking dances of his "wild girls" illustrate the very characteristic which Lewis wants to emphasize. As Edmund says, "There's a chap who might do anything—absolutely anything." Without a ruler nature will be nothing but a bonfire of energy. Its antics will be unpredictable and frightening. Susan expresses Lewis's point here. "I wouldn't have felt very safe with Bacchus and all his wild girls if we'd met them without Aslan."

But a redeemed nature who has heard the voice of its maker and who recognizes his viceroy, man, as its ruler, is a servant who can produce a life-giving wine for the aged nurse and provide an abundant feast for the whole population of Narnia. The wild energy will still be there, but it will be controlled for the delight and benefit of all the land.

VI.

The Voyage of the "Dawn Treader" is the only story of The Chronicles which does not take place at all in Narnia. It may come as a surprise to the reader when, in The Silver

Chair, Eustace stands in the courtyard at Cair Paravel and says, "I don't know whether this is Narnia," but as we think back, we remember that when he fell through the picture along with Edmund and Lucy and was hauled dripping out of the sea, Caspian and his crew had already passed the Seven Isles and were heading for the Lone Islands. And as Eustace does not make the return trip in the *Dawn Treader* but goes back home through the door in the sky at the utter East, he could truly say that he had never been in Narnia even though he had been in the world which Aslan had created.

That he needed to breathe the air of that world and receive the self-knowledge that the great lion could give is apparent in the first paragraph of the book. Perhaps Lewis's childhood dislike of his own name, Clive Staples (which caused him to rename himself "Jack"), was part of the reason for fastening "Eustace Clarence Scrubb" upon the boy who "almost deserved it." Most children like common first names, and "Pete," "Sue," "Ed," and "Lu" no doubt strike the note of ordinariness which gives the child reader the confidence that these will be safe guides into unknown lands.

So, anyone who is called Eustace Clarence by his parents and Scrubb by his teachers can be expected to be a disagreeable and untrustworthy person: a "record stinker," to use Edmund's phrase. But, as we know from the outcome, his case is not hopeless. Lewis believed in the depravity of boys but not in their total depravity. A part of one's nature can sometimes be blamed on someone nearer than Adam. Eustace had the misfortune to be born to "modern parents."

The description of their home is partly for comic purposes, but we can be sure that the author did not approve of the child's calling his parents "Harold" and "Alberta." In the address on "Membership" alluded to earlier Lewis refers to the "perverse" notion that children should call their parents by their Christian names. It ignores, he says, the organic unity of the family and teaches the child that his mother is only a fellow-citizen in a featureless society. It is the attitude of the collective toward the individual—one more counter to be added to the total. But the family, like the church, preserves for the individual a unique relationship which,

167

through interaction with "the body," encourages the true growth of his personality.

Perhaps it is because Eustace had not experienced the benefits of membership that he is introduced to the Narnian world on board a ship. The crew of a small sailing vessel such as the *Dawn Treader* illustrates the necessity of subordination of each for the good of the body and the fulfillment of each as he makes his indispensable contribution to the common goal. But Eustace knew nothing of the joy of being part of a team.

It would be distorting Lewis's purpose, however, to imply that all of the boy's faults can be explained by his environment. The technique used to delineate his character indicates that Master Scrubb is a free soul who is shaping his own character by his attitudes and actions. Although the author begins with the direct method and tells us immediately that we are about to be introduced to a bully and a braggart, in the main he allows us to come to our own conclusions. The indirect method of characterization in which the reader listens to what the character says (and thinks), sees what he does, and hears what others think about him has the advantage of portraying his traits without interrupting the action and gives us the illusion that we have arrived at an independent judgment.

Thus, although Lewis is in complete control of the materials of the story, our own "deductions" contribute verisimilitude to the character. We hear the know-it-all attitude of Eustace, expressed to most of the people on the ship. We see his selfishness and conceit portrayed in his diary, and we see his dishonesty as he tries to steal some of the precious drinking water at night. In addition to his own words, thoughts, and actions, the character of Eustace is illuminated by the opinions of the members of the crew. Rhince's private speculation about the dead dragon that perhaps "it ate the little brat and died of him: he'd poison anything," although not exactly charitable, probably expresses the feelings of others as well.

The problem of "the little brat" is, I fear, too much of what Lewis calls the great sin—pride. In *Mere Christianity* he says that pride is the universal vice; no one is without it. It is essentially competitive. The proud person looks down upon everyone else and imagines himself to be vastly superior. He seeks the company of others, but it is only in order to lord it over them. Although an attempt to characterize Eustace brings all sorts of vices flocking to the mind—his complaining, rudeness, cowardice, etc.—his constant attempt to degrade everything and everyone in order to enhance his own self-image seems to overshadow and make mild all his other faults.

And so, when Eustace goes to sleep on a dragon's hoard of treasure after being about as obnoxious and dragonish as possible, he wakes up as a dragon himself. I think we can say that the boy is turned inside out. His inner life is put on display, is dramatized. And the audience for this morality play is Eustace himself. It is when he looks into the pool and sees the horrible transformation that he discovers the ugliness of his true nature. Just as the pool mirrors his dragon-shape so the dragon-shape mirrors his inner self.

But there is some hope for a person when he begins to see himself as he actually is. We are told that Eustace realizes that he is a monster cut off from the whole human race, and an appalling loneliness comes over him. But he had been that sort of monster before he became a dragon; it takes the change in form to make him see the monster within. And when he reveals himself in all his ugliness to the others and hears them wrestling with the problems of what to do with a friendly dragon on board ship, "poor Eustace realised more and more that since the first day he came on board he had been an unmitigated nuisance and that he was now a greater nuisance still."

Such a humbling realization makes him ready for the sort of surgery which Aslan performs on him. The painful operation takes place in a garden on the top of a mountain. A similar mountaintop garden is described twice elsewhere in *The Chronicles,* once in *The Magician's Nephew,* and again in *The Last Battle.* As Eustace had discovered no garden-crowned peak in his aerial exploration of the island, we must assume that Aslan transports the boy by magic to the same green hill that appears in the other stories, whose position might be described as "east of the sun and west of the moon." In the other books the garden is arrived at by travel- ing westward, but it is, we are told, a spur of the topless mountain beyond the Utter East which is known as Aslan's country.

Within the garden is a spring of living water, an image associated elsewhere with Aslan. We have already noted the spring that flows from the great lion's footprint after he re- veals himself to Shasta. The flowing water appears again in *The Silver Chair* first as satisfaction for the thirsting soul of Jill and then as the gift of eternal life for Caspian. In the story of Eustace it seems to suggest the baptism which heals and transforms. Again we must remind ourselves to resist the temptation to see allegory where Lewis meant only examples and illustrations. These are adventures in another world which convey truth in their own terms. The illustrations may at times run parallel to earthly parables but must not be taken as mirror images of them.

The process of "undragoning" Eustace expresses a truth which most adult readers probably recognize immediately. Man's unassisted efforts to change himself always result in failure. Eustace tries to take off his ugly covering, but under- neath each layer is another one just as bad. He needs a divine miracle in order to get rid of his dragon-nature. The process is excruciating—in fact, Aslan's first blow seems to go right into the heart. But that is the spot where the change must begin. And, when the water of regeneration has done its work, and Eustace is a boy again, Aslan dresses him in new clothes. Just as the Christian is not dressed in the filthy rags of his own righteousness but in the righteousness of Christ, so Eustace loses his dark and knobby dragon-skin and gains garments appropriate for his new nature. Or to paraphrase Paul's statement in First Corinthians: he is sown a natural dragon; he is raised a spiritual boy.

VII.

THAT THE problem of Eustace is central to the plot of the first half of the book is obvious. And when we remember that he is an important character in both *The Silver Chair* and *The Last Battle*, we need not apologize for spending some time discussing his reformation. In the second half of the story, however, he subsides to a minor role in the action. But another character whom we must notice maintains a position of importance in both halves of the story; in fact, he might be called the spirit of the *Dawn Treader*.

We have already met Reepicheep, the mouse, in the preceding book. At the Battle of Beruna the "ground level" attacks of the High Mouse and his troops are a decisive factor in the victory over the army of Miraz. After the battle he is made a Knight of the Order of the Lion. In many ways he represents the ideals of knighthood. He is the soul of courtesy and good breeding. He is the first to rise from the table at the approach of the star's daughter and the first to put his trust in her story and begin to feast at Aslan's Table. His kindly nature expresses itself in the hours he spends with Eustace while the boy is still suffering from the reptilian enchantment.

The mouse is a wise counselor in times of crisis. His advice saves the *Dawn Treader* from the Sea Serpent. His insistence that they must not avoid the Dark Island out of fear results in the rescue of Lord Rhoop. And his rebuke of Caspian at the end of the book, concerning the responsibility of kings who must not leave their thrones in order to sail beyond the end of the world, states a fundamental principle which Lewis treats in several ways in his writings.

Reepicheep is also the soul of honor—probably the word which comes most frequently to his lips. There are two aspects of honor which Lewis illustrates in the person of the mouse. One is the outward, the respect due to a person simply because he is a person. Each of us wishes to be accepted as having the worth of an individual. Of course, such self-esteem can become excessive and result in vainglory. Aslan sounds a caution to Reepicheep in the earlier story when he says, "I have sometimes wondered, friend, whether you do not think too much about your honour." But he goes no further. When the mouse points out that if he and his troops did not defend their dignity, their small size would make them the butt of unpleasant humor by those who measure worth in inches, the lion offers no rejoinder.

But we should not think of Reepicheep as a swashbuckling braggart looking for affronts to his honor. His most frequent use of the word expresses its inward meaning—a keen sense of ethical conduct. It represents his integrity, the ideal he holds up for himself. He will sit all night at Aslan's Table because the greatest danger is to leave a mystery unexplored through fear. Not to sail into the darkness of Dark Island because of cowardice would be no small impeachment of their honors. It is worth noting that each time Reepicheep advises courage for the sake of honor, it turns out that this is the wisest course to follow.

He is also concerned for the honor of others. He tells the invisible monopods that anything done against the honor of Lucy will bring about a fight to the death. But when he hears what they want, he concludes that it would be a noble and heroical act "in no way contrary to her Majesty's honor." He is willing to hazard his own life for any worthy cause, but his inner vision of right conduct is a white plume which he never soils with words or actions unbecoming of a Knight of the Order of the Lion.

Perhaps most important of all is that Reepicheep *is* the dawn treader. Caspian and his crew sail east until the water becomes too shallow. Edmund, Lucy, and Eustace go on until their boat is grounded. Reepicheep, alone, actually treads the dawn. As a seeker after adventure, whether it is fighting in the forefront of the battle or sailing over the edge of the world, the mouse, from nose to tail, is the personification of the questing spirit of man. Like the Ulysses of Tennyson's poem he is eager to sail beyond the utmost bound of human thought. Like him he admits that the gulfs at the edge may wash them down, but the momentary glimpse of what is beyond the world will be worth it all.

But the trip on the *Dawn Treader* is a "glorious adventure" for him not simply because he will be able to see strange sights. Reepicheep is a spellbound character. He is a seeker of enchanted lands beyond the horizon. His is the restless heart that is not content with anything less than the land of heart's desire—Aslan's country. When Ramandu explains that to break the spell upon the sleepers at Aslan's Table, one of the ship's company must sail into the utter East and never return, Reepicheep replies, "That is my heart's desire."

It had been so ever since his birth. The promise of the Dryad's rhyme spoken over his cradle that in the utter East he will find all that he seeks had been a spell on him, he says, all his life. The pursuit of all that we seek is hope. And hope is one of the supreme virtues of the mouse's character. In *Mere Christianity* Lewis describes hope as that desire for one's true country which the Christian expects to find after death. But he also says that you seldom find one virtue without the accompaniment of some others. The maintenance of hope requires fortitude, which includes determination to continue toward the goal. When there is some possibility that the ship will turn back at Ramandu's Island, Reepicheep says that when the *Dawn Treader* fails him, he will paddle in his coracle. "When she sinks, I shall swim east with my four paws." If he does not reach his goal, he says, he will sink with his nose to the sunrise. Here is the singlemindedness of Paul, who says to the Philippians, "This one thing I do, forgetting those things which are behind, and reaching forth unto those things which are before, I press toward the mark for the prize of the high calling of God in Christ Jesus."[3]

But Reepicheep does not need to swim that last mile. Before entering his little coracle, he takes off his sword and throws it into the Silver Sea where it lands point down and stands there as a marker like a cross in the water. This is the end of the battle for the little warrior. Like Paul he has fought a good fight. Trembling with happiness he climbs into his little boat and disappears over the standing wave. For him this is the road to Aslan's country. And we know that he arrives there safely. In *The Last Battle*, when King Tirian and his party climb the green hill to the garden at the top, the one who comes through the golden gates to greet them and welcome them in the name of Aslan is Reepicheep.

The other main characters of the book we have met before, and not much more needs to be said about them. Caspian confirms our expectations that he will be an able leader of men. Considerate of both his crew and his guests and yet decisive in times of emergency, he shows his mastery of difficult situations in his speech to his men at Ramandu's Island.

His faults are largely those of immaturity, as when he unwisely leaves the ship to walk across Felimath Island and falls into the hands of Pug and his slavers, or under the spell of the Silver Sea needs the rebuke of Aslan for planning to accompany Reepicheep to the utter East. The solid qualities of Edmund and the adventuresome and warm-hearted characteristics of Lucy are consistent with their earlier actions and require no further comment except as they have a bearing upon the plot.

VIII.

THE PLOT can be divided into eight episodes and like most travel books has a constantly shifting setting which contributes to the reader's interest in the story. Although we cannot say that the structure of the plot is tightly bound together—most of the events occur simply because the ship has arrived at a different place—there is a sense of continuity because the fate of each lost lord is discovered as the journey progresses, and because the ship gradually draws nearer to the utter East. Our main interest is not in these unifying threads, however, but in the immediate episode and whatever conflict it produces. However, it is true that most of the episodes contain a barrier or danger to the accomplishment of the goals of the voyage.

The first two chapters establish the settings and characters as Eustace, Lucy, and Edmund are dropped into the sea and rescued by Caspian, and then the *Dawn Treader*, the moving stage of the story, is explored by the new arrivals. The hostility of Eustace toward Reepicheep opens the way for the conflict in which the mouse shows his swordsmanship while being swung by his tail, and his opponent discovers that honor is a commodity not to be treated lightly.

The second episode, in which slavery is abolished in the

Lone Islands and a new regime established, reveals the whereabouts of the first of the seven lords. As His Sufficiency, Governor Grumpas, is relieved of his office and Lord Bern is made Duke of the Islands, Caspian demonstrates his quick thinking and decisiveness in dangerous situations. Although the spotlight in this episode is upon the young king of Narnia, it should be noted here that he is not the protagonist, or leading character, of the entire narrative. Sometimes it is Eustace's story, sometimes that of Lucy or Reepicheep, and, perhaps most often, it is an event in which all of the main characters participate equally.

All of *The Chronicles* display this characteristic. While Ransom is clearly the leading character of *Out of the Silent Planet* and *Perelandra,* Jane and Mark Studdock each the protagonist in their halves of *That Hideous Strength,* and Queen Orual the center of our attention in *Till We Have Faces,* Lewis used a different technique in the Narnian series. In each of the seven tales at least two and sometimes five humans work together as a unit, and always there is at least one other Narnian "creature" who, like the Beavers, or Bree, or Reepicheep, is an important part of the team which is striving to defeat witches, thwart tyrants, or sail to the world's end.

As Lewis has said elsewhere, the fairy tale does not lend itself to the detailed study of a single character. The reader is pleased to find himself in the midst of a group whose varying voices and opinions give color and depth to each decision and action. It should also be noted that in each story the team always includes at least one boy and one girl. Narnia was not created for the interest of one sex alone.

The third episode takes place in chapters five, six, and seven, and includes the storm and Eustace's adventures on Dragon Island. We should not think of the storm as a separate episode. It is described very briefly, and most of chapter five consists of the self-revealing diary of Eustace and the beginning of the adventure which transforms him. And, of course, the storm is the immediate cause of the water-shortage which illuminates the character of Eustace, and of the long stay for repairs at Dragon Island while the boy becomes "undragoned." It should also be remembered that the second step in the search for the seven lords is accomplished here when it is discovered that the gold band which causes so much pain to Eustace's foreleg is the arm-ring of Lord Octesian.

Chapter eight reveals the fate of the third lord as the landing party at Deathwater view at the bottom of the pool the golden form which once was Lord Restimar. This chapter contains three events—the stop at Burnt Island, where Reepicheep obtains his coracle, the encounter with the Sea Serpent, and the discovery of the Midas-water whose curse not only destroyed Restimar but also throws its bewitching influence over the group from the *Dawn Treader*.

This chapter serves as a unifying device, for in each event we see the five major characters acting as a unit. The conversation shifts from one to the other, and Eustace is praised even though his attack on the Sea Serpent did no good. The end of the chapter is almost the exact middle of the narrative. So with the problem of Eustace solved we can give our attention in the last half of the story to monopods, fear of the dark, and a star's daughter.

IX.

THERE IS a marked difference between the first and second halves. Slavery, storms, enchanted dragons, and sea serpents are real dangers which need energy and intelligence to combat. But the ominous situations of the last four episodes turn out to be largely psychological. Although the monopods and magician seem fearsome, the little jumpers turn out to have no harm in them, and Coriakin, as Lucy says, is "a brick." The Dark Island proves to have "nothing to be afraid of," and the supposedly "enchanted food" of Aslan's Table actually had not been touched by the enchanted sleepers. Lewis is, perhaps, suggesting that the enemy within is the last antagonist to be conquered.

The fifth episode continues to display the close unity of the group now that Eustace has been integrated into the body, but it is Lucy who steps into the lighted circle and receives most of our attention. It is she who hears the invisible voices planning to cut off the party's retreat to the ship. She is the one called upon to "risk the magician"and read from his book of magic. It is to her that Aslan reveals himself and to her is given the doubtful privilege of convincing the monopods that they have not been uglified.

The three chapters are arranged like many stories with an ascending mood of danger and suspense and then a relaxation of tension to a state of harmony and goodwill. Lewis shows his mastery of the storyteller's art particularly in his handling of the technique of delay. Wilkie Collins's formula for writing a story was "Make 'em laugh, make 'em cry, make 'em wait." And the reader is certainly made to wait as Lucy receives her instructions from the chief voice and then begins the climb to the mysterious upper regions where the magician may be lurking or lying dead.

It takes Lewis almost six hundred words to propel her up the stairs and down the hall to the room where the book of magic sits on its reading stand. Part of the reason for the effectiveness of this account is that it is told with Lucy as the central intelligence. The words are the author's but the feelings are those of the girl. As the tick-tock of the grandfather clock fades away and she hears nothing but the beating of her own heart, we travel with her and participate in the atmosphere of peril which Lucy's fears project upon the masks and the doors and the bearded mirror.

Although our heroine pushes on past her fears and accomplishes the task as we would expect her to do, she does not come through completely untarnished. It takes the sudden appearance of Aslan's angry picture to prevent her from making herself beautiful "beyond the lot of mortals," with its cataclysmic results, and she perversely eavesdrops on a friend with the help of magic and like many greater sinners suffers the results of her ill deed. Lewis illustrates here, as elsewhere, that character is formed through hard choices and that failure is often as profitable as success in teaching the lessons of life.

In a poem called "The Adam Unparadised"[4] Lewis imagines Adam and Eve after the fall encountering various pre-human monstrosities outside of Eden—dwarfs, giants, trolls—creatures destroyed in the flood but remaining in the racial memory to become the source of the mythology and folklore of ancient cultures. And one stanza speaks of the couple waking at night to "a thumping shock as of piles being driven" and fleeing in terror until the sunrise reveals "the bouncing Monopods at their heels." Lewis also refers in an article titled "Religion and Rocketry" to St. Augustine's question regarding "the theological position of satyrs, monopods, and other semihuman creatures."[5]

But the monopods of Narnia, like its other inhabitants, have breathed the transforming air of this world. Few literary figures exude the charm of cheerful stupidity as do these living pogo sticks. As leaping monuments to the comic imbecilities of the human race, they can be an embarrassment to the reader who examines them too closely. Who has not remembered with inner cringing his own social chitchat no more substantial than "Ah, you've come over the water. Powerful wet stuff, ain't it," or "When chaps are visible, why they can see one another"? And who has not laughed at his own humiliating rational blackouts when, like the monopods, he moved the milk out of the dairy instead of the cat?

If the monopods are any more than delightful entertainment for the reader—and for the Narnians—the key to their meaning is, perhaps, in the conversation between the magician and Aslan. Coriakin admits that although his charges are very stupid, there is no real harm in them. But he sometimes is impatient for "the day when they can be governed by wisdom instead of this rough magic." And to his question Aslan says that the time for the revelation of himself to the Duffers is a long way off. The lion's appearance now would only terrify them.

This passage suggests that the monopods will eventually develop some intelligence and some courage, but until that time arrives, they must be ruled like children and disciplined when their foolish stubbornness would do them harm. Lewis seems to be saying that God is no respecter of persons. He loves stupid people just as much as smart ones, but His dealings with each are tailored to the individual needs of each. Fuller revelations of His nature are withheld until our capacities have been adequately enlarged.

X.

THE SIXTH episode is treated in one chapter and need not occupy much space here. The Dark Island is a place where nightmares "come true." But they only come true in the imaginations of the crew. They have no existence in the real world, and no two are alike. Eustace hears giant scissors opening and closing. Rynelf hears "them" coming up the sides of the ship. Another hears gongs beginning. But when they have rescued Lord Rhoop and have been guided out of the darkness by the albatross, the island and its surrounding night completely disappear.

The theme of this chapter has to do with groundless fear—the fear of bad dreams, darkness, and the unknown. And although we should not minimize the terror generated by imaginary evils, the message of this episode is, Fear not. When Lucy's prayer to Aslan is answered and they are in the daylight again, they all realize that "there was nothing to be afraid of and never had been."

We should be cautious, however, about making the theme of each episode our main concern. Lewis probably thought that an adventure to a nightmare island would make a good story and give Reepicheep a chance to chastise the humans for their poltroonery. His stiff bow and statement, "It is, then, my good fortune not to be a man," was, no doubt, remembered in Narnia as long as the events of this trip lived in story and song.

With the rescue of Lord Rhoop from Dark Island and the discovery of Lords Revilian, Argoz, and Mavramorn on Ramandu's Island the tally of seven is completed. But as the enchantment of the three sleepers cannot be lifted unless the *Dawn Treader* sails to the end of the last sea, the two quests (that of Caspian and of Reeicheep) are united.

But the seventh episode—the events on the island of the retired star—has to do with more than the completion of the quest. The romantic element introduced here, although only lightly touched, had been prepared for earlier. When Lord Drinian in chapter two relates the events which took place on the trip prior to the unexpected arrival of the children, he tells of the week they spent at Galma and says,

> "We thought the Duke would have been pleased if the King's Majesty would have married his daughter...."
> "Squints, and has freckles," said Caspian.
> "Oh, poor girl," said Lucy.

And that is all. Nor is the Duke's daughter ever mentioned again. This exchange is a "plant," a detail introduced early in a story which has a bearing upon a future event, but which does not reveal that relationship. Because the earlier fact or comment had been "planted," the event which it foreshadows seems natural even though it is a development we had not expected. Drinian's comment tells us that Caspian is of marriageable age and makes more acceptable later the attraction the young king feels for the beautiful daughter of Ramandu, who eventually becomes his queen. As there is no love element in the story except for this very late bloom, it would seem rather incongruous without the early plant.

But what are we to make of Aslan's Table, the rich and ornate board where a king's feast is set every day? In some ways it seems to represent the central feast of the Christian faith—the Lord's Table. The Stone Knife which lies alongside the food is the instrument used to kill Aslan at the Stone Table. Just as the sacrament is taken by believers "in remembrance" of Christ's sacrifice, so anyone coming to this table would be reminded of Aslan's sacrifice which ransomed Edmund and freed Narnia from the evil power of the Witch.

Such an interpretation also explains the three sleepers. Ramandu's daughter tells Caspian and his party that the three lords quarrelled, and one of them seized the sacred knife which he should not have touched. At that moment the enchanted sleep fell upon them. Lewis is, perhaps, remembering the warning of Paul to the Corinthians that they must not come to the Lord's Table irreverently. "For this cause," he says, "many are weak and sickly among you, and many sleep."[6]

But to say that partaking of the food here enacts a Narnian Holy Communion goes too far. The Table is not presented as a place of worship. Perhaps Lewis intends it as a comment upon the rich feast provided for the soul by Christ's sacrifice. The subtleties of sacramental theory are not offered to either the child or adult, but the spiritual sustenance which Christ's death provides is illustrated for all.

Here again is the temptation to discover "the mare's nest by the pursuit of the red herring." It is easy to find more meaning than Lewis intended. In fact, the allegorist would, no doubt, make the entire voyage a spiritual journey with slavery at its inception and triumphal entry at its end. But, although the episodes at times illustrate spiritual truths, they do not fit into allegorical slots. Placing Aslan's Table where he does instead of, say, immediately after Eustace's transformation suggests that the author intended to make the task of the allegorist more difficult. Lewis knew that his first business was to tell a story which would live in the mind of the reader. The "messages," if the story is to be effective, must be subordinate to the action.

The final episode, the journey across the last sea, is one not so much of events as of atmosphere. A sense of wonder settles upon the crew as the ship sails into waters where no one has gone before. The strange constellations, the submarine hunting party, the "sweet" water so powerful it is called "drinkable light," the Silver Sea of lilies, and perhaps, most of all, the sight and sound of Aslan's country create a strangeness as if the travelers are close to the line which divides the here from the hereafter. As the small boat with the three children and the mouse come closer and closer to the green wave which bounds their world, the stronger is the feeling that beyond is the country they are searching for. The intense longing for "home" of those who feel like sojourners here in this world is beautifully expressed in the passage just before Reepicheep goes on alone in his little coracle. As they look beyond the sun into Aslan's country, a breeze comes from the east and with it a smell and a musical sound. Of this indescribable experience Lucy could only say, "It would break your heart." It was the music from home, and the longing it created was so intense that it hurt.

The last scene of the book is, perhaps, Lewis's clearest statement of the identification of Aslan with Christ. A lamb, the animal most frequently used to represent Christ, appears as the children come ashore and invites them to come and dine upon fish which are roasting upon a fire. Then he changes into the golden form of the great lion. The meal of fish on the shore reminds us of the last appearance of Christ recorded in the Gospel of John in which He invites His disciples to "come and dine" upon fish after they had been out all night upon the Sea of Galilee. It is at this time that Aslan makes the statement already referred to as the purpose of the entire *Chronicles*. Speaking of the children's world he says that he is to be found there also but there he has another name. "You must learn to know me by that name. This was the very reason why you were brought to Narnia, that by knowing me here for a little, you may know me better there."

XI.

AFTER COMPLETING *The Voyage of the "Dawn Treader"* Lewis wrote *The Horse and His Boy* and then decided to hold the latter book back from publication and issue the further adventures of Eustace first. So *The Silver Chair* appeared in 1953 and the story of Bree and Shasta in 1954. This arrangement not only presented to the public the Caspian Triad in chronological order, but also allowed Lewis to tantalize the reader by letting Eustace and Jill hear the tale of the lost prince of Archenland on their first night in Narnia. Lewis says in an aside which we have come to recognize as the voice of the raconteur, "I haven't time to tell it now, though it is well worth hearing." Such a tactic surely did not dampen the anticipation of his audience for the story when it appeared.

Although there are some similarities between *The Voyage*

and its sequel, there is no dramatic transformation of character in *The Silver Chair*. Jill, who is most often the central intelligence, is introduced in a state of tears because she had been bullied by "them." Our sympathy is aroused (which it was not when the preceding story opened with Eustace). We soon discover that Jill has some faults to be corrected, but her personality problems do not dominate several chapters as did those of Master Scrubb.

Jill has a tendency to look down on anyone who does not possess her talents—such as being able to stand on the edge of cliffs. But after the disastrous event on the mountain of Aslan, which separated her from Eustace, she displays her honesty by confessing to the lion, "I was showing off." And, of course, as she learns later, Eustace's acrophobia or fear of high places is no more to be despised than her own claustrophobia or fear of enclosed places as she is forced to crawl through the dark passages of Underland. Lewis could sympathize with such psychological weaknesses. In fact, he was afflicted with the same phobia as Eustace. In a letter he lists among other things which he fears most, "the tops of cliffs."[7]

In the first half of the story Jill is somewhat short-tempered and quarrelsome and tends to push herself forward and demonstrate her place of importance in the business at hand. Puddleglum has to interrupt her or she would have revealed their whole purpose to the Green Witch at the giant bridge. The "sparring and snapping" of Eustace and Jill is often cut short by Puddleglum, who observes in his gloomy fashion that adventures like this often end with the companions fighting and knifing one another. But it is not until the self-centered decision to apply for lodging at Harfang and the subsequent discovery that they had muffed the second and third signs that Jill faces up to her faults and takes the blame for their failures. Like the experience of other characters in the series, her admission of her shortcomings brings about a correction of them. In the second half of the book her honesty, bravery, and good sense predominate.

As we have thoroughly explored the character of Eustace in the preceding pages, it will not be necessary to say much more about him here. The change that took place on the trip to the utter East seems to have been a permanent one. Eustace is at times irritated by Jill, and he yields to the temptation of warm beds and hot baths at Harfang and misses the second sign, but in the main his record as a faithful follower of Aslan's orders is good. He shows a little more maturity here than he did on the *Dawn Treader* and acts with more authority and confidence. We will meet him again when even greater demands are made of his courage and skill as he joins King Tirian in his last battle.

XII.

PUDDLEGLUM IS the only character in *The Chronicles* who is consciously patterned after an actual person. The inspiration for his creation, Lewis admits, was Fred Paxford, his gardener at The Kilns, who was a person of great integrity, but given to gloomy predictions even though inwardly an optimist. But the marshwiggle is certainly more than a copy of anything. He is an original. One of Lewis's most successful creations, he ranks with Reepicheep as also one of the most popular.

Puddleglum—what more appropriate name could be concocted for this denizen of marshes whose "bright side" is that, if we break our necks on the crags, we won't be drowned in the river? We have already noted the fitting sound of the names of Screwtape's colleagues. This propriety is to be found in most of Lewis's fiction, but especially in Narnia. Reepicheep and Peepiceek could only be mice, and Pattertwig is obviously a squirrel. Bree and Hwin are names for horsey throats to pronounce (in fact, Bree is a shortened accommodation for human lips of Breehy-hinny-brinny-hoohy-hah). Rumblebuffin is what a giant mother would call her giant son, and Charn, the snarling name of the world of evil from which came the Witch who tyrannized Narnia with one hundred years of winter. By sound and association Lewis forges words which illuminate these creatures of an alien land.

However, he did not hesitate to borrow and adapt a name when it served his purpose. Clodsley Shovel, the mole who assists at the feast in *Prince Caspian*, has a name which sounds like the invented ones, clod and shovel being proper associations for a natural digger. But Lewis named Clodsley after a famous British admiral of Queen Anne's reign with the irresistible name of Sir Cloudsley Shovel.

And so, the gloomy world of Puddleglum can be found, Jill and Eustace conclude, under a wet blanket. That is not the whole story, but it is true that the marshwiggle not only always predicts and concludes the worst possible results, but seems to believe that a contemplation of the dire possibilities of the future is the best way to prepare one for this vale of tears. As he says, "I'm a chap who likes to know the worst and then put the best face I can on it."

But the "best face" is usually not an optimistic conclusion but a stoical acceptance of things as they are. For this reason his "bright sides" are not exactly flashes of encouragement. He observes that although it looks like an early winter, they will probably hardly notice the weather—with enemies and mountains, losing their way, next to nothing to eat, and sore feet. When they find themselves in absolute darkness in Underland, he concludes that the good thing about being trapped here is that it will save funeral expenses.

Although the extremes of Puddleglum's cheerful gloom move us to laughter, does he not touch a common chord? Faced with the hostilities of this life, who has not been reminded that "this world is not a friend to grace to help us on to God." During the horrors of World War II Lewis wrote to his brother that the best thing would be "waking up and finding yourself safely dead and not quite damned"[8]—a statement almost worthy of the marshwiggle.

And a serious view of life has its advantage when going on adventures. Puddleglum never loses his temper despite the bickering of the children. In fact, he proves to be a very wise counselor to them. He stops Jill from telling their plans to the Witch at the giant bridge. He extracts a promise from his companions not to tell their mission at Harfang. He wisely calls the signals on their escape from the palace of the Gentle

Giants. It is his advice that they should be present when the prince is in the silver chair. And it is he who reminds the prince that he must choose between seeing the Land of Bism and seeing his father.

Although he always downgrades himself—lamenting that he was "born to be a misfit" and insisting at the end of the adventure that nothing had happened to him "worth talking about"—it is his courage that snatches victory from defeat in the Witch's house when he stamps out the fire with his bare foot. In fact, wherever danger lurks he shows what Eustace calls "pluck and cheek," whether it is in the off-hand way that he expresses his determination to accompany them on the trip or his undaunted attitude after capture by the earthmen.

But perhaps the key to Puddleglum's character is that he is wise in the ways of Aslan. If a moral decision is called for, he always chooses right. His faith expresses itself at several crucial points in the story. When they discover that they had walked right over and into the second and third signs (the ruins of the giant city and the writing in stone) but had ignored them in their eagerness for the glowing windows of Harfang, he insists that "Aslan's instructions always work: there are no exceptions." If they had been looking for the signs, they would have found a door or a tunnel of some other way under the ruin.

In fact, it is significant that in spite of his gloomy predictions, Puddleglum never seems to show discouragement. After the three have been captured by the earthmen and are being taken on their long sunless journey across the underground sea, he encourages Jill by reminding her that they are on the right track again—under the city and following the signs.

Nor is he dispirited when the enchanted prince explains that the writing is only a fragment of a much longer statement about some ancient giant king. Puddleglum declares, "There are no accidents." Aslan's plans may include a new meaning for old words, but he always guides aright. And when they hear the last sign (a request in Aslan's name), it is the marsh-wiggle who points out that their business is to obey the sign even though it may mean their deaths. They must free the prince from the silver chair regardless of their fears. As he expresses most clearly some of the ideas of the story, we will have to return to him again.

XIII.

THE PLOT of the story, like that of *The Voyage of the "Dawn Treader,"* is organized as a quest. *The Silver Chair,* however, is more tightly constructed. Most of the episodes grow out of preceding ones and contribute to the excitement of later events. The travelers to the north are not seeking adventure but following orders. The difference between the two plots is illustrated by the *Dawn Treader's* exploration of the Dark Island simply because it is a great adventure and the failure to explore the Land of Bism by the other party because it would interfere with their central purpose of bringing the lost prince back to his father. The reference to Reepicheep by Eustace as they gaze down into the glassy-bright colors of Bism emphasizes the fact that even matters of honor and adventure must give way to the business of achieving the goals which have been set for one in this life.

At the beginning and end of the plot, serving as a frame to the action, are the scenes at Experiment House and on the mountain of Aslan. The narrative proper is divided into two equal parts—the trip above ground as far as Harfang, and then the trip below ground until the seekers have accomplished their mission and reappeared in Narnia.

In the overland travel the tension builds as the task becomes more difficult and dangerous. The muffing of the first sign means that the children must enter the forbidding northern country with no help but that of Puddleglum. The haphazard peril of the rock-throwing giants is supplanted by the Green Witch's allurement of baths and beds at Harfang, a temptation which is made almost irresistible by the misery of the wind and snow in the northern mountains. The greatest danger of all is revealed, of course, after they see from the windows of Harfang that they have muffed the second and third signs and then realize that the purpose for which the Witch had sent them to the Gentle Giants was for them to be man-pies at the Autumn Feast.

But the confession and remorse of Jill and the others that they have not been diligent in repeating and looking for the signs is the turning point in the story. It is a turning point not only in the unraveling of the plot but also in the geographical course of the story. Although the travelers have no sense of direction while in Underland, their long trip through caves and tunnels and across the lifeless ocean to the Witch's city is steadily southward. When the "green worm" is slain and they escape through the underground pathway, they are only a few miles from the breakthrough into Narnia.

So, ironically, the earthmen, who capture the three overworlders for the Queen of Underland, bring them to the prince they are seeking and make it possible for them to return to Narnia without the arduous trip through the northern winter. The underground actions, of course, contain tensions and mysteries—notably in the decision to free the prince because he utters the fourth sign, and in the struggle against the last enchantment of the Green Witch. But throughout this half of the story there is a sense that, as Puddleglum says, "We're back on the right lines." The plot is reaching its climax and denouement.

A part of the final unraveling or denouement is the liberating of the gnomes. Here is another species which Lewis borrowed from folklore and transformed into a uniquely Narnian being. In folk tales the gnome is described as a misshapen creature, a type of dwarf who knows where the gold and gems of earth are to be found. This, no doubt, accounts for the grotesque appearance of the Narnian ones, some a foot high and some taller than men, some with horns and some with beards, some with twelve toes and some with none. And they not only know the location of the treasures of earth but are natives of a land where living jewels grow out of its fiery soil.

They are the dwellers of the Really Deep Land, the Land of Bism, far below the shallow caverns of the Green Witch.

And here again by Lewis's inventive imagination we are introduced to another far country. In the preceding story we viewed the mysterious landscape of the utter East. Now we peer a thousand fathoms down to the bottom of the world where the central fire flows in streams and the salamander utters witty and eloquent sayings (the other meaning of the word *gnome*).

Here, the dazzling riches of the earth are vibrant and alive—rubies that can be eaten and diamond-juice that can be drunk. The hot breath of Bism is rich, sharp, and exciting, and the blaze of its colors is like the tropical sun through stained glass windows. The intensity of its existence is represented by the liberated gnomes, who cast off their enchanted gloom like an oversized coat and amid the firecrackers and rockets merrily turn cartwheels and fling themselves into the fiery mouth that has opened for them.

We are given only a glimpse before the bright canyon becomes a crevasse, then a slit, then a thread, and then blackness, and Bism is lost to us forever. But now we know that there is a world within the world—at least in Narnia. This episode illustrates, I think, the reason for the success of the entire series. Although Lewis's confessed purpose is to "steal past watchful dragons" with Christian truth, this is really only a partial statement. It is the purpose of Lewis-as-Christian.

But Lewis-as-gifted-storyteller intends for us to gaze through "magic casements opening on the foam of perilous seas in fairy-lands forlorn." He speaks to the imagination of the reader who has dreamed of life deep within the earth. The child who has longed to ride on the wings of the wind sails with Jill on the breath of Aslan, or satisfies another desire by traveling on the back of Glimfeather. And each of these adventures is described with a certain gusto which suggests that the author is enjoying them as much as the reader.

And, of course, the setting contributes as much to the atmosphere of mystery and adventure as the action. From the colored birds of Aslan's land, who sing rather advanced music, to the gathering of owls with its Chaucerian touch (the chapter title comes from the poet's *Parliament of Fowls*), and on to the grim northern countryside and harrowing Harfang, the setting echoes the diminishing and bleak prospects in the plot.

Then from the utter darkness of Underland to the phosphorescent glow around the sleeping dragons and Father Time (who will awake in the next story), the setting brightens to the lighted apartments of the prince and the glare of Bism's eternal day and reflects the progress of the plot toward its resolution. And we know that we are home when we visualize the Great Snow Dance with its dryads and fauns and intersecting snowballs and hear the merry cheers and kindly help as the travelers are literally dug out of the earth. The austerity of the foreign lands and the warmth and charm of Narnia are all important parts of our experience.

XIV.

THE SILVER CHAIR is the only one of the seven *Chronicles* in which Aslan appears nowhere but at the beginning and end of the story. In fact, with the exception of his brief entrance at Cair Paravel to take Jill and Eustace back home, he does not reveal himself outside his own mountain country. And yet this very absence from the action contributes to the theme of the book.

Aslan's relationship to the theme is linked to the significance of the "signs" which he gives to Jill. Their importance is inherent in the action and is emphasized repeatedly. The lion's statement after he teaches Jill the four guidelines or commands which will make their quest successful gives the clue to their meaning. "But, first, remember, remember, remember the Signs. Say them to yourself when you wake in the morning and when you lie down at night, and when you wake in the middle of the night."

These words appear to be a biblical allusion. Moses orders the Israelites (Deut. 6:7–8) to keep the commandments and statutes of the Lord constantly before them and to "talk of them when thou sittest in thine house, and when thou walkest by the way, and when thou liest down, and when thou risest up. And thou shalt bind them for a sign upon thine hand. . . . " And just as Moses exhorts the people to keep the commandments diligently, so Aslan says, "Let nothing turn your mind from following the Signs." Remember and obey.

As there never is any thought by the children of disobeying the commands, it seems safe to say that Lewis is thinking of the importance of mastering Christian truth and making it a part of one's life. It may be that he did not want the reader to conclude that he believed one should rely on visions and dreams (the appearances of Aslan) for guidance in this world. God has left us the Law and the Prophets, the Gospels and the Letters for our guidance. When He seems absent, we still have His Word.

And so Aslan is strangely absent from the journey. But his "signs" guide the travelers unerringly to the appointed goal. It is only when Jill allows her longing for the flesh pots of Harfang to turn her from her morning and evening ritual that they are led astray. The actual signs (greeting the first friend seen in Narnia, finding the ruined city, following the directions of the writing there, and obeying the request in the name of Aslan) seem to be relevant only for the story. I doubt that Lewis intended them to have a "message." It is the diligent attention to the instructions which receives emphasis.

Another idea which is developed toward the end of the narrative is the question of reality. When the present is grim, it is easy to imagine that our memories of past happiness are only wishful imagining. During the long trip over the silent sea the travelers begin to feel that they have always been in the darkness and to wonder if the bright overworld had been only a dream. This problem is elaborated in the final enchantment of the Witch. She persuades them that all their memory of the sun and even of Aslan is a dream, a dream woven from the lamps and cats of Underland.

What does one do when the world of reality seems a dark pit, and faith in God and hope of heaven are called wishful thinking and pie in the sky? Lewis comments in the essay "On Obstinacy of Belief" that if what Christians believe is a delusion, "then we should have to say that the universe had produced no real thing of comparable value and that all explanations of the delusion seemed somehow less important than the thing explained."⁹

And it is Puddleglum whose ringing affirmation states the principle in relevant terms. For he makes it a moral matter instead of a logical one. "I'm on Aslan's side," he says, "even if there isn't any Aslan to lead it." He chooses the right (the *Tao*) whether it exists in the real world or not. To quote Tennyson again, "We needs must love the highest when we see it." And Puddleglum chooses the highest even if it only exists in a dream world. "I'm going to live as like a Narnian as I can," he declares, "even if there isn't any Narnia." In this dark world, Lewis implies, the voices of skepticism may create an atmosphere in which faith finds it difficult to breathe, but one can still take sides with that which ought to be. In fact, such a moral stand will breathe fresh strength into one's faith.

There are a number of other ideas which are touched on briefly, but perhaps only the two scenes in Aslan's land which bracket the quest need further comment. In each scene the stream of living water plays an important part. Jill is invited to drink although in doing so she must put herself at the mercy of the lion, who makes no promise not to do anything to her. With the addition of a drop of Aslan's blood the stream washes away the evidence of death and decay from Caspian and presents him before Eustace in the flower of his youth.

The first scene clearly presents an image of the living water which Christ promised to the Samaritan woman at the well. Jill discovers that it satisfies her thirst almost immediately. But she also learns that there is no other stream and that after the quenched thirst comes obedience to the lion's will. The second scene reminds us, by the tears of Aslan, that Christ shared the sorrow of the mourners at the grave of Lazarus even though he was about to drive back the forces of death and corruption.

But perhaps most significant is the image presented of death as a minor event in Caspian's transformation into a citizen of Aslan's country. Lewis did not believe that death should be pictured to the child or adult as a triumphant monster. He did not regard being killed as a great evil. Of his experiences in World War I he commented that if he and a young German had shot and killed each other simultaneously and met afterwards, they would probably have laughed about it. He describes the death of "the patient" in *Screwtape* as simply a homecoming. Other characters describe their own death as an "unstiffening" of old joints and a cessation of old pains. But, most of all, for the followers of Aslan it is an entering into a new joy.

And so the Caspian Triad has illustrated the proper attitudes one should take to combat the doubts of what Lewis called our post-Christian age. It has displayed nature as most completely fulfilled when man assumes his responsibility as its ruler under God. It has showed questing man as reaching beyond the safe world of his own neighborhood into mysterious lands where none have walked before. It has declared what guides will be trustworthy when such quests lead into paths where the light does not extend beyond the next step. And it has indicated that transformations as deep as the heart are necessary for true happiness, and goals as high as God's throne for entering into the life to come.

CHAPTER 8
FIRST AND LAST THINGS:
THE MAGICIAN'S NEPHEW
AND *THE LAST BATTLE*

I.

BEGINNINGS MAY be no more impressive than the small crack in a speckled egg that is soon to hatch a nightingale, and endings may occur "not with a bang but a whimper." But Lewis was well aware of the potential emphasis in first and last things. The Genesis and Revelation of Narnia take full advantage of their chronological positions. Both contain mind-stretching elements which are lacking in the other five books. The extinction of Charn and the birth of Narnia have an almost Miltonic quality about them, and the events which bring the days of Narnia to a close fill the mind with something of the immense scope of the book of endings which inspired it—Revelation.

Not only were these two completed after the other tales were written, but they each presuppose a knowledge by the reader of the characters and conflicts which are sandwiched between these two stories. I do not mean that it is necessary to know the other adventures in order to understand these, but the full enjoyment of both is in part dependent upon a knowledge of what has already been told. Tirian, the last king of Narnia, meditates upon the history of his country and finally in the concluding pages of the book meets most of the heroes of antiquity in the great and final homecoming. The reader's enjoyment of these passages is enhanced if he already knows these heroes.

The forward look of *The Magician's Nephew* is expressed in the opening paragraph in which we are told that it will show "how all the comings and goings between our world and the land of Narnia first began." And the last chapter assumes knowledge of *The Lion, the Witch and the Wardrobe* when it speaks of "another child" finding the lantern still burning in Lantern Waste when, centuries later, she found her way into Narnia on a snowy night.

Although some of *The Chronicles* were quickly forged in the white heat of inspiration, *The Magician's Nephew* did not take shape as easily. Lewis's first attempt to explain the lantern in Lantern Waste, as already noted, was unsuccessful. He apparently returned to the task after *The Silver Chair* was completed in March, 1951. Later in the year he again became dissatisfied with the story, and laid it aside. Then perhaps sometime in 1952 he revised it and completed it to his own satisfaction. It shows the evidence of careful craftsmanship.

Although it has its own story, it is quite clearly also a book of explanations. In addition to explaining the origin of the lantern, it also reveals how the animals become talking animals; what disastrous events admit to Narnia its greatest enemy, the White Witch; why the wardrobe possesses its magic qualities; and, when Lucy discovers that magic, why Professor Kirke is such an understanding adult.

II.

DIGORY KIRKE, who grows up to become a famous professor, shows some of the qualities as a boy which, no doubt, make him famous as a man. His inquisitiveness about the empty house on the block, about the history of Charn, and about the future kingdoms which will surround Narnia, indicate a mind thirsty for facts. He is "the sort of person who wants to know everything." But a questioning mind is a spirited horse which needs a bridle. An appetite for information, like that for food, can be excessive, and the proverbial advice, "Put a knife to thy throat, if thou be a man given to appetite,"[1] although intended for one eating at a king's table, applies to food for the mind as well. Digory is "wild with curiosity" to read what is written on the pillar in the Hall of Images. And his craving to know what will happen if he strikes the magic bell causes the fight with Polly and the unfortunate events which follow. But the question of whether barriers should be built across fields of investigation is a matter of broader implication than the light it sheds on the character of Digory and must be returned to later.

The boy is also rather thin-skinned about any implied or stated reproach. Polly's remark that "Digory" is a funny name evokes the response, "It isn't half so funny as Polly." And the first serious quarrel occurs when she criticizes his thoughtlessness about leaving the homeward pool unmarked in the Wood between the Worlds. In fact, as we are told later, he is always more fearful of "looking a fool" than Polly.

But these flaws are far overshadowed by his merits. One of the most clearly delineated of the characters who visit Narnia, he shows both superior intelligence and stalwart virtues. Not only does he discern Uncle Andrew's trap with the rings (although too late to save Polly), but he also does better than his uncle in figuring out the working of the rings and the significance of the Wood between the Worlds.

He has a sense of responsibility for the potential havoc which Jadis can create in London, and, at considerable danger to himself, accomplishes her eviction. Also, although sorely tempted by the Witch, his sense of honor and faithfulness does not fail him as he stands outside the golden gates of the garden with the apple of life in his pocket. And his statement to the Witch that he does not want eternal youth, but would rather live an ordinary life and then die and go to Heaven indicates that his religious choices have been properly made.

Perhaps his most winsome quality is his warm and sympathetic nature. In spite of their quarrels he and Polly develop a strong and lasting friendship. His reaction to the story of the Deplorable Word is, "But the people?" His feelings immediately go out to the victims destroyed by the fanatic tyranny of the Queen. And, of course, his intense desire to see his mother return to health is not only a character trait but also one of the motivating forces in the plot.

Of the four girls whom Lewis introduces to Narnia, Polly is the most aggressive and competitive. Her repeated, "I'm game if you are" and her challenging "I'll go anywhere you go" demonstrate her refusal to play Dr. Watson to Digory's Sherlock Holmes. The characteristic does not seem to be the product of conceit. She simply will not allow Digory to be any more daring than she is. She is also rather outspoken, telling Digory on their first meeting that he has a dirty face and bluntly labeling as "absolute bosh" the Queen's explanation of the purpose of their trip to Charn. She is a little more practical and cautious than her companion and does not let the excitement of exploration make her forget the pathway home. She insists on testing the green rings in the homeward pool and prevents a disaster by stopping Digory from running off without marking their own watery exit.

Although not as inquisitive as the boy about the acquisition of facts, she is imaginative and creative, with her "smugglers' cave" in the attic and the story she is writing there. This is the sort of childhood entertainment that Lewis approved of. He complained to his brother in a letter that "modern children are poor creatures."[2] The "poor creatures" referred to are the "evacuees" who stayed in Lewis's house during World War II and were the source, no doubt, of the opening situation in *The Lion, the Witch and the Wardrobe*. But their repeated question was, "What shall we do now?" Lewis exclaims, "Shades of our childhood!" by which he does not mean that their childhood was similar but just the opposite. The inventiveness of the brothers as children apparently left no room for adult assistance in killing time. In fact, the Belfast house of Lewis's boyhood gave him several details for the opening chapter of *The Magician's Nephew*. But his own "study" in the attic and his boyish narratives of "Animal Land" convinced him that Polly could be alone without being lonely.

Like Digory, Polly feels a sense of responsibility to rid London of "the Terror of Charn" and a sense of loyalty not to leave him when they are supperless in the Western Wild. Like him also her sympathies go out to the common people who were destroyed by the Deplorable Word. She even feels sorry for Uncle Andrew and hopes that Aslan can say something to "unfrighten" the old sinner. Both Digory and Polly are "strong personalities," each with a keen sense of right and wrong and the sort of delight in the works of Aslan that make them at home in Narnia.

III.

"GLORY BE! I'd ha' been a better man all my life if I'd known there were things like this." Such is the reaction of Frank, the cabby, to the beauty of the singer's voice and the blazing chorus of song as the stars sing an accompaniment to their creator's music. This moral response to all that is lovely gives us the key to the character of the man who is to be the first king of Narnia. His English is not that which would serve in Buckingham Palace, but a cockney accent does not disturb his new subjects on Narnia's day of creation. His kind words to everyone, even to Jadis after she has smashed his cab, indicate the native benevolence which will characterize his reign. His firm and comforting remarks in the darkness of Narnia's uncreated night and the hymn which he leads just before Aslan begins his song suggest that there will be harmony between the creator and his viceroy. In fact, the lion's first words to him are, "Son, I have known you long."

And it is not surprising that this young married man, who used to sing in the choir back home and who says that death is nothing to worry about if you've led a decent life, should find this new land "a fair treat." His delighted reception of the "moosic" of creation, his sympathetic conversation with Strawberry about the life of a London cabhorse, his affirmative but humble answers to Aslan's catechism for kingship, all suggest that he will fill with honor the place which has been prepared for him.

Lewis presents King Frank with, here and there, a touch of humor, such as the remark that the harvest hymn sung by the cabby in the darkness was hardly the song for a place where nothing had ever grown. But it is the warm humor of approval which smiles at human inadequacies. Uncle Andrew is much more comic, but our smile of approval here is for the chastisement received by a selfish old scamp.

The dabbler in magic appears as a rather formidable figure when he first rises from behind his high-backed chair "like a pantomime demon coming up out of a trap-door." He seems to be the master of the conflict with Polly and Digory, as first one and then the other vanish at the touch of a yellow ring. But his mastery deteriorates very rapidly when the children bring back the Queen of Charn to his study. From this point on he supplies most of the humor of the story as we see him reaping the result of his foolish meddling with powers which he only half understands.

Lewis was concerned that Uncle Andrew might turn out to be the sort of comic character who would entertain the adult reader, but not the child. And there are probably subtleties in his amorous imaginings about Jadis when she is out of sight ("a dem fine woman") that would be lost on the younger reader.

But, as we have noted earlier, much of the humor of Narnia is visual. The old gentleman probably comes closer than any other figure in the series to imitating (unwillingly, to be sure) the slapstick comedian. The muffled noises and struggle out of the top hat that was smashed down over his face, the fall into the muddy brook with his white vest and frock-coat, the planting and watering by the kind animals when they thought he was a tree, the honeycomb in the face donated by the charitable bear—surely these are scenes which any audience of children would appreciate.

But the other magician of the story is no laughing matter. Although Lewis quite clearly did not have the Queen of

Charn in mind when he created the tyrant who kept Narnia in winter's grip for a century, he works backward from the White Witch and not only sculptures a terrifying form in Jadis, but also shows the corrosion of individuality which evil wreaks upon its possessor. He, perhaps, had in mind Lord Acton's famous dictum: "Power corrupts and absolute power corrupts absolutely." The Empress is a figure of evil grandeur. Even as an old man Digory still said that she was the most beautiful woman he had ever seen. Tall and of superhuman strength she towers majestically over the ruins of Charn, and in the London streets, even without her magic, displays a sort of splendor in her scorn of the mob.

But when we meet her as the White Witch, her grandeur is gone. It is true that she has regained her magic powers, but her use of them is defensive. Hers is a holding operation, guarding against the threat of the four unfilled thrones at Cair Paravel. Served by dwarfs and wolves in her small and gloomy castle, she leads a miscellaneous army of hags and incubuses, wraiths and efreets, wooses, orknies, and ettins. Gone is the glory of the Queen whose troops laid waste the great cities of Felinda, Sorlois, and Bramandin. The White Witch with a face the color of salt is a hollow ghost of the full-bodied woman who uttered the Deplorable Word.

IV.

BUT THE Queen of Charn is almost as important to the setting as she is to the plot. Without her identification of the dungeons and torture chambers and her description of the annihilating struggle of its last days Charn would be nothing but another heap of the rubble of antiquity. Knowing, however, the insane reach for power and the contempt for human life in the House of Charn, the reader feels a certain awe at the bleak desolation surveyed by the lonely star and the red eye of the cold sun at "the end of all the ages."

However, the most memorable scenes in the book are those set to music. Taking his cue, no doubt, from the Book of

Job that when the Lord created the earth, "the morning stars sang together and all the sons of God shouted for joy," Lewis presents the good and happy land of Narnia as rising into being to the song of Aslan. The pools of green grass that spread out from the lion and ripple over the hills and vales, the primroses that suddenly dot the landscape, the beeches and pines that spring out of the soil like little green geysers, all make visual the melodies of life which burst from Aslan's mouth.

Earlier the poet Dryden had written,

> From harmony, from heavenly harmony,
>   This universal frame began.[3]

But Lewis's vision for his own harmonious land hardly needs the inspiration of the music of the spheres and other tuneful myths. Once the reader has caught the spirit of the country, he feels that it could not have happened any other way.

It would be surprising if the man who wrote *A Preface to Paradise Lost* showed no influence in this book from the creation scenes of Milton's poem. But Lewis pictures the great lion as pacing the ground and being intimately involved with his creation, while Milton describes the Creator as uttering the divine fiat from without, projecting His creative power down into the new universe; so the two accounts are not as parallel as one might expect.

In the description of the appearance of animals, however, the impact of the poem upon the prose is quite obvious. Both writers imagine the beasts literally coming out of the earth. Milton says,

> ... out of the ground up rose
> As from his Lair the wild Beast ...
>
> The Tawny Lion, pawing to get free
> His hinder parts, then springs as broke from Bonds,
> And Rampant shakes his Brinded mane. ...[4]

And he describes the other animals as coming up like the mole above "the crumbl'd earth." Milton's stag, like the Narnian one, "from underground bore up his branching head."

But, of course, Milton was using his imagination to flesh

201

out the brief account of Genesis. Lewis was under no such limitation. The Narnian creation at a few points shows the influence of the epic, but elsewhere it displays the unique invention which we have come to expect in Narnia. In addition to the song that creates its vegetable and animal life and the living stars, the flash of fire and wild creative call seem an appropriate and impressive act as Aslan raises the selected animals to self-consciousness and intelligence.

V.

BUT THE scenes in Charn and Narnia also indicate the structure of the plot. The book is divided into two almost equal parts. The first describes the chain of evil choices which brings Jadis from her world of death to Narnia. The second reveals the strategy which gives the young land a bright morning of many centuries before it is darkened by her hundred years of snow. For the reader who has read the next story the relationship of the two parts is obvious, but even for one who begins with this story the two halves become a unit through the comic adventures of Uncle Andrew in both London and Narnia and through the critical illness of Digory's mother and the gift of healing which he brings back for her.

In fact, this latter thread of the plot is the longest in the story. It begins when Digory's face goes "the wrong sort of shape" as he tells Polly that his mother is dying. His longing rises to an intense hope after he discovers that there are other worlds and that there might be a land of youth with a fruit to cure his mother. In the young land of Narnia his hope is dashed when Aslan tells the animals that the boy is responsible for the presence of Jadis in their new world. Then the suspense reaches its climax at the garden on the green hill when the Witch tempts him to steal the apple and take it home to heal his mother. His resistance of the Witch brings about a rapid resolution to this thread when Aslan gives him an apple, and it does its magic cure.

Although this part of the narrative does not occupy our

attention as often as other matters in the story, it is skill-fully woven into the tapestry of the plot and, in fact, becomes the connecting link with the adventures of the Pevensie chil-dren. The tree that grows from the core of the apple furnishes the wood for the wardrobe which becomes to the next genera-tion the gateway to Narnia.

The plot as it deals with the Queen of Charn develops in three steps. The selfish desire of Uncle Andrew to conduct his "experiment" at the expense of the children's safety sends them out of the world. Digory's selfish desire, in the face of Polly's objections, to satisfy his curiosity concerning the magic bell awakens Jadis from her charmed sleep. And the queen's lust for power and determination to conquer the world bring her to London and to the fight in the street. Then the force of those evil choices is blunted as the timely inter-vention of Digory and Polly transfers Jadis to Narnia where a magic more powerful than her own forces her to flee from that land. But, of course, the evil has not been destroyed but only postponed. In *The Lion, the Witch and the Wardrobe* we learn the terrible price that must be paid for her final defeat.

The second half of the story as it concerns the Witch is not a struggle so much as it is a preparation for her appear-ance in the next story. The only conflict is that between Dig-ory and Jadis concerning the use of the apple, and the choice which he faces is whether to keep his promise to the lion or to steal the apple for his mother. The future of Narnia is not a factor in his thinking. But, of course, the story of the planting of the tree of protection explains the long delay in the return of the Witch and looks forward to the conditions which Lucy found centuries late when she stepped through the ward-robe.

VI.

THE EDUCATION of Uncle Andrew concerning the dangers of experimental magic is, perhaps, not a thread of plot in that his adventures create very little tension or suspense. Once Jadis arrives, there is no doubt that from now on he will be an ineffective and futile figure. But Lewis uses him to illustrate some of the problems of the first day of creation. The animals receive intelligence and speech from Aslan. But information will come with experience. As the cabhorse says, "But, please, we don't know very much yet."

And so their innocent speculation as to whether Uncle Andrew is something of the tree sort or "the Neevil" which Aslan mentioned demonstrates humorously one of the themes of the story—the superiority of love over knowledge. The welfare of others must always be placed ahead of the acquisition of facts. Without experience the animals make some amusing errors regarding Uncle Andrew, but their efforts are well-intentioned and actually turn out to be just what the old rascal needs.

Frank, the cabby, confesses to not much "eddycation" and feels inadequate for the job of king, but Aslan's questions indicate that the requirements for a Narnian ruler are as follows: showing kindness and fairness to everyone, having no favorites, allowing no exploitation, and being a courageous leader in war, an industrious worker in peace, and a father who trains up his children to the same kingly conduct. Whatever knowledge is needed will, no doubt, come with the passage of time.

But Uncle Andrew places knowledge first. He admits to being like Mrs. Lefay, his fairy godmother, who disliked "ordinary, ignorant people." Humans and animals, he thinks, are there to be exploited for his own selfish purposes. The children who arrive in his study are just what he needed. The guinea pigs which he bought are his to be tortured or killed for his experiments. Rules of honesty are proper for little boys, but do not apply to great scholars, who must follow "a high and lonely destiny." And, of course, this phrase links him with Jadis, who says the same thing of the destiny of rulers. She too lived to control others. The difference between her and Uncle Andrew is that she has more knowledge and therefore more power. She has ruthlessly searched and found the knowledge of absolute destruction—the Deplorable Word.

As the book was written within a decade of World War II, the description of the effects of the Deplorable Word no doubt reflect something of the pessimism and fear which were generated by the development of the atomic bomb. The public warnings that man may be about to commit racial suicide probably influence Lewis's description of the power-mad queen and the totalitarian state of Charn. That he intends it as a warning is made explicit toward the end of the story when Aslan accompanies the children as far as the Wood between the Worlds and points to the dry hollow that had once been the entrance into Charn. "Let the race of Adam and Eve take warning," he says.

But between those who place kindness first and those who place knowledge and power first stands Digory, who is to become a famous professor. His experiences in Charn and Narnia show him what must be the order of his priorities. Of course, Lewis approved of the pursuit of knowledge. He does not imply that any knowledge of itself is evil—the children travel by the rings that Uncle Andrew had made. But he seems to be saying that any search for truth or fact that is Christian and not devilish must be guided by a concern for others and a desire for the apple of healing rather than the word of destruction.

Another idea illustrated by the story is related to the mysterious Wood between the Worlds. This place which is not a world but leads to all worlds, a crossroads of creation, is described by Digory as a rich place, "as rich as plum-cake." Lewis tells us that the Wood is very much alive. One can almost feel the trees growing. But it is also a place where nothing has ever happened and where Polly and Digory almost forget their past life and feel like drowsing there forever. The dozens of pools, each apparently the entrance to a different world (and "world" here does not mean planet, but universe), represent another attack by Lewis on our narrow and limited notion that the only reality is that which belongs to our own universe. Not only is there the different time and space of Narnia, but perhaps myriads of other times and spaces as well.

But the Wood itself seems to be the root or source of all

life. The pool by which the children enter Charn is just a puddle, and before the end of the book there is no water left in the grassy hollow. The source of life for that world had dried up. By such a device Lewis is able to say that man's existence and that of his world are dependent upon decisions of the Creator and not the creature.

The universe in which we live will someday be rolled up like a scroll. As Lewis says in the essay called "The World's Last Night," Christians find it hard to remember and others find it hard to believe that human life in this world is "precarious, temporary, provisional." But Scripture teaches that our race will end through a "sudden interruption from without." We do not know whether we are in the first or last act of our drama, but we do know that we have been ordered to be as faithful servants as if "this present were the world's last night."[5]

But the Wood also serves as a divider. Digory, Polly, and the cabby are at home there. Even Strawberry is benefitted. His ears come up into their proper place and his eyes lose their fire. But the Witch is stifled and terrified, and Uncle Andrew trembles with fear. The latter two have chosen death rather than life and find the Wood contrary to their natures.

Their reaction is much the same to the song of life which creates Narnia. Uncle Andrew wants to creep into a rat-hole. The song makes him think and feel things that he does not want to remember. The Witch hates the song. "She would have smashed that whole world, or all worlds, to pieces, if it would only stop the singing." But the two children and the cabby—and even the horse—drink in the music with open mouths and shining eyes. The food for those who affirm life and righteousness is poison to those who deny it.

We have seen Aslan as redeemer, teacher, and guide. In this story, of course, he is presented as creator. As a representation of Christ he is acting according to Scripture, for the writer to the Hebrews tells us that God made the worlds through the Son. Aslan as the son of the Emperor-over-the-sea is functioning as both the revelation and executive of his father. But his concern is as much for the welfare of his creatures as for their creation. The mission on which he sends

Digory is for the protection of the newly created world, but it is also for the boy's own good. When he returns with the apple after the conflict with the Witch, Aslan's "Well done" indicates that the lion knows that he has won a battle.

And face to face with Aslan, Digory "felt absolutely content." In "The Weight of Glory" Lewis speaks of that time in the future when the redeemed soul will hear God's "Well done" and discover "that she has pleased Him whom she was created to please.... With no taint of what we should now call self-approval she will most innocently rejoice in the thing that God has made her to be." And so Digory without conceit rejoices in the commendation of Aslan.

VII.

READERS, NO doubt, differ in opinion as to which is the best of *The Chronicles,* but it is the final story which received the Carnegie Medal as the best children's book of 1956. Completed in 1953, it clearly indicates that Lewis intended with his seventh tale to let night fall over Narnia forever. The first sentence begins, "In the last days of Narnia," and Tirian is introduced as "the last of the Kings of Narnia." *The Last Battle* includes a number of final things, and among them a last judgment. In addition to being redeemer, teacher, guide, and creator, the great lion is judge of his world.

The central theme of the book is stated by Jewel, the unicorn: "All worlds draw to an end; except Aslan's own country." Lewis often reminded his readers that we live in a linear universe, one which is moving in a straight line toward dissolution. On this point, he says, science and religion agree, "for the universe, they tell us, is running down, and will sometime be a uniform infinity of homogeneous matter at a low temperature." And so Narnia comes to an end as the stars fall, the sun and moon are put out, and High King Peter with his golden key locks the door on a frozen waste that is no longer a world.

The subject of last things dominates the story so com-

pletely that it lacks some of the characteristics which we have
come to expect in the series. For instance, there are no glaring
faults to be corrected in travelers into Narnia from our world.
In fact, character delineation is not as sharp here as in the
previous stories. Eustace and Jill have been tried in previous
crucibles and demonstrate that the refining process was successful. They move through the story as untarnished heroes.
Jill shows her wood-craft and skill at archery and Eustace his
improved swordsmanship and his good sense. They both
show the warm attachment to each other which such adventures generally create and a loyalty to this alien land which all
the friends of Narnia demonstrate.

Tirian is a young king when we meet him, and as the
duties of government have already settled on his shoulders,
he shows the early maturity which responsibility often
brings. But his youth has not been entirely outgrown, for
there is an impetuosity at times in his conduct which an older
person would have held in check. Although he does not have
as many individualizing characteristics as some other Narnian characters, his courage, kindness, and steadfastness
shine forth in all of his actions. We are not surprised when
Aslan pronounces the divine accolade of "Well done" upon
the last king of Narnia.

Perhaps the best illustration that Lewis is more interested
in action and ideas in this story than in characterization is in
the delineation of Jewel, the unicorn. Described as a "lordly
beast" and "one of the noblest and delicatest" of the talking
animals, it is several times pictured "with its neck bent round
polishing its blue horn against the creamy whiteness of its
flank." And the fierceness of its attack in battle is illustrated
when in the charge on Stable Hill the unicorn is described as
"tossing men as you'd toss hay on a fork."

But these are actions and appearances. The inner view
which displays attitudes and characteristics is not as clear. We
get to know Reepicheep and Puddleglum by what they say.
But Jewel's longer speeches are often summarized rather than
quoted. The unicorn's talk with Jill in which he gives us the
only historical review we have of the centuries between
Frank, the first king of Narnia, and the Golden Age of High

King Peter is accomplished in one page-long paragraph which compresses a much longer account. But as Lewis does not present it in Jewel's own words, it lacks the flavor of personality which we savor in Mr. Beaver's explanations to the children or Glimfeather's greeting of Eustace and Jill.

However, it would not be correct to say that the unicorn's words are always muffled by summary. Some of the most memorable sayings of the book come from his mouth. We have already noted his statement which sums up the theme of the story. His faith is expressed in the advice that they go back to Stable Hill "and take the adventure that Aslan sends us." When he is facing almost certain death, he tells his beloved King and companion, "I would choose no other life than the life I have had and no other death than the one we go to."

And to Jill's trembling question, as the grim mouth of the Stable becomes a more certain eventuality, he replies, "Nay, fair friend. It may be for us the door to Aslan's country and we shall sup at his table tonight." But, perhaps, the statement which reverberates longest in the memory is his declaration after they have all come through the Door and have breathed the delightful air of Aslan's land: "I have come home at last!... I belong here. This is the land I have been looking for all my life, though I never knew it till now."

Such statements illuminate the unicorn's mastery of the subtleties of language as well as his gentleness, wisdom, courage, and devotion to Aslan. But these are statements which speak for all of Aslan's followers. They do not set him apart as a unique individual in the way that Bree's or Hwin's words set them apart.

Perhaps the characteristic which is emphasized most is his unity with Tirian in both attitudes and actions. When the dryad arrives with the report that the talking trees are being murdered, Tirian and Jewel both become too angry to think clearly. When events seem to indicate that Aslan is not the kind King of the Woods whom they had believed in, they both agree that they have lived too long. At the brutal beating of the talking horse, rage comes over them at the same time. And when they realize that their rash attack had been against unarmed men, they both surrender to what they expect to be the judgment of Aslan. The "one mind" which a life-long friendship can create is well illustrated in the devotion of each to the other.

Poggin, the Dwarf, is another example of the less sharply drawn characters of this book. He uses the plain, somewhat rustic language which we have learned to associate with the sons of earth. His advice is sensible and his loyalty to Aslan and the King unshakable. But there are no "beards and bedsteads!" or "giants and junipers!" in his speech. He does not, like Trumpkin, stand clear from the crowd.

I do not mean to imply that this lack of individualizing details is a flaw in the book, but it illustrates Lewis's concern in this story for broader issues and vaster panoramas than those which are produced by human decisions and actions. We have seen in the earlier adventures that choices growing out of virtues and vices shape one's destiny. Now we see that those choices align one with the larger destiny of worlds either divine or demonic.

VIII.

THE PLOT arranges the action into two equal parts. The first eight chapters describe the events which lead to the end of Narnia. The last words of chapter eight are Tirian's lament: "Narnia is no more." The last eight chapters deal with the end of all life here in this "shadowland" and with the new life in the new land where every day "is better than the one before." The pattern of action begins in chapters one to four with Shift's plan to gain power through his false Aslan and with his success in fooling the Narnians and taking captive the King and the unicorn.

Then the next four chapters record a temporary setback for the ape as otherworldly help in the persons of Jill and Eustace frees the King and rescues Jewel and Puzzle. But it also records the final triumph of the enemy, as the Dwarfs reject both the true Aslan and the true King, Cair Paravel falls to the Calormenes, and the god Tash occupies Narnia. Religiously and politically the forces of evil seem triumphant.

But their triumph is only apparent. As God makes the wrath of men to praise Him, so Shift and his co-conspirators are made a part of the divine plan to bring the faithful home and roll the curtain down on a world whose millenniums have all been spent. Chapters nine to twelve speak mainly of death, as each member of Tirian's party looks the grim monster in the face and conducts himself with courage and firmness. For them the Stable Door seems to be dark jaws into the unknown, but on the other side it is revealed as an entrance to the land of heart's desire.

And the last four chapters present the other side of the door. Aslan's face becomes the divider for all races in the Narnian last judgment, and the reversal of nature returns the world to its darkness and void. The rest of the plot is not so much conflict as discovery. The revelation that nothing which was good in the old world has been lost and the great reunion which marshals the heroes of the past before our imagination assure us that we have only read the title page of "the Great Story, which no one on earth has read: which goes on for ever: in which every chapter is better than the one before."

IX.

MOST OF the ideas which are illustrated in the story have to do with what the theologian would call eschatology, things related to the end of the world. Conditions in the last days of Narnia are characterized by counterfeit religion, atheism, and demonism. Shift's plan to exploit gullible Puzzle for his own profit suggests that false cults and antichrists arise when ordinary people allow clever people to do their thinking for them. Lewis did not believe that limited mental capacity excuses one from using what brains he has. As he says in *Mere Christianity*, "God is no fonder of intellectual slackers than of any other slackers."[6] As Eustace tells Puzzle, he should have spent less time saying he wasn't clever and more time trying to be as clever as he could.

The false Aslan not only creates terror and misery among the Narnians, but allows the atheists, Rishda Tarkaan and Ginger, to spread their deadly doctrine among the Dwarfs. With the revelation of the counterfeit Aslan they throw aside their belief in the true one. But as their fate is different from that of the evil triumvirate (the ape, the Calormene, and the cat), we must assume that their attitude is different. The Dwarfs demonstrate the self-blinding disease of cynicism which causes them to regard all kindness as humbug and to be interested in nothing but their own tight little circle—"The Dwarfs are for the Dwarfs." As Aslan says, "They have chosen cunning instead of belief. Their prison is only in their minds, yet they are in that prison." Cynicism can blind one to the blessings of both the here and the hereafter.

But there is not only a true Aslan; to the surprise of many, including Rishda Tarkaan, there is also a real Tash. Perhaps, taking a hint again from Milton, who makes the chief officers of Satan's army the false gods worshiped by man, Lewis presents the god of the Calormenes as a real demon representing every vice and corruption—in fact, all that is opposite to Aslan. Claiming that Tash and Aslan are one and the same thing—and present in the Stable—Rishda invites the god he does not believe in into the game of deceit. When Tash manifests himself with earthquake and blue fire, fear makes a believer of the Tarkaan. Lewis did not believe that the satanic world was a figment of man's childish imagination. One cannot play with the fires of Hell without bringing disaster down upon his own house.

But what can we say of the righteous in the last days? Lying prophets, fake miracles, and false Aslans may confuse the faithful for a while. Tirian and Jewel are overwhelmed by the uncharacteristic behavior ascribed to Aslan. The little animals who bring food and drink to the captive King are fearful that even this kindness may be wrong. But conduct still divides the good from the evil. Heads may be confused, but lovers of righteousness will still act righteously. Nor will they be deceived for long. Because he knows the character of Aslan, Tirian soon realizes that the "Tashlan" in the Stable is nothing but a cheat.

The Last Battle is about death—the death of a world and the death of individuals, both good and bad. As children are included in the circle of Lewis's listeners, he does not give us the pictures of violent endings which we saw in *That Hideous Strength*. In fact, the death of the wicked is treated with great restraint. Ginger, the cat, for his work in the betrayal of Narnia to the Tisroc of Calormen is given a glimpse of Tash and then loses the gift of self-consciousness which made him a Talking Beast. His reversion to being a dumb animal is a death to his selfhood. Shift and Rishda are carried away by the monster (the ape apparently in his stomach), but we are not treated to any gory details.

However, we must not assume that among the King's companions the grim reaper is treated lightly. Jill and Eustace admit to each other that they are terrified as they approach the last battle. But like Lewis's other heroes they ignore the body's cowardice and move straight into the danger. And Jill speaks for the author when she says that she would rather be killed fighting for Narnia than to grow "old and stupid" in England and then die anyway. A life that is spent on a worthy cause wisely invests a coin which no one can keep forever.

Tirian and Jewel, who have faced death in battle before, make their farewells to each other and express no regrets as the end draws near. As we have noted, Jewel suggests that the "deadly door" of the Stable may be the entrance for them into the delights of Aslan's country. Later we hear the description of their own deaths by the Professor, Polly, and Edmund. As the train wreck was apparently sudden and violent, their deaths were instantaneous and painless. The older ones only felt a release from old age, and Edmund lost a painful knee injury. And the experience of Tirian, Eustace, and Jill, as they are forced through the Stable Door, is nothing but stepping from darkness into marvelous light. If there is a message here, it surely is that death must be prepared for and not ignored, but for those who are prepared, it is simply a passage through the portal to a better world.

213

X.

BUT THE panorama of death extends beyond the individual to races and nations and to the world itself. As we would expect, there are allusions here to the Apocalypse and to Christ's account of the last judgment in Matthew. But just as the creation and redemption stories are uniquely Narnian, so in this book we have only hints and reminders of scriptural eschatology. Appropriately, the world that is discovered through a wardrobe expires while being watched through a stable door. But there is a last trump, as the giant, Time, whom Jill and Eustace had seen sleeping underground, raises his horn to his lips and blows a high and deadly taps for a world whose lights are to be put out.

The giant's name, while he lay dreaming, was Time. But Aslan says that now he will have a new name. As the angel declares in Revelation, time shall be no more. Perhaps his name will be Eternity. Although the different currents of time in Earth and Narnia do not run parallel—so that returning to the merry land after a year in England, one may find that he has missed his friends by several centuries—yet each stream seems to flow in a normal course. While in either place, time seems to pass in the same way and at the same speed.

But the waking of the giant and the changing of his name implies a change in the quality of time. We are told that the parade of creatures past Aslan's face may have taken five minutes and it may have taken years. It is hard to measure such time. And after the great reunion with the heroes of antiquity Lewis says, "About half an hour later—or it might have been half a hundred years later, for time there is not like time here...." Beyond the Stable Door "Time's winged chariot" is at rest. He is no longer a taskmaster.

And so the last trump causes the stars to fall, "even as a fig tree casteth her untimely figs." As in the biblical account the heavens depart "as a scroll when it is rolled together." But, of course, the Narnian stars are not like those in our universe. They are living creatures who sang the song of creation with Aslan on Narnia's first morning. We met two of them on the trip to the utter East. Coriakin, the magician who benevolently ruled the monopods, was a star removed from the sky for some unknown misdemeanor, and Ramandu was a spent star who waited on his island until his diet of fire-berries from the sun would renew his youth. Also, we must not forget that the blood of the stars ran in Tirian's veins, for his ancestor, Caspian the Seafarer, had married Ramandu's daughter.

With its breathing stars, its talking trees and beasts, Narnia has been a world bursting with life and consciousness. All of it must be called to its creator before the world dies. And so, we hear the distant wail of the nations as the living and the dead are called to face the face which is the watershed of eternity. As Lewis says in "The Weight of Glory," "In the end that Face which is the delight or the terror of the universe must be turned upon each of us either with one expression or with the other, either conferring glory inexpressible or inflicting shame that can never be cured or disguised."

Like Christ's description of the division of the sheep on His right and the goats on His left, those who hate Aslan turn to his left and into the dark shadow. Lewis goes no further with this group than to say, "I don't know what became of them." But those who love their creator turn to his right and come "in at the door." In this scene Lewis presents a skillful blending of the figures of Christ as the judge of the nations and Christ as the Good Shepherd acting as the door to the sheepfold.

But the death-throes of the planet seem to follow a reversal of creation. It is true that there are still a few hints from the Book of Revelation as the dying sun and its blood-red moon cast their gruesome color across the waste of waters. But the destruction of all vegetation by the prehistoric creatures who die and leave skeletons which look like fossils many millenniums old, and the rising of the sea, which finally covers all and swirls up to the door but not beyond ("here shall thy proud waves be stayed"), suggest the undoing of the web which is woven in Genesis and in the words of the Lord to Job. In fact, after the giant reaches across the sky and squeezes the sun like an orange, the primal darkness rests upon the face of the deep. But when Peter closes the door of death upon a dead world, he also locks out death itself. In the new world death shall be no more.

XI.

IF THE theme for the faithful who pass through the Stable Door is "O death, where is thy sting?" the theme for the life which they find beyond it is "O grave, where is thy victory?" Awaiting them are friends both new and old, delicious fruits free for the taking, and joy inexpressible in the knowledge that Aslan's home is now their home. One of the most moving episodes in *The Chronicles* is the account of Emeth, the young Calormene soldier, who finds himself in Aslan's land. In *Reflections on the Psalms* Lewis tells us that Emeth means "truth." The young Tarkaan, for whom Jewel wishes "a better god than Tash," is, no doubt, Lewis's picture of the "Gentile" whom Paul describes in Romans as doing by nature the things contained in the law, "which show the work of the law written" in his heart.[7]

Emeth is, like Psyche (whom we will discuss in the next chapter), an *anima naturaliter Christiana,* a naturally Christian soul. In a letter written near to the time when he was working on *The Last Battle* Lewis says, "I think that every prayer which is sincerely made even to a false god ... is accepted by the true God and that Christ saves many who do not think they know Him."[8] He goes on to point out that in the parable in Matthew of the sheep and goats the sheep do not seem to know that they have served Christ. And so Emeth tells Aslan that he has been the servant of Tash. But the lion assures him that all worthy service is done to him and all vile service is done to Tash no matter what name is used, and that without knowing it, Emeth has been seeking him all his life. "For all find what they truly seek."

One of the reasons why this episode is a passage of great power is that the elevated style of the words of Emeth give a poetic tone to his story. But an even greater reason is the sense of wonder which he conveys as he speaks of the "Glorious One" whose beauty surpasses that of all the world "as the rose in bloom surpasses the dust of the desert." The incredible joy at being accepted by the lion, as he says, "weakens me like a wound. And this is the marvel of marvels, that he called me, Beloved, me who am but as a dog."

Where does a writer go after he has lifted the reader to such heights of feeling? What device will ease him back to the level of narrative action? One method is to insert a little comic relief. One of the dogs in Tirian's party objects to the last phrase which Emeth uses. But an older dog reminds him that they call their puppies *boys* when they misbehave.

> "So we do," said the first Dog. "Or, *girls.*"
> "S-s-sh!" said the Old Dog. "That's not a nice word to use. Remember where you are."

Lewis was amused that although *cow* is a perfectly respectable word for female cattle, *bitch*, which is the correct word for a female dog, is regarded as rather vulgar in polite society. If dogs could talk, would *girl* be a disreputable word in mixed company?

But the repeated cry in this happy land is "Further up and further in!" "Up" and "in," however, do not lead to an attainable peak or the central point of a circle. Just as the inside of the Stable is vastly bigger than the outside, so the deeper and higher one goes in Aslan's land the larger it becomes. The garden at the top of the green hill turns out to be not a garden but a world. When one goes farther in, as Mr. Tumnus tells Lucy, it is "like an onion: except that as you continue to go in and in, each circle is larger than the last." Measurement in the world beyond the Door is not limited by the boundaries of our three-dimensional universe. Just as time is of a different quality, so is space. Here again Lewis stretches our imagination so that we can think of possibilities beyond the logic of our own length, width, and thickness.

But the inner world is like the outer one except that it is more real and more beautiful. The new Narnia beyond the Door should not surprise us if we have had the proper education, for, as the Professor says, "It's all in Plato." Lewis presents the Narnian heaven as made up of levels of platonic reality extending into infinity. Nothing that was good in the old world is ever absent in the new. As Peter looks across a gap, he sees the England of this new world and in it the Professor's house where their adventures began. Probably young readers will agree that this is the way Heaven ought to be. For many, Grandmother's house with its Christmas fragrance and its mysterious upstairs halls and parlor and library should have a permanent place among the mansions of the New Jerusalem.

And the reason the Professor's house can be seen is that each discovers that he has telescopic vision. Lewis refuses to leave the inhabitants of Aslan's land with old bodies in a new world. Paul speaks of the glorified bodies of those who are called from the grave to everlasting life. Lewis does not presume to know what they will be like, but he does give each of the Narnian saints, even Poggin and Puzzle, the ability to outrun the wind, to swim up waterfalls, and to skim across lakes and rivers. It is only a hint of what lies ahead when, as Lewis says in *Miracles*, the laws of the new creation will apply. When Christ walked on the water, and Peter, for a moment, did also, we are given, he says, a "foretaste of a Nature that is still in the future."[9] In the new creation, bodies will not be a problem or burden.

Like most literary masterpieces this story does not leave us looking backward but ahead. The curtain is drawn because "the things that began to happen after that were so great and beautiful that I cannot write them." As Aslan speaks to them he no longer looks like a lion. The reader closes the book feeling that the author has drawn the imaginary story as close to reality as he dares. If we agree with his theology, we can step easily from the mountain of Aslan to the City of God.

THE WAY TO
THE TRUE GODS

CHAPTER 9
TILL WE HAVE FACES

I.

LEWIS TELLS us that *Till We Have Faces* had been in process of composition, at least in his mind, since undergraduate days. Twice he attempted to put it into poetic form but gave up after writing only small fragments. And then, as his last creative effort in the realm of fiction, he found, as he says, "what seemed to be the right form."[1] The book was written in 1955 and '56, after the Narnian tales had been completed. His books in the following years are all nonfiction.

As the full title indicates, it is *A Myth Retold*. The myth is the Cupid and Psyche narrative whose earliest known version is a story within the story of *The Golden Ass* by Apuleius, a Latin writer of the early part of the second century A.D. However, Lewis's tale is much more than a retelling. He changes a number of the significant details of his source, adds other plots and themes, and makes one of the sisters his protagonist instead of Psyche. In fact, of some of the changes which he makes he says that this is the way it "must have been," which raises a question concerning Lewis's view of myth.

In a book written some years later, titled *An Experiment in Criticism,* he devoted a chapter to myth and defined it as a story which is not dependent upon literary excellence or even upon exciting narrative movement, in which the characters seem remote and otherworldly, the story impossible or supernatural, and the tone always grave and awe-inspiring. Whatever the myth meant in antiquity, modern man often views it as meaningful or representative even though not historical.

And so when he says that his version is the way that the Cupid and Psyche myth "must have been," he perhaps means that it approaches much closer to the ideal as exemplified by the other great myths of our heritage. As we would expect, his changes give the story a religious meaning very different from that of the version of Apuleius. But his chief concern is not to clean up or rescue the myth from the later contamination. It is to show that God is ever seeking in all nations those who will turn to Him. By telling of the struggle in a pagan culture of one who, even in the darkness of polytheism, finds the victory which comes through surrender to the true God, Lewis is following a path which he knows well. For Queen Orual was also "surprised by joy."

It is not my purpose to compare the version of Apuleius with that of Lewis, but any unbiased reader would agree that the latter writer has raised to an acceptable level what in some details of the Latin version was a ridiculous story. (An example is Psyche's being persuaded by her sisters that her husband was a serpent after she had slept with him many nights and had become pregnant by him.) But we must remember that some of the events of the story are the heritage which Lewis received from classical literature. He, no doubt, felt an obligation to include certain essential details of the original in his narrative even though he does clothe some of them with meaning which is not apparent in his source.

II.

BUT WE can hardly say that the entire book is a treatment of the Cupid and Psyche affair. In fact, that is a minor part of the story. What Lewis gives us is a legal document—a deposition of Queen Orual. Part one, written as carefully as any statement under oath, is her charge against the gods. Part two, only about one fifth the length of the other, is her account of the gods' answer to her charge.

So we must focus our attention on the Queen of Glome, who writes her deposition with the hope that it will be heard in a court of Greek wise men who will judge between her and the gods. But from the gods she expects no answer. Twice on the first page she makes this statement, and part one ends with the phrase "no answer." Orual is an angry plaintiff who despairs of justice, but wants the world to know that the gods are the worst plague ever to come upon mankind.

The book is all written in the last weeks of her life—part one immediately following her progress through neighboring kingdoms, and part two in the last four days, when she knows she is dying. In fact, her death interrupts her manuscript. Critics have often commented on the difference in style between this and Lewis's other stories, but the reason is easy to discover. The voice here is that of the queen of a barbaric little kingdom of the ancient world. In all of Lewis's other fiction, with the exception of *The Screwtape Letters*, we hear his own voice either as omniscient author or first-person narrator. With such a point of view the writer feels no limitation except that which concerns the subject matter. But a first-person narrator who, unlike that of *The Great Divorce*, is not the author, confines the writer to the physical, mental, and emotional world of that other person. So Lewis must clothe himself, as it were, with the mind and feelings of Orual and look at life as she would see it.

The first page, in which the Queen states her purpose, might suggest to the reader that the tone of the book will be bitter, but this is not entirely so. There are bitter comments from time to time, and the tone is predominantly somber. In order to accuse the gods, she must tell the story of her own life, and so, the reminiscence touches upon joys as well as sorrows. Also, Orual is a very honest person, who tries to set down her evidence impartially, whether it tells against herself or against the gods. It is true that she is self-deceived, but her discovery of that fact is the main theme of part two, and is set down as honestly as that of part one.

Although the first-person point of view eliminates some of Lewis's talents which the reader has come to appreciate, it gives the book the great advantage of authority. The very voice of the chief character tells us not only of characters and events but also of motives, her own and others. Like David and Solomon she was for many years both ruler and judge of her little kingdom and had become very perceptive in discerning the desires that move men to action. Nor does she hesitate to lay bare the inner workings of her own life as she understands them. Her narrative has the magnetic power of private "confessions," which no omniscient author's voice could create.

Also, Orual is an effective storyteller. Although at times in part one she makes judgmental comments which remind us that the story is told from the perspective of a person disenchanted with life, she relates the events and her feelings about them as if they had just happened. She keeps to a strict chronological order and does not destroy suspense by revealing outcomes before actions. The reader usually feels that he is there observing and listening rather than hearing the voice of an old woman reminiscing. Even when she tells of fancies and passions and then concludes, "But I am ashamed to write all these follies," she still writes them in the even reportorial style which allows the reader to look directly into her mind as it was as that time.

III.

AS WE would expect from the point of view, the plot is organized around the life of the Queen. The entire structure is built to illustrate what, as Orual says, the god of the Grey Mountain "has done to me." But, as she learns in the end, what the god had done was divine surgery for her own good, and so the plot also illustrates the condition which desperately needed the cutting and grafting.

There are several ways to describe the plot. The exterior story might be divided into nine parts:

1. Eden—the happy love of Orual, Psyche, and the Fox.

2. The Accursed—the worship of Psyche and ruin of the kingdom.

3. The Great Offering—the sacrifice of Psyche and the salvation of the land.

4. The Bride of the God—Psyche's story of her divine husband and Orual's rejection of it.

5. The Judgment of Orual—the destructive power of Orual's demonic love and the sentence of the god upon her.

6. The Establishment of the Queen—the events which settle Orual firmly on the throne.

7. The Works of the Queen—the brief summary of her deeds over many years.

8. The Lying Myth—the Queen's progress into neighboring lands which reveals the false story of Psyche and causes her to write her book.

9. The Revelation—the events and visions which change Orual from bitterness to beauty.

As the story is primarily concerned with inward ugliness and inward beauty, we can also describe the structure in terms of Orual's inner life. It is significant that Lewis intended to call this story *Bareface*. The publisher objected, suggesting that it sounded too much like a Western. Although Lewis's second offering was finally accepted (which also emphasizes the countenance), he still liked *Bareface* better. And so, using this motif as a guide, one might describe a plot structure in which the first part of the story, up to the destruction of Psyche's palace, is called "Love Barefaced," showing the progress from Orual's open and childlike love for the Fox to the intense and possessive love for Psyche—a love which on the mountain is displayed "barefaced" as closely akin to hatred.

After this disaster Orual wears a veil for the rest of her life, and, figuratively, the remainder of part one could be called "Love Veiled." Although her love for Bardia is a passion which extends over most of the years of her reign, it is deeply hidden. The veil is lifted only to Ansit, Bardia's wife, and then only after his death. Also Orual is veiled behind her position as Queen. She tries to turn her back on the affections, let the woman die, and be all Queen. But the veiled love expresses itself in the works of a benevolent ruler who frees slaves, improves working conditions, and moves her barbarous little kingdom several leagues in the direction of enlightened civilization.

Completing this structure is part two, which would be called "Orual Barefaced." It is here that the veil is stripped from her eyes and she sees in herself the ravenous love which had devoured the three who had loved her most deeply. Her love had sent Psyche weeping through the world bereft of her marital happiness; it had held the Fox in Glome when he longed to return to the Greeklands; and it had worked Bardia to death when he could have enjoyed years of retirement with his wife and family. But it is to Orual's credit that she recognizes her bare face. As she is the one who says, "I am Ungit," so she is the one who hears the god say, "You also are Psyche." But these are matters of theme and must be discussed in greater detail later.

IV.

IN THE introductory note (not present in the American edition) Lewis refers to one of the themes of the story as "the straight tale of barbarism."[2] From this statement and from ample evidence in the book we must conclude that the setting is more than a background for the action. Glome is a small kingdom less than two days' journey from the north to south. It is located several hundred miles northeast of Greece, probably south of the Ukraine (the Wagon Men come from the steppes) and not far from the Black Sea. (From a ridge of the Grey Mountain Orual sees far away a gleam of "what we call the sea.")

North and east of the capital, which is also called Glome,

is the Grey Mountain, which is close to the border. North of Glome is another small kingdom called Phars and farther north yet probably Germanic tribes from which blonde, big-boned, hard-handed Batta had been captured. West is the country of Essur, whose borders extend along those of both the other two kingdoms. To the south is the much larger kingdom of Caphad from which Psyche's mother came.

Then twenty kingdoms or more farther south is the land of books, free discussion (even of the gods), philosophy, and poetry—the land of the Fox—post-Socratic Greece of perhaps the fourth century B.C. We should imagine Glome as just on the edge of the area of Greek influence. Its barbaric king wanted his offspring to be brought up in the wisdom of Greece, as he tells the Fox, but before the Greek slave arrives, apparently no one in Glome could read Greek.

The barbarism of Glome is best personified in its ruler, King Trom, whose word is law and whose law is often but the expression of his brutal moods. His palace is partly of wood and partly of brick, with its wall hangings of skins, its uneven stone floor, and its great mirror in the Pillar Room. It houses his slaves, his bastards, his legitimate family of three daughters, and his armed guards. The degree of social amenities to be found here is summed up in Orual's description of the banquet which follows her victory over Argan— "the gobbling, snatching, belching, hiccuping, the greasiness of it all, the bones thrown on the floor, the dogs quarrelling under our feet."

But perhaps more significant than the table manners is the superstition and dark idolatry which governs the lives of the people of Glome. At the center of this sort of barbarism is the House of Ungit, a divine brothel and slaughter-house with its temple prostitutes and sacrifices—both animal and human. The old priest with his "Ungit smell"—of blood and burned fat and singed hair, of wine and incense—sums up what Orual calls "the horror of holiness." Ungit is identified by the Fox with the Greek Aphrodite and the Babylonian Ishtar, both goddesses of love. Whatever else Ungit is, her position as a goddess of love contributes most significantly to the ideas of the book.

227

Although Ungit spreads the smell of her greedy holiness over the entire city, a fresh wind blows when the setting is shifted to the countryside. The idyllic days of Psyche's childhood, when the Fox and Orual spend so many hours with her on the hilltop overlooking the town or under the blossoming almond and cherry trees, suggest that there are pleasures beyond those stimulated by the ugly fertility goddess.

In the introductory note already referred to, Lewis lists as one of the themes "dark idolatry and pale enlightenment at war with each other and with vision." This three-way conflict is, of course, expressed in other ways than through the setting, but it is during those summer days on the hilltop, as they gaze across at the Grey Mountain, that Psyche dreams of her gold and amber palace on its highest ridge and imagines herself as the bride of its great King. And as her imaginings turn out to be prophetic, we must conclude that they come from this third world which is neither dark idolatry nor pale enlightenment. The "good dreams" which, Lewis believed, come from God to the sincere pagan worshiper speak to Psyche of a reality which is behind nature—which is supernatural. And to it she responds with longing.

The same voice comes to Orual when she makes her first trip to the Mountain with Bardia. The sun shines on the morning dew making the grass jewel-bright, and the vast tumble of hills and forests and lakes create a colored world of breathtaking beauty around the mystic Mountain. And within her is a voice which says, "Why should your heart not dance?" The delight which is a response to beauty seems to draw her on and to offer her "strange and beautiful things, one after the other to the world's end."

Here is the voice of vision, of a reality not included in the rationalism of the Fox or the blood sacrifices of Ungit. Through the setting Lewis evokes the voice which he called "joy," the voice from beyond the stars, which speaks through beauty and invites us to the world where we shall receive the morning star and put on the splendor of the sun. And although Orual struggles against the voice and rejects it and destroys the palace, she finally knows that it was true vision.

228

V.

ALTHOUGH THERE are some dozen and a half characters mentioned by name in the story, only half that number are of continuing importance. They can be divided into a triad of threes—the barbarians: King Trom, Batta, and the old priest; the enlightened counselors: the Fox, Arnom, and Bardia; and the images of love: Redival, Psyche, and Orual.

The King, the nurse, and the priest illustrate the foulness of home and religion in the childhood of Orual. The father, who was a figure of fear and hatred, was no father to her. She tells the Fox, "You are ten times my father." The roaring King with his blustering red rages and his murderous white rages calls one daughter "the young whore" and the "salt bitch," another "the hobgoblin" whose face will sour the morning milk, and the third his own chattel to be offered to the Shadowbrute to save his throne. There is not one expression of affection in all his words and actions concerning his daughters, even though one is beautiful, another is courageous, and the third is radiant.

But we must remember that the picture we get of the King is projected through the lens of Orual's experience with him. Although his obscene and rowdy tyranny is a burden which the palace must carry, we get a glimpse of another side from the remark of Bardia that the King is not a bad master to soldiers, shepherds, huntsmen, and others of the rough world of men. In King Trom Lewis seems to be presenting barbaric man as bullying male: tyrannical, vindictive, capricious, and untouched by the humanizing effects of charity or even affection.

Batta, the nurse, is the only thing maternal which Orual knows, and she is drunken, bawdy, and vindictive. Her first recorded words are a threat to the two sisters. "Only wait till your father brings home a new queen." She seems to enjoy creating fear in the children. When the Fox arrives to teach them, she promises lots of whippings, ear pullings, and hard work. Her involvement in the plot is always related to gossip

229

and tattling. It is her story that brings about the castrating of Tarin. She is also, no doubt, involved with Redival in carrying the story of the worship of Psyche to the old priest. And, as Orual finds in her first year as Queen, Batta had sent many slaves to their death in the mines by her lying tales. Her malicious gossip is a club by which she extorts her share of all gifts which the palace slaves receive.

The burden of her presence upon the childhood of the three sisters is something like that of the King upon the palace. Orual remembers in later years her loving moods— the huge, hot, strong, yet flabby hugs from which the child fled to the garden to be freshened and cleansed. And Psyche on the mountain in thinking of the ugly past that she has left behind mentions Glome and the King and Batta.

It is significant that Orual sees an image of Batta in Ungit. In the old stone with its lumps and furrows and gobbets of blood she sees a face "swollen, brooding, infinitely female." It reminded her of her old nurse with her "smothering, engulfing tenacity." In Batta Lewis seems to be representing barbaric man as degenerate female: a busybody, a cheat, and a wine-sodden old woman whose only maternal instincts are sentimental possession and control.

The old priest, the interpreter of the gods, also creates in Orual only fear and hatred. The voice of Ungit, as he calls himself, not only is responsible in her eyes for the sacrifice of Psyche, but is a figure synonymous with "holiness." And "holiness" means the smell of blood and death and the obscene rites of the fertility goddess.

The girl's fear of him is representative of the special meaning which the term "god-fearing" has in Glome. In the Old Testament "the fear of the Lord," which is the beginning of wisdom, includes both reverence and love. But in Glome a god-fearing man is one who scrupulously makes the sacrifices required and participates in the rites demanded, because he fears the anger of the gods. The King claims to be a god-fearing man. Bardia lists the religious practices which he himself observes as evidence of his piety, but concludes: "I think the less Bardia meddles with the gods, the less they'll meddle with Bardia." Earlier he had referred to the part of the

Mountain beyond the Holy Tree as the bad part. "I mean the holy part," he says. Here is no desire to "dwell in the house of the Lord forever."

But the old priest is more than a figure of fear. Although the Fox regards him as nothing but a clever politician maneuvering the superstitions of the people to his own advantage, Orual realizes that the blind old man is more than a trickster when he sits calmly and speaks with perfect self-control while the King's dagger-point is at his ribs. As Orual says, "He was sure of Ungit." His confidence grew out of belief in the reality of his god.

His speech indicates that he is intelligent—that his religious beliefs are not simply traditions handed down to him which he mouths without understanding. He has what might be called a philosophy of mystery. "I, King, have dealt with the gods for three generations of men, and I know that they dazzle our eyes and flow in and out of one another like eddies on a river, and nothing that is said clearly can be said truly about them."

In one sense he comes closer to the truth about the divine nature than the Greeks with their superhuman gods with human hates and lusts. Lewis seems to be suggesting that the Greek myths as they have come down to us have often become too understandable, have lost their supernatural mystery. To use the similes of the old priest, they are clear and thin like water when they should be dark and thick like blood. Certainly Lewis's treatment of the Cupid and Psyche story is closer to the view of the old priest than to that of Apuleius. In fact, one of the themes of the book (which is implied in the title) is that man in his present state cannot "by searching, find out God." Only by revelation can he know the divine nature. And even that is impossible until man's nature is changed. We cannot meet God face to face "till we have faces."

But the old priest is blind, perhaps illustrative of the confused darkness in which his idolatry moves. He knows that there must be sacrifices and expiation for sin. But in his description of the Great Offering there is a mixture of figures which both suggest and contradict Christian doctrine.

Lewis did not believe that all pagan religions were completely empty of truth. In an essay titled "Religion without Dogma" he speaks of the mass of mythology which has come down to us as having many sources mixed together—from history, allegory, ritual, and so on. But he suggests that some of the sources may also be supernatural—in fact, both diabolical and divine. The latter, he says, may be a *praeparatio evangelica*, a divine hint in the ritual or poetry which shadows forth the central truth declared clearly and historically in the incarnation.[3] As already noted, he refers to these divine hints as the "good dreams" which God had sent to man prior to the full revelation in Christ.

In the Great Offering the victim is led up the Mountain to the Holy Tree, suggesting the *Via Dolorosa* to the "tree" at Calvary. The victim must be perfect—like the passover lamb and therefore like Christ, whom Peter describes "as a lamb without blemish and without spot." But the victim, if a woman, is said to be the bride of Ungit's son. And here we have a confusion of the bride of Christ, the church, with the Bridegroom, Christ, who gave His life for the church. Also the human victim is called the Brute's Supper suggesting the Lord's Supper except that the roles are reversed—the human is offered to sustain the Shadowbrute instead of the divine offered as food for the believer.

And then, as the worship of Ungit is a fertility cult, the man lies with the goddess or the woman lies with the god. Here, Lewis may be suggesting not only confusion but even diabolical inspiration to darken and corrupt the "good dreams." In *Perelandra* Ransom speaks of mythology as being "gleams of celestial strength and beauty falling on a jungle of filth and imbecility." And so, the old priest with his broken truth and obscene error is a powerful image of barbaric man's religious conceptions.

VI.

WE HAVE already noted Lewis's statement of the three-way conflict between dark idolatry, pale enlightenment, and vision. Of the enlightened counselors the Fox is most important and most clearly drawn. Next to Orual he is the most fully-rounded character in the book. Orual describes him on first sight as a short, thick-set man, very bright-eyed, with reddish hair and beard which is already turning gray.

Although the philosophy of the Fox is an important part of the theme, it is not only as a philosopher that he has a place in the story. In the vision of judgment in part two the Fox says that he is the one who should be punished because he fed Orual upon words, upon "a prattle of maxims." But she insists that it is not true, that he had fed her upon love—upon what is costliest of all. And the love of the old Greek slave and tutor for the ugly little princess is probably more important than his philosophy. His tenderness in singing, "The Moon's gone down, but Alone I lie," as he recognizes that romantic love will probably never come to Orual is parallel to his long vigil by her bedside when she is desperately ill.

But of the many instances of the "Grandfather's" self-giving love for the "Daughter" the greatest is his voluntary exile from the Greek lands for which he longed. The scene in which he is made a free man and conjures up in his mind a return to those delights which mean "home" is presented very movingly. But after an agony of struggle he responds to Orual's despairing cry, "Do they mean you'll leave me?" and remains, a limb in the socket where he is placed. That this is his greatest expression of love for her is recognized by the Queen in the final vision when she tells him that his reasons for staying were only disguises for his love.

Just as deep, no doubt, although not illustrated by as many instances is his love for Psyche. Orual says that he was like a true grandfather. His love for the baby was "wonderful." He regarded her beauty as "according to nature"—as an expression of the ideal form which nature ought to produce but usually misses somehow. And the depth of his feeling is revealed when he tries to speak to Orual of Psyche's death and then breaks down and leaves weeping.

In fact, Orual pictures him as a very sensitive person, tears coming to his eyes easily. He shudders in horror at the description of human sacrifice in the House of Ungit. He is also very modest, being shocked that the women of Glome go unveiled, and embarrassed at Redival's exposure of herself. He never complains of his present state or boasts of his past life, although he apparently had been very well-educated in the culture of Greece, especially in its literature. But in Glome he is still inquisitive, thirsty for knowledge from whatever source.

In regard to his philosophy something is lacking. But Lewis's phrase, "pale enlightenment," which obviously refers to the Fox, should not be taken as a severe criticism of him. His enlightenment is pale because it is not complete. As Psyche tells Orual the night before the sacrifice, it would be dark as a dungeon without his teaching. But "the Fox hasn't the whole truth." His is the paleness of early dawn, in some ways better than the darkness of Ungit, but still not the blaze of clarity which the Sun of Righteousness will bring. However, this figure is misleading for it suggests progress from Ungit to the Fox and then to Christ. As we will see shortly, this is not Lewis's idea.

The Fox, of course, does not represent all of Greek thought. Psyche speaks of "other masters" than those he followed, who taught of an afterlife(the reference is to Plato). But he had come under the influence of "the porch" or *Stoa*. The Stoics taught that all reality is matter and that the divine nature is a universal working force which pervades all matter. They tried to live "according to nature," that is, consistently with the system of things, and stressed avoiding passion, unjust thoughts, and indulgence of the senses.

Such principles account for the Fox's opposition to anything supernatural. The myths and the gods are all "lies of the poets." He insists that Psyche's story of the god and the palace are hallucinations and that the blessings Glome received after the sacrifice came by chance. He was convinced that, as the divine nature is neither envious nor jealous, there is no danger in comparing Psyche to Aphrodite, and as there are no deadlands beyond this world, to depart from an undesirable life by suicide is "according to nature."

It is significant that Lewis makes the Fox a Stoic rather

than a Platonist. His antisupernaturalism creates a much sharper opposition both to Ungit and to true vision, and therefore increases the tension of the plot. It is also probable that Lewis felt that through the rationalism and naturalism of the Stoics the Fox could be used as a criticism of the skepticism of the present age. But we should not regard the Fox as narrowly philosophic. He has the same faith in knowledge as Socrates. Evil men are to be pitied. Their acts are the result of ignorance. If they knew better, they would be better. And his statement, in the face of the King's scorn, that all men are of one blood has a breadth similar to that of Paul, who says on Mars' Hill that God "hath made of one blood all nations of men."

His position as Orual's "Virgil" or guide through the deadlands in part two, gives Lewis the opportunity to let the Fox criticize his own former philosophy. As he admits to Minos, the judge of the dead, the old priest got something from the mystery of his dark house, and the people got something from the ugly black stone which he never got from his trim sentences and no one ever got from the statue of the Greek Aphrodite. The maxims and the statue were too simple imitations of life.

What is lacking in the philosophy of the Fox is a provision for the possibility of the supernatural. In the vision of Psyche's labors, the Fox calls her to come back from the journey to the deadlands to his world where all is "clear, hard, limited, and simple." One can simplify life by ignoring, as the Fox had, everything that is not clear, hard, and limited, but such a system does not account for all reality.

In a paper called "Christian Apologetics" Lewis classifies all religions, like soups, into the "thick" and "clear." The thick ones are those with orgies, ecstasies, or mysteries, and the "clear" are those which are primarily ethical and philosophical. He points out that Christianity is both thick and clear—both mystical and ethical. When the orgies of Ungit and the ethics of the Fox are supplanted by the mystery of redemption and the Sermon on the Mount, then, as Lewis says in the paper, God will have "both the savage and the citizen, both the head and the belly."[4]

235

VII.

THE ONLY time that we hear the real name of the Fox is when Arnom says, "More than you think, Lysias." The affinity between the man who inherits the priesthood when the old priest dies and the representative of Greek culture is demonstrated almost as soon as Arnom appears in the book. They understand each other well and think in the same patterns. Arnom is an "enlightened" priest. He not only opens more windows in the dark House of Ungit and scrubs it after each sacrifice, but learns to talk about Ungit in a rationalistic way as "signifying" the earth, the mother of all life.

When Arnom moves the worship of Ungit a little closer to the "clear" religion of the Fox, he also loses some of the mystery of the "thick" old cult. Orual reports that she knew the old priest was dead because Arnom came into the room wearing the bird mask and other insignia of the office. But, she says, "He was only Arnom." There was no awesome atmosphere such as had surrounded the old priest and made one feel that the holiness of Ungit moved with him.

When the first books are imported from Greece, Arnom is the Fox's first pupil in the study of its language and literature. It is Arnom who sets up the figure of Aphrodite in the temple in front of the shapeless Ungit. And, significantly, when he adds the final note to Orual's manuscript, he does not refer to himself as the priest of Ungit, but of Aphrodite. He had been Hellenized.

In the figure of Arnom, Lewis shows the impact of rationalism upon mystery. Man insists on explaining what is unexplainable. The priest's agricultural explanation during the rite of the year's birth sounds reasonable until Orual asks herself why such a mystery should be made of the fact that the rain falls out of the sky and makes the earth fertile.

That Ungit is not simply a personification of such ideas is made clear by the two episodes which follow Arnom's explanation. The peasant woman who comes with her offering and her burden and leaves strengthened and sustained does not find her strength in the Greek notions of religious symbolism.

She has reached through the darkness and touched a mystery which Arnom knows nothing of. Here as elsewhere Lewis uses a character to say that God hears the prayers of those who do not know that they know Him.

The reaction of the people to the rite of the year's birth also gives the lie to the philosophic explanation. When Arnom hacks his way out of Ungit's house with his wooden sword as he had done for many years at this season, the people rejoice with an enthusiasm which cannot be explained as a reaction to an allegory of the circling year. They show a spontaneous excitement which can only be the result of faith in a mystery which, as the old priest had said, is "more than letters written in a book."

Although much in the primitive worship of Ungit is false, in fact, diabolical, yet, as the Fox says, speaking from the illumination which death brings, the way to the true gods is more like the House of Ungit than like the cold, clear sentences of Arnom's new philosophy. Or as Lewis says in a letter, speaking of Christianity, "we are now approaching something which will never be fully comprehensible."[5]

VIII.

AND THAT it would never be comprehensible is taken for granted by Bardia, the third of the Queen's counselors. As we have already noted, the captain of the guard is a god-fearing man, but no mystic. He accepts the gods as a fact of life to be taken into consideration when necessary, but he shows no inquisitiveness to explore them beyond the requirements set by the gods themselves. Although, as Psyche says, he is wise in his own way, he is a man of action rather than of thought. He calls the Fox a word-weaver and shows no evidence of being influenced by Greek culture. But as a soldier, a diplomat, a practical leader of men he serves the Queen well where human relations are concerned. He knows men and knows how to direct their movements to the Queen's advantage.

His position in the story is similar to that of the Fox—it relates to both love and religion. When Bardia is in his last illness, Arnom tells the Queen that he is "your loyalest and most loving subject." Although a faithful and affectionate husband to Ansit, he is also a loyal and loving servant to the Queen. The two loves do not overlap or conflict. At first, his attitude toward Orual is admiration for the courageous young girl who attacks him with a sword. Then, it is interest in her as his talented student in swordplay. And, finally, it is friendship with her as his Queen and warrior-companion in the field.

Two years after this book was published Lewis was writing a series of radio talks which later were published as *The Four Loves*. Of the four (affection, friendship, eros, and charity), Lewis identifies friendship as that love which is built upon common interests. The beginning of common interest between Bardia and Orual is, of course, her natural talent with a sword. But as she takes over the reins of government and concerns herself with military, diplomatic, and domestic affairs of state, the base of their friendship broadens considerably.

However, when the friendship is between a man and a woman, as Lewis points out in the talks, it may pass into erotic love if there is no hindrance. For Orual there is none, and it changes very shortly into that passion. But on Bardia's side there is the barrier of his love for his wife, as well as the ugliness of the Queen. There is no hint anywhere that the deep love he has for her as Queen and friend is at all tinged with the erotic. After the first meeting with Psyche when the two are forced to spend the night on the mountain together, Bardia suggests, with some embarrassment, that because of the cold they sleep "back to back, the way men do in the wars." And Orual comments that she discovered that "if you are ugly enough" men will soon forget that you are a woman. It is this attitude which defends Bardia from any conflict between his hearth and the palace.

The night before the sacrifice of Psyche, just before Bardia lets Orual into the room to see her, he says, "I wonder, do the gods know what it feels like to be a man." Here is a remark that with some adjustment could appear in the Old Testament. It expresses the need for the incarnation. Lewis suggests that it is hard for man to believe that the divine nature can know and feel the limitations and longings of humankind. God is so completely "other" that His infinity seems to limit His understanding of the incomplete and the fallen.

But Lewis says in *Miracles*, "The union between God and Nature in the Person of Christ admits no divorce."[6] In the humanity of Christ is the permanent assurance that God can and does accommodate Himself to the lowest level of His creation. Christ's reply to Philip, "He that hath seen me hath seen the Father,"[7] is the answer to Bardia's question.

But he lived before the incarnation. He represents the pre-Christian attitude of the common man toward the supernatural. As Jacob whispers "How dreadful is this place"[8] after his vision of God, so Bardia remarks of their necessary sleeping place on the mountain, "Not where a man'd choose; too near the gods." And just as the Israelites cry out to Moses, "Let not God speak with us, lest we die!"[9] so earlier he had expressed his extreme terror at the sight of Psyche, the bright-faced bride of the god.

Lewis makes it clear that Bardia's aversion to any intimate association with the gods is not because of immoral actions or attitudes. He is a wholly admirable man, loyal, honest, tender, and brave. Rather, it is because he believed that the gods are bad for man—they are a different species"; one must avoid them or be hurt. And as Lewis did not believe that Bethlehem cancelled out the thunders of Sinai, we should examine later the sense in which Bardia is right.

IX.

BUT WE cannot say that Redival's aversions are unrelated to immoral actions or attitudes. Feather-headed, wanton, and spiteful, she seems during most of the story to represent the person whose outward beauty covers up a natural tendency to evil. However, the episode in part two which Orual calls the first snowflake of her own winter is also for the reader a spotlight which changes the color of Redival's motives.

In writing of the early days Orual remembers the companionable sister with whom she caught tadpoles, built mud houses, and did a thousand other things which children enjoy. And she thinks, how terribly Redival had changed. Then, as if the divine surgeons, as she calls them, are already at work, she learns the reason for the change. From Tarin, the young lover of Redival, now a fat and powerful eunuch of the great king to the south, she learns that her own thoughtless abandonment of Redival for the Fox and then for Psyche was the cause of the change. "First of all Orual loved me much; then the Fox came and she loved me little; then the baby came and she loved me not at all."

As Lewis says in *The Four Loves*, "As soon as we are fully conscious, we discover loneliness. We need others physically, emotionally, intellectually."[10] Redival is robbed of the companionship and love of her older sister by invasions of their happiness in which she can have no part. Born without intellectual capacities, it is no wonder that she hates the lessons of the Fox and fills her lonely hours by plaguing him and encouraging others to do the same. And the arrival of Psyche, who robs her of what love Orual still has for her, is, no doubt, regarded as the final collapse of her world.

Is there any wonder that, looking on her little half-sister as the usurper of her own place in her sister's affection, she becomes spiteful? And then, when puberty comes and Redival feels the change in her body which young womanhood brings, what more natural response for the abandoned teenager than to find comfort in the handsome young guard. And when Tarin is snatched so violently and brutally from her, is it surprising that she should turn back to the malice of her nurse and the bawdy and gossip in which the old barbarian delighted?

In the tragic decay of the golden-haired sister's character Lewis illustrates the results of frustrated need-love. Although in the book mentioned he puts love into four categories, he also identifies in each a need-love and a gift-love. The gift-love is a self-giving which, like God's grace, is not the result of the merit of the recipient, but of the nature of the giver.

However, such a high level of love is rare. Most of our loves, he says, are need-loves—like hunger, the response of an emptiness in our being to that which can fill it. He compares need-love and gift-love to the mold and the shape which it produces. It is not until Redival is given in marriage to Trunia as a means of cementing the friendship between Phars and Glome that the mold of her need-love is filled. As we should expect from such a history, she talks of nothing but her children when Orual visits her and asks about no one in Glome but Batta.

To say that Redival "represents" need-love would be misleading because she is much more than a symbol, and the story is not an allegory. As we have already noted Lewis preferred "instance" or "case" to "symbol" in discussing characters or events in his narratives. If there is verisimilitude in the person, we should feel that she has a life of her own and, therefore, has a larger bulk in the story than the word "symbol" implies.

X.

IN A letter to Clyde Kilby of Wheaton College, Lewis calls Psyche an instance of the *anima naturaliter Christiana,* the naturally Christian soul. He says that she is always being guided toward the true God, but that she is "under the cloud" of the pagan religion in which she has been raised.[11] And she certainly appears to the reader to have all the qualities of perfection, within and without, which can be expected of a mortal woman.

Although Lewis here is following his source in regard to physical beauty, he fleshes out her character and includes virtues which are quite foreign to the Psyche of Apuleius. From Orual's description of her, Lewis's Psyche seems to be the platonic ideal of what a person should be from childhood to young womanhood. She has at every age the proper beauty for that age. It is such a "natural" beauty that the beholder is not astounded at it until the girl is out of sight. In her presence it seems what one should expect from nature.

Her inner qualities are no less ideal. As the Fox says, Virtue herself has put on a human form in Psyche. Truthful, obedient, loving, forgiving, brave, it is difficult to find any fault in her. Although she inherits her father's hot temper, it only shows when others are in trouble. Such perfection would probably be difficult for the reader to accept if she were the central character. We do not like our heroines to be inhumanly flawless. But it is only after we know that she is to be the Great Offering and the bride of the god that most of these character traits are presented directly to the reader. Prior to that we know her primarily through the praise of Orual or the Fox or the people of Glome.

However, in the conversation of the last night before Psyche is sacrificed, we get a clear picture of her perfection. And at this point we can accept it, for now we are approaching the supernatural. In fact, Lewis makes some very pointed associations between Psyche and Christ. We must not say that she is a symbol of Christ, for he says in the letter already referred to that Psyche is like Christ in some ways because every good man and woman is like Christ.

But the association is made explicit when Psyche says to Orual, "How can I be the ransom for all Glome unless I die?" And she seems to echo Christ's first words on the cross when she forgives Redival with the comment, "She also does what she doesn't know." Like the High Priest's remark at the judgment of Christ that "it was expedient that one man should die for the people,"[12] the King says, "It's only sense that one should die for many." And when Orual tells her, "You healed them, and blessed them, and took their filthy disease upon yourself," this not only suggests the ministry of Christ but also echoes the messianic statement of Isaiah, "Surely he hath borne our griefs and carried our sorrows . . . the chastisement of our peace was upon him; and with his stripes we are healed." And the statement of the Fox that at the Holy Tree she did not cry out even when they left her, reminds us again of Isaiah. "As a sheep before her shearers is dumb, so he opened not his mouth."[13] So Psyche, who is to become a goddess, reflects the image of Christ.

But we must understand what Lewis means by goddess. One of the reasons for the difficulty of this book is that it lives in two worlds—that is, as a pagan story with Christian themes it contains two value systems. In the original narrative Psyche literally becomes a goddess—a part of the Greek pantheon. And there is something of the divine about her in the closing pages of this book. But as Lewis says that she is an *anima naturaliter Christiana*, we must conclude that she becomes a goddess in the sense that every Christian becomes a child of God and will inherit the likeness of Christ. In "The Weight of Glory" Lewis says, speaking of our relationship with our neighbors, "It is a serious thing to live in a society of possible gods and goddesses."

We must be careful not to read any more into Psyche than Lewis intended. Her remark that by dying she is to be the ransom for all of Glome could be understood to mean that she actually is a symbol of Christ Himself. But Lewis's statement about her in the letter makes such an interpretation impossible. We must assume that her remark is an expression of the demands of the heathen religion in which she was raised, but put in a form so that it will remind the reader of her Christlike character. Her relation to the gospel is "sacramental" rather than symbolical.

So we must follow the old Greek myth, or, at least, as much of it as the author uses, and at the same time recognize the use which he makes of it to convey Christian truth. Because the words of the book are all those of the pagan Queen of Glome, he can give us no direct comments on the story's relationship to the gospel. But such biblical parallels as we have just noted show at least something of his intent.

Psyche, then, is "according to nature"—perfect in beauty, perfect in virtue—in fact, Christlike. What does it mean? The Psyche of Apuleius was of surpassing beauty. This is the starting point—the material which Lewis had to work with. But she was also a rather silly girl and at times vindictive—with a lie she brought about the death of her wicked sisters. We could hardly call her a model for Lewis's character.

But there is another Psyche. At the end of the story Orual is told, "You also are Psyche." And the two Psyches who stand side by side reflected in the pool, both beautiful but each different, give us the key to the youngest sister's place in the story. She is the ideal pattern for the Christian soul. (In fact, the Greek word *psyche* means soul.) She is the likeness of Christ promised to every believer. It is for this reason that she has an otherworldly quality about her. Like the bride of Christ, made perfect in Him, she has something of the character of the church triumphant. Or, as the redeemed soul who stands before her Creator, she learns, as Lewis says in "The Weight of Glory," "that she has pleased Him whom she was created to please."

But beside the ideal stands the actual, Orual, who has come through bitterness and rebellion to surrender and to a similar beauty. If Psyche is the pattern, Orual is the process, an "instance" or "case" of the blows of chisel and hammer which the ugly child of Adam must undergo before the Divine Artist sees in His work the image of His Son.

But before discussing Orual there is something more to be said of Psyche. In their last interview before the sacrifice she says that she has had, all her life, a sort of longing for death. Not a longing which grew out of unhappiness, but just the opposite. It was when she was most keenly aware of the beauty of this world that she longed to go to the beauty which is behind it. Through the beauty of this world, she says, that which is beyond seemed to call her, "Psyche come."

Here she speaks quite clearly for Lewis himself. In a letter to a friend he speaks of this longing for his *patria*, his home, and says that it is strongest when life here seems closest to Heaven. "All joy... emphasises our pilgrim status.... Our best havings are wantings."[14] In "The Weight of Glory" he elaborates on this idea, as we have noted in the first chapter. We are not satisfied with merely seeing beauty, "we want to pass into it." We want to *be* that beauty. But in this world that is impossible; we cannot get in. "But" (to repeat his figure of speech), "all the leaves of the New Testament are rustling with the rumour that it will not always be so." Someday we will pass beyond nature, "into that splendour which she fitfully reflects."

This is another characteristic of the Christian soul. Psyche's longing to reach the Mountain and the gold and amber house which the greatest King of all is going to build for her is a longing for home—for her own country. She says that it feels "not like going, but like going back." Psyche, like the worthies listed in the Letter to the Hebrews, desires "a better country, that is, an heavenly," and places no high value on a long life in this present world. The summons from beyond the stars makes this whole universe a waiting room.

XI.

BUT AS we have already indicated, this is Orual's story. In the introductory note Lewis lists "the mind of an ugly woman" as one of the four themes of the book. And in the letter to Professor Kilby he says, "But of course my interest is primarily in Orual." It is her conception of herself, her loves, her attitude toward the supernatural which are at the center of the story. Intelligent, loving, brave, a born leader, Orual has many qualities which make her a very attractive person. It is easy for the reader to identify with her and to become involved with the tensions of her life. As a child she seems happy and carefree, except when the two ogres of her childhood—her father and the old priest—intrude on her activities.

Significantly, it is at the time of the arrival of the bride who is to be Psyche's mother that Orual first becomes aware of her own ugliness. And with the awareness comes fear. Redival has the golden curls and the beauty. She will be loved, she thinks, but the ugly stepdaughter will be hated. She says that while the girls are singing the Greek wedding hymn (which they do not understand) pictures of the cruelties of stepmothers in stories are dancing in her head.

245

Thus, early in life her expectations of love are lowered. Her ugliness makes it difficult to believe that anyone really loves her. She loves the Fox, and his loving nature would make it hard for anyone to doubt him. But when she gives him his freedom and then realizes that he may leave her, she concludes, "It was Psyche he loved. Never me." The love of Psyche, also, is all that an older sister could desire, but in that last night before the sacrifice, when Psyche speaks of going to the Mountain and to her lover, Orual's response is "I only see that you have never loved me." And when Bardia asks permission to leave to assist his wife, who is in labor, she believes that he regards his home as his true life and his service to the Queen as simply his day's work.

So when she determines to go to the Mountain a second time and force Psyche to act, she tells herself, "You are alone, Orual." Everyone else follows his own concerns—the Fox to his sleep, Bardia to his wife. But much of Orual's sense of being solitary is self-imposed. Because she is ugly, she assumes that she generates love in very few people.

Actually, there is ample evidence in the story that her tender and considerate nature creates love in most of those who serve her. Not only do the deep loves represented by the Fox, Psyche, and Bardia stand out as rare gems which could be exhibited by few people, but also, her servants and the people of Glome show a love for her which is a response to her kindliness and benevolent wisdom as ruler. Her servants weep at her wounds, show faithful gratitude at her gift of freedom, and display much love at her return to her kingdom after the trip into neighboring lands. Yet in the last few moments of her life she thinks it strange that Arnom and the women weep. "What," she asks herself, "have I ever done to please them?"

It is, perhaps, because of her ugliness that the love she has for those dearest to her is all need-love. As we have already noted, she knows nothing of the gift-love which thinks only of the welfare of the loved one, even it it means separation from oneself. Ansit, Bardia's wife, illustrates this sort of love when she speaks of her son Ilerdia, who is growing up and is daily less his mother's child and more his own, involved in the world of affairs. She says, "Do you think I'd lift up my little finger if lifting it would stop it?" This is a love which does not cling to its object, but rejoices in the joys of the other, even though it means a separation. But Orual, as Lewis says in the letter, "is (not a symbol) but an instance, a 'case' of human affection in its natural condition, true, tender, suffering, but in the long run tyrannically possessive and ready to turn to hatred when the beloved ceases to be its possession."

And Orual's possessive love, most terribly illustrated in the ruin of Psyche's happiness, is displayed in all its devouring ugliness as she reads her complaint against the gods before the vast concourse of the dead. It had been hinted at the night before the sacrifice, more clearly seen on the first trip to the Mountain, and dramatized on the second trip, but when the true word is dug out of her, as she says, and presented for all to hear (not the complaint she had written but the one she had felt) we realize how close to hatred it had become.

As Lewis says in *The Four Loves*, affection alone "will go bad on us."[15] We need the intervention of a higher sort of love in order to keep it pure. And so, when Orual speaks in her true voice, she tells the gods that she would rather have seen Psyche torn to pieces by the Shadowbrute than for her to have "some horrible new happiness" which she had not given her. Like the possessive mother in *The Great Divorce* she harps upon the word "mine." "The girl was mine." And later, "She was mine. *Mine!* Do you not know what the word means? Mine!"

XII.

WE HAVE discussed three of the four themes which Lewis lists in the introductory note: barbarism, the mind of an ugly woman, and the three-way conflict between idolatry, enlightenment, and vision. The fourth is "the havoc which a vocation, or even a faith, works on human life." By "vocation" he means, of course, a special call to missionary work or other Christian service—or Psyche's call to a supernatural and separating relationship. And the "havoc" is not an evil but the inevitable sword of division which Christ becomes between the person and the family and friends who do not sympathize with the conversion or call and who view it as a robbery of the family unity or pagan serenity which had existed before.

It is impossible to make a clear-cut distinction between Orual's possessive love and her aversion to the "unnatural and estranging" religious experiences of Psyche. Like the gods they flow in and out of each other. But quite clearly, in the meeting of Orual with Psyche the night before the sacrifice and in the two confrontations on the Mountain Lewis illustrates the separating power of God's call. On the night in the tower Psyche tells her sister that she feels that she has been divinely chosen for the sacrifice. "I am the one who has been made ready for it ever since I was a little child in your arms, Maia. The sweetest thing in all my life has been the longing—to reach the Mountain, to find the place where all the beauty came from—"

Orual can only say to this vision, "Oh, cruel, cruel. Your heart is not of iron—stone, rather." And on the first trip to the Mountain when Psyche assures her sister that the god, her husband, will somehow make her see Psyche's palace, Orual cries out in rage, "I don't want it. I hate it. Hate it, hate it, hate it. Do you understand?" But, of course, the most dramatic illustration of the dividing power of a vocation and the "havoc" which it can create is at the second meeting on the Mountain when Orual uses Psyche's love for her as a tool to get her own way and in doing so destroys the happiness of both.

But Orual's opposition to the world of Psyche's husband begins long before her sister is named the Great Offering. Her dread of the supernatural appears early in life. Her fear of the priest, she says, was different from her fear of her father. It was the holiness, the Ungit smell and the Ungit clothes of skins, dried bladders, and the bird mask which made him terrifying. And, of course, when Psyche is dedicated to death, the fear turns to hatred.

Although Orual was the student of the Fox and in some sense "enlightened," she never completely accepted his skepticism or rejected a belief in the gods. As she tells Psyche before the offering, the Fox thought that either there were no gods or they were better than men. But it turns out that they are viler than the vilest men. The only defense against them (and she says it is a frail defense) is to love no one, listen to no music, never look at nature, and labor incessantly.

Against this bitterness come three voices of the supernatural different from that of the old priest. First is the voice behind nature which speaks of beauty and joy. As she says when she describes the first trip to the Mountain, the huge and ancient silence, the mystic quality of the Mountain, the sense that the heart of nature danced for joy, made it very difficult to believe in ugliness, her own or that of the world. Through this beauty and through her longing to wander beyond the world's end the voice speaks of a reality in the supernatural which is beyond the experience of either the priest or the Fox.

Second is the inner voice which repeatedly tells her to leave Psyche to the gods. The figure of speech used with its first appearance is significant. "A thought pierced up through the crust of my mind like a crocus coming up in the early year." And this flower is that Psyche is worthy of the gods, that it is fitting that they have her. And again, later on the same trip, the thought comes to her that Psyche is happy. Why should Orual mar what she cannot make? And a third time, the picture of Psyche bright-faced and overflowing with joy tells her not to meddle. She realizes that she is among marvels which she does not understand. But still her pride and possessive love cause her to go through with her destructive plan.

The third voice comes with the direct appearance of the god to her at the time Psyche's palace is destroyed. The beauty of his face was so intense that, she says, it was not possible for her to bear it for more than a split second. But in that flash she knew that the supernatural world is not a fable. She had refused to hear the other voices, but she cannot shut out his words. She does not know, however, the meaning of

249

the sentence which the god passes upon her—that she will know herself and her work, and that she also will be Psyche. As it turns out, the statement is actually a promise rather than a judgment, but Orual understands it as some sort of mysterious doom.

What does it mean? The reader might at first suppose that the "work" referred to is her accomplishments as Queen. Arnom in the concluding note to the book describes her as "the most wise, just, valiant, fortunate, and merciful" of rulers in that region of the world. But the queenship to Orual is simply a means of filling up the sandy waste that is her life after she has ruined Psyche's happiness. Lewis seems to be illustrating that a life without love or faith, no matter what the accomplishment, is vanity of vanities.

In fact, the description of the emptiness of her life is probably influenced by the tone of boredom in the Book of Ecclesiastes. Just as the writer planted gardens and orchards and made pools of water to water them and got possessions of great and small cattle, but concluded that all was vanity and vexation of spirit, so Orual makes cisterns, improves the stock, builds bridges, and then asks, "Who cares?" She wonders who sends "this senseless repetition of days and nights and seasons and years?" And, as the biblical writer speaks of the circuits of the wind, the repetition of the days, the return of the waters from the sea,[16] so she speaks of the days and months and years as going "round and round like a wheel" until they become a burden she can hardly bear.

XIII.

SO WE MUST not conclude that the deeds of her queenship are the "work" referred to by the god. Orual does not completely know herself until she reads her true complaint before the audience in the deadlands and therefore does not understand her "work"—that is, what she had done to others. But this brings us to part two of the book, which many readers find very difficult to understand.

Perhaps the most important fact to remember is that this concluding addition to the story is written by a very different Orual. Instead of cursing, she blesses the gods. She speaks of the "divine surgeons" who were at work upon her. Almost her last words are, "I know now, Lord, why you utter no answer. You are yourself the answer. Before your face questions die away." Like Job she finds the divine presence eminently adequate for all her needs.

The key to Lewis's purpose in adding part two is to be found in the probes or surgical incisions by which the "divine surgeons" lay bare the cancer at the center of her being.

First, are the words of Tarin which reveal her "work" on Redival—the desertion of one who needed love as much as she did. In spite of her golden curls Redival is the handicapped one whose need-love would never be able to reward Orual as do the rich and costly loves of the Fox and Psyche. But such limited ones make possible the expression of that gift-love which asks for no rewards—which "seeketh not her own" but loves because love is the expression of its nature.

Second, as she says, the gods used her pen to probe her wound. The very writing of her story causes her to see motives and attitudes which she had not been aware of. The sorting of pretext from true reason is represented in her dream of the seeds which had to be sorted and in which she is sometimes an ant laboring to complete the impossible task. Through her book she understands herself a little more clearly. But to discern all the purposes of one's own heart is a task beyond anyone's ability. In order to come before God, man must know something of his need, but such knowledge is not obtained by self-analysis alone.

The third probe is in the searing words of Ansit, who reveals to Orual what she has done to Bardia. Her demanding love had weakened him until he was brought to his death by an illness which a strong man would have been able to resist. His wife tells the Queen that her love is like that of the Shadowbrute, loving and devouring at the same time. And when her anger cools, Orual has to admit to herself that she had loaded him with work to keep him in her presence. She worked him early and late because of her pleasure in seeing him and hearing his voice. As the god had promised, she begins to see more clearly herself and her work.

These three incisions of the divine scalpel show Orual her inner self and prepare her for the vision in which she descends with her father to the depths of the earth (where Ungit originated). Here she sees her face in the mirror and confesses, "I am Ungit." Her love is the all-devouring, barren thing which receives but gives nothing back. But her attempt, first by sword and then by drowning, to cease being Ungit is thwarted by the second statement of the god, that she must die before she dies.

When the ugliness of one's fallen nature is revealed to a person, he may cry out with Paul, "Who shall deliver me from the body of this death?" Of course, since the setting of the story is pre-Christian, Lewis cannot go on with Paul and say, "I thank God through Jesus Christ our Lord."[17] The cryptic statement that there is another death which must take place first causes Orual to attempt a life of virtue—of death to the passions and other vices. But, like Paul, she discovers that what she would, she does not, and what she hates, she does.

This truth, that man cannot obtain the beauty of holiness by his own efforts, is illustrated by a second vision, that of the golden rams of the gods. Orual desires beauty so that she will no longer have the face of Ungit, but her efforts to obtain it are disastrous. Her direct approach to the golden ones brings nothing but the terrible force of their horns and hooves. She realizes, however, that her defeat is not because of the anger of the rams, but because the divine nature, simply by being what it is, is destructive to natural man. The Lord told Moses that no man can see His glory and live. Only through the mediation of the Son of Man can we partake of His holiness.

Orual clings to one last rag of self-righteousness, however. Her love of Psyche had been virtuous. And so the gods send her a third vision in which Orual seeks the water of death. Here before the vast concourse of the dead she dies before she dies as her true complaint is "dug out" of her. When she confesses the loathsome nature of her love for Psyche and then throws herself from the pillar on which she stands, she surrenders herself to the judgment of the gods.

It is only when she realizes that, as the Fox says, Psyche "had no more dangerous enemies than us"—that they had been in league to keep her "from being united with the Divine Nature"—that Orual recognizes the ugliness of her true voice and is ready to receive the casket of beauty brought back from the deadlands by Psyche herself to "make Ungit beautiful." After she is "unmade," she hears the divine words, "You also are Psyche." The beauty which she had tried so hard to obtain is hers by the gift of another.

Here again is the theme of vicariousness which is stated in *Perelandra*. As the King says, "The best fruits are plucked for each by some hand that is not his own." And the Fox tells Orual while they watch the panorama of the labors of Psyche, "We're all limbs and parts of one Whole. Hence, of each other. Men, and gods, flow in and out and mingle." This statement is an expression of the doctrine of co-inherence which Lewis learned from his friend Charles Williams—that through love one can share and literally lighten the sufferings of another. Williams called it "the practice of substituted love."

In fact, Lewis told his colleague, Nevill Coghill, that during his wife's intense suffering from cancer he had been able to receive into his body her pains. "It was crippling," he confessed. "But it relieved hers."[18] In a letter he suggests that this principle may be fundamental to all creation. "Is it so very difficult to believe that the travail of all creation which God Himself descended to share, at its most intense, may be necessary in the process of turning finite creatures (with free wills) into—well, into Gods . . . ?"[19]

In this doctrine is the explanation of a statement of the Fox which has puzzled many readers. He tells Orual that she bore the anguish of the tasks which Psyche achieved. The tasks were easy for the sister because Orual suffered at sorting the seeds, seeking the golden fleece, and searching for the water of death.

Lewis explains this "law of exchange" in his essay on "Williams and the Arthuriad." Love, he says, does not even need a mutual compact. "We can be their beneficiaries without our own knowledge or consent."[20] Love works below the

253

level of consciousness and shares the burdens of another without being aware of it. And as the Fox says later, speaking of Orual's destruction of Psyche's happiness, "She bore much for you then. You have borne something for her since." As burden-bearers we flow in and out and mingle with each other. It was not necessary for either Orual or Psyche to know that their anguish eased the load of the other.

The steps of this co-inherence are, in part, governed by Lewis's source. In the account of Apuleius Psyche is given four labors to perform. Each is represented in Lewis's story both in the life of Orual and in that of Psyche. Orual's efforts to sort the seeds, to obtain the golden fleece, and to receive the water of death are repeated in the panorama in which, because of Orual's anguish, Psyche easily sorts the seeds, obtains the fleece, and receives the water of death. The fourth labor, that of bringing the casket of beauty from the land of death, is done by Psyche and received by Orual as evidence that the divine transformation has taken place. Ugly Orual is dead. In her place is a second Psyche, different, but also very beautiful.

For those readers who still feel that there are loose ends in the story which should have been tied up, let me observe that the book is not a novel, and it is not a myth explained. It is "a myth retold." As Lewis says elsewhere, a good myth is "a story out of which ever varying meanings will grow for different readers and in different ages."[21] So, this is the myth as it "must have been," not thin and clear like water, but dark and thick like blood. Let each reader find here the meaning that speaks to his condition.

Perhaps all that is necessary to be said in conclusion is a comment on Orual's question, "Why must holy places be dark places?" That is, why don't the gods speak plainly and say what they want us to do. She complains, "I had to guess. And because I guessed wrong they punished me." Before she made her second trip to the Mountain, she prayed at length for a sign from the gods. But no sign was given.

Lewis is, here, dealing with the problem of human freedom and moral responsibility. As he says in a letter, "The love we are commanded to have for God and our neighbour is a state of the *will.*"[22] God may thunder at Sinai to underline the seriousness of the law, but He more often speaks with the still small voice which we can listen to or ignore. One cannot be frightened into a moral choice. And so, like the rest of us, Orual is given elbow room to make her choices from moral grounds. She is given enough light to make the right choice, but not enough to terrify her into a decision against her will. Her "guess" that Psyche's husband is not a god comes from her will: she does not want him to be a god.

But when the "divine surgeons" had done their work, when she sees herself, and her will is changed, then the approach of the god as she stands with her sister beside the pool is a new terror but also joy and overpowering sweetness. Although she now loves Psyche more than ever before, it is not she who counts. The love of God enriches all other loves. As Lewis says in *The Four Loves*, "By loving Him more than them, we shall love them more than we do now."[23]

A PANORAMA
OF LANDSCAPES

CHAPTER 10
THE TAPESTRY OF SPUN TALES

I.

ALTHOUGH JACK Lewis, like Eustace Scrubb, was afraid of "the tops of cliffs" (as he admitted), he loved to travel afoot on the rural byways of Britain. And a fear of high places does not prevent the memory from climbing a hill to view the land traversed. Reliving in letters the vacation hikes he took with friends, he describes their walks down into stream-threaded valleys, their pauses at little grey churches to read a portion of Scripture, and their pre-arranged stops at some quiet farmhouse for a night's lodging. Part of the joy of travel is the backward look.

And so, as we come to the end of our journey through Lewis's landscapes, it is pleasant to remember again the muted hues of Malacandra, the tossing horns and prancing hoofs of Heaven's unicorns, or the sizzling welcome of bacon and eggs and mushrooms as Shasta is served his first Narnian breakfast by Duffle, Rogin, and Bricklethumb. Also a survey of the panorama of ideas with which his tales have stimulated our thinking might help to remind us that the ground from which they came was a deeply plowed and carefully tilled countryside.

But great ideas do not automatically create great literature. What is there about Lewis's style and literary technique which make his stories such an effective stage for dramatizing his ideas? The style of a writer is difficult to define. Perhaps the shortest definition of style is Jonathan Swift's, "Proper words in proper places." And probably the most complex is, "The style is the man." I will not attempt to illustrate the one definition by an analysis of the sentences nor the other by a psychoanalysis of the man. But before going further I would like to point out a few characteristics of his written word.

Most scholarly books are written in a very impersonal style. If the author must refer to himself, it is to "the present writer," and the student or fellow scholar he is writing to is always "the reader." But in *The Discarded Image,* one of Lewis's last works (in fact, it was published a few months after his death), there are few, if any, references to "the present writer" or "the reader." There are, however, nine hundred and forty-three first and second person pronouns referring to Lewis and his audience. The *I's* and *me's,* the *we's, you's,* and *us's,* even in this scholarly work on medieval and renaissance literature, remind us that here is a man projecting his ideas as an encounter with another person—"a man speaking to men." Looking back at the tales we have discussed, I think that perhaps this speaking voice is the warp of the narrative fabric, the background thread which makes a single tapestry of the varying texture of bright islands and gray cities, of dancing dryads and bloody offerings to the Shadowbrute.

It is true that the point of view (the eyes through which we view the action) does not allow Lewis to project himself into all the stories with the voice of the raconteur which we noted in the spinning of Narnia. But the conversational quality and eye-level encounter with the reader in his expository style, which shows so clearly in such works as *Mere Christianity,* emerges in his narrative style either by the creation of a narrator who is consciously speaking to an audience, or a leading character who, as central intelligence, is the window through which the storyteller can view the action and discuss it with us. That is, the tales contain very little impersonal narration. If the voice is not Lewis to the "child," Screwtape to Wormwood, or Orual to the Greek audience she hopes for, it is Lewis commenting on Ransom's resentment at Much Nadderby or on Jane's shattered self-composure when she meets the Director at St. Anne's. The speaking voice is still firmly woven into the loom.

Another characteristic of his expository style which reappears in his narratives is the concrete image. In Lewis's essays the concrete is usually attained through analogy. The abstract idea is given a body through an apt illustration. The Germanic and Celtic barbarians "were not in the least like Hottentots dressed up in bowler hats." The *Summa* and the *Divine Comedy* are "as crowded and varied as a London terminus on a bank holiday."

We hardly need to illustrate this same picture-creating trait in the tales. Each reader will supply his favorite scene—perhaps faraway Cair Paravel shining in the setting sun "like a great star resting on the seashore"; or the description of the rose-red valley between the peaks, Tai Harendrimar, the Hill of Life, where Tor would rule the coming generations of Perelandra. Sometimes the descriptions are built with sense-evoking adjectives, but more often with figures of speech—metaphors and similes which like the expository analogies give concreteness through comparison—"great matterhorns clothed in flowers... shaped something like a lily but tinted like a rose." The vividness of the scene, often coupled with the awe or delight of some traveler within the tale, makes us feel that it must have actually happened.

Another example of vividness is in the strange characters which populate these distant landscapes. Lewis more than once condemned the science fiction which carries the reader light years into the Milky Way to observe ordinary people falling in love or fighting wars which could as easily have been staged in our own atmosphere. Distant planets and worlds beyond wardrobes are for surprises. Sometimes the

261

surprises are biological—the stilt-like *sorns* and translucent *eldils*—and sometimes they are psychological—the queenly innocence of Tinidril and the ill-adjusted antiquity of Merlin.

But although strange in outer fur or inner tensions, Lewis's characters all display the recognizable traits which set them apart as individuals. As we pointed out, however, in discussing the Narnian "creatures," he does not use his omniscient powers as author to peer into the minds of his nonhuman characters. We are told directly of Ransom's internal struggles, but not of those of Hyoi or Trinidril. And so most of the characters display their individuality through their speech. This dramatic quality of the tales—characteristic conversation for each participant—is one of the most effective devices of Lewis's narrative technique. Each person speaks like a unique individual. No one would mistake Puddleglum's voice for that of Reepicheep or Weston's rude words for the smooth evasions of Deputy Director Wither.

The inventiveness of Lewis's imagination is not exhausted, however, by his many-tongued crowd of characters. As we think of the lands we have visited—the canyons and islands of space, the lilting birth and solemn death of Narnia, the infernal grit and stench of Hell, the celestial solidity of Heaven which his genius has discovered to us—we must admit that much of the pleasure of his books has come from our journeys through delightful or breathtaking landscapes. And not the least of the delights of those landscapes are their denizens, the singing beasts, the thumping monopods, the ghostly trippers who contribute a strangeness which gives new dimensions to the word *otherworldly*.

The concreteness and inventiveness of the tales remind us that Lewis was a poet. But that he was also a logician is apparent when we recall the balance and order of his plots and characters. The logical structure of *Perelandra* with its central temptation section and coordinated preceding and succeeding chapters, or *The Last Battle* with its theme, "Narnia is no more," at the exact center of its plot, illustrate the precision with which Lewis organized the action of his stories. Also, the use of the same number of characters from the N.I.C.E. as those representing the Company, or the three triads of persons in *Till We Have Faces,* demonstrates again a mind which admired the symmetry of logical arrangement.

Integrated with the neatly arranged characters and actions and the otherworldly scenes are, of course, the ideas. But before summarizing these we should remind ourselves again of Lewis's method of integration. He received a number of letters from readers who wrote of the characters of his stories as "symbols" of ideas and the plots as "allegorical systems." He always denied that these terms should be applied to his tales. Referring to his characters as "cases" and "instances," not "symbols," he pointed out that his narratives are "supposals" rather than allegories. "What if," on another planet, a race like ours began with a temptation, but successfully resisted it? Such a story would be free to imitate the Genesis account at times and go its own way at other times as the author wished.

It is this freedom which the allegory lacks and which probably caused Lewis to abandon the form after writing the early and rather difficult allegory, *The Pilgrim's Regress.* He may have felt that the technique makes the character a prisoner to the meaning he represents. The allegory or system of symbols shackles the symbolic character to the theme, which dominates the action, and we feel that he is being moved over the chess board according to the prescribed allegorical pattern.

Elsewhere he points out that words are arbitrary symbols for things and have no necessary similarity to that which they symbolize. The sunlight on a landscape in a painting, however, is not a symbol. Its relation to reality is based on similarity. It has something in common with actual sunlight even though not nearly so rich in characteristics.

It is this similarity between fiction and reality which he calls "sacramental" rather than symbolical. Aslan, the lordly lion, is not a symbol, but a sacrament of Christ because, although not as lordly as the Lion of the Tribe of Judah, he has, on a lower level, something of the character of Christ. The Christlikeness of Psyche, which we noted, is another instance of the method.

The sacramental character receives some of his character

traits from the other world which he reflects, and yet is free to be an individual and act as a well-rounded fictional person according to the "just suppose" or "let's pretend" of the author. Just suppose Christ came to a world like Narnia. Might He not have taken a form something like Aslan? Let's pretend that Psyche is a good pagan seeking the true God, who finds Him and is made perfect in her Redeemer. She is an instance of the redeemed soul, but she is not a symbol of all redeemed souls. Therefore she is still free to be Psyche, the loving sister of Orual. It is this freedom which gives the great literary advantage to the sacramental over the symbolical in conveying ideas through fiction.

It should be pointed out, however, that in Lewis's earlier discussion of the sacramental and allegorical methods in *The Allegory of Love* he does use the word *symbolism* to represent the sacramental as opposed to the allegorical. But later he employs *symbol* in the more conventional sense to mean a person or object which stands for an idea, one of the units within an allegory.

The Christian terms and examples used to describe the sacramental method should not blind us to the fact that the source of the idea is Greek. That Christians reflect the image of Christ is, of course, a New Testament doctrine, but, as Lewis admits, the concept that a literary figure reflects on a lower plane something which is more real and rich at a higher level is the application of Plato's doctrine of "Ideas" to literary theory.

II.

A FEW of what we called "recurrent ideas" in Lewis's works were discussed in the introductory chapter. But now that we have walked through the various countrysides which make up the panorama of his fiction, it is time to summarize the themes he has chosen to present "sacramentally" through his characters and their actions.

From Aslan and Maleldil to "the Enemy" and "the true

gods" we have a spectrum of views of the nature of divinity. And the hostile and polytheistic visions are just as useful to the author as the orthodox and sympathetic ones. Perhaps we should first note the emphasis upon the incomprehensibility of God, the doctrine that there is nothing about Him which man can grasp by the powers of his intellect alone. By Screwtape's exasperated, "What is He up to?" and the repeated, "He's not a tame lion," Lewis makes it clear that he has no map of "the Abyss of the Father." Man cannot build a road into the divine mystery.

But a corollary to that principle, which receives even greater emphasis, is that God is self-revealing and approachable. We can know nothing except what He reveals, but His revelation through nature, through law, through the incarnation fills our wandering paths with more signposts than we care to take notice of. The approachableness of Aslan to those who know him, Tinidril's delighted walk with Maleldil, the unquenchable joy of Sarah Smith, bathed in a divine love which her ghostly husband's theatricals cannot diminish—these are sacraments of the divine humility which accommodates itself to every level of need.

The supreme example of that accommodation is the incarnation, accomplished by Maleldil the Young, as the *hrossa* call the Second Person of the Trinity. But "the Word made flesh" is most completely delineated, of course, by Narnia's great King of the Woods. There are few doctrines of Christology which are not mirrored in the words and actions of Aslan. Of the shorter episodes are the thrice-repeated "Myself!" expressing to Shasta the self-existence of the Trinity; the revelation to Bree that the lion is a "true beast," just as Christ is a true man of flesh and blood, not a divine apparition; and the painful but loving chastening of Aravis, whose red welts evidence the concern of a father for the moral health of his child.

But the acts of Aslan which we remember longest are those which change worlds. Not only does he illustrate the truth that Christ is Creator; the lion also suggests by his comings and goings and the Wood between the Worlds that God may have created myriads of universes in addition to the one which we so naively regard as all reality. And although *The*

265

Magician's Nephew shows a world coming into being complete with its stars, flowers, and talking beasts in less than a day's time—a telescoped Genesis account—we must not forget that Lewis gives us another picture of creation. *Perelandra* reveals the last part of the sixth day of creation shortly after man has been placed in his garden planet. And the days of creation on Perelandra are eons of time. Tor, the King, speaks of long ages in which the ruling *eldil* had been the very hand of Maleldil in preparing the planet for this morning day in which two creatures made in the image of their Creator will begin their reign as the rulers of nature. Lewis, of course, is not presenting in the two creations historical choices, but, as he says, "possibilities" to lift our imagination out of its provincial and materialistic rut.

Christ as Redeemer is also depicted imaginatively in almost every world which Lewis has created. The story of redemption which Oyarsa "desires to look into" is followed in its sequel by the statement regarding Maleldil's death in "the Wounded World" for each man individually. The appeal of the solid saint to the Big Ghost to "ask for the Bleeding Charity," and Psyche's willingness to die as a sacrifice for "all of Glome" remind us, each in a different way, of the atonement.

But few would disagree that the most effective and affecting account of the cost of salvation is that which relates the death at the Stone Table. In spite of the freedom which the sacramental method gives him, Lewis follows the gospel narrative closely enough that any child or adult who is aware of the scriptural record will be able to recognize the representation. And the joy and wonder of the resurrection could hardly be presented better in terms a child would appreciate than in the stormy romp of Aslan with Lucy and Susan.

Lewis also illustrates the fact that God is at work in His world. The divine surgery, as Orual calls it, which gives her a heart transplant; the wrestling-Jacob chapter, when Ransom discovers the meaning of his name; the numerous appearances of Aslan in which he instructs or guides or removes a dragon skin demonstrate the profound statement in the hymn on Perelandra's Hill of Life that all of God is in the smallest seed and all of creation is within Him who is in the seed. Not an electron spins around its nucleus without the energy of His presence.

And then Lewis completes his presentation of the major tenets of the Christian faith with his eschatology. Tor speaks of last things as he looks forward to the overthrow of Earth's Dark Lord and the remaking of the Silent Planet into the paradise which it had been intended to be. *The Last Battle* displays the renewal in a different way. The new heaven and new earth described by the Revelator are divided from the old in Narnia by a stable door. The old world drops back into the lightless void, and the door of death is closed forever, but for those who look into Aslan's face and love him the new world lies ahead with joys unending.

The indescribable joy with which *The Last Battle* ends is, I think, the theme of themes of Lewis's fiction. The principle that at the heart of the universe there is pleasure shines forth in scene after scene of his tales. The ecstasy of delight that Ransom feels as soon as the space ship lifts him above this world's atmosphere illustrates Lewis's contention that we of this Earth live in an evil pocket of a good universe. On Malacandra the *séroni*, the *hrossa*, and the *pfiffltriggi* live in happy harmony even on a dying planet. Perelandra is an Eden of love and joy for all creatures from singing beasts to worshipping King and Queen. At the borders of the celestial land where the solid people meet the tourists from the Gray City, on the ghostly side there is fear and trembling, but from the hills of light come the thundering feet of those who are bathed in rapture. And it is not out of place to subpoena old Screwtape to grudgingly witness to God's "hedonism" at whose right hand are "pleasures for evermore."

When we think of Narnia, although we cannot close our eyes to the Tisrocs and green worms with which our heroes and heroines must contend, we still can call it a merry land where feasts and frolicking far outnumber the occasional tests of character. And even the bitter Queen of Glome ends her life in "overpowering sweetness," saying to the Lord, "You are yourself the answer. Before your face questions die away." The holy mirth which Lewis extolls in his comments on the Psalms is a river of joy which divides and flows through the delta of his many landscapes.

Delight is an essence of reality beyond this evil pocket because love is also an essence. Within the pocket we must have justice because our deeds fall below justice. But in the sinless worlds beyond, all is gift. And even here God rewards us not according to our rights, but according to His love. Love is an intricate bond which unites all creatures, as well. Each is enriched by the love and labors of another. This principle of grace and vicarious love is stated clearly by Tor as he accepts his office of Oyarsa of the young planet and acknowledges it as a gift from many hands. And the reverse of the principle is stated by the Big Ghost as he demands his "rights" and turns his back upon the offered grace. The death of Aslan for Edmund is a sacrament of the vicarious love of Christ, and the labors of both Orual and Psyche illustrate substituted love or co-inherence as it applies to human relationships. The network of love leaves no creature untouched.

The network of love touches all, but all do not respond in love. There is the bent will which rejects reality and "casts itself into the Nowhere." The nature of evil, the existence of Satan, and the tragic results of sin are topics which Lewis believed should be forced upon the consciousness of this skeptical age. In spite of the humor of *The Screwtape Letters* and the fantasy of *The Great Divorce* he makes it clear that he believed in supernatural powers of evil and in a Hell in which man's own choices can confine him. The nature of Satan and his cohorts is illustrated in the character of the Bent Oyarsa of Thulcandra, part of whose history we learn through the words of the Oyarsa of Malacandra. Some of his characteristics are represented in the Un-man, who is, perhaps, possessed by that very spirit. Of the same evil brood are the *macrobes* who give orders to Frost and Wither through the head of Alcasan.

The nature of evil is demonstrated by the anti-life attitude of the leaders of the N.I.C.E. and by the destructive practices of the Un-man, who tells the Lady that he has come to make her acquainted with death. But in the devilish strategy of Screwtape and the obsessions of the citizens of the Gray City we see the inward-turning, ego-admiring nature of creatures who have turned their backs on their Creator.

In fact, Lewis uses several characters to illustrate that sin is self-destroying. The degeneration of Jadis from the Queen of Charn to the White Witch of Narnia demonstrates the principle, as does, perhaps more vividly, the ghostliness of the trippers to Heaven's borders. And the emptiness of evil is most dramatically depicted by MacDonald's hairline crack as a measurement of the dimensions of Hell. That which turns from God and "casts itself into the Nowhere" will eventually find its existence tempered with nothingness.

The wrong choices which are produced by man's fallen nature are like leprous growths which corrupt the vital organs of the individual. Lewis demonstrates in *The Great Divorce* that each ghost who turns his back upon Heaven has destroyed by previous wrong choices the power of choosing good for himself.

It would be pointless to list every sin whose self-destroying work can be found in the tales, but a few sinners who are worth mentioning here include the cynic who has "seen through" everything and therefore can see nothing, the mother whose love has degenerated to mere possession, the role-player whose identity is swallowed up by the parts he played, the shopkeeper whose only interest in the reality of Heaven is in its commercial value, and the bishop who has conformed to the spirit of the age until his mind is no more than a personified evasion.

Among the social evils which the fallen race has produced, Lewis attacks "inner rings" through Mark Studdock and the N.I.C.E., nature worship through Weston's espousal of life-force philosophy, and the theory of "cure" rather than punishment for criminals, in the treatment of Ivy Maggs's husband by the N.I.C.E.

But too much emphasis upon sin and evil would falsify the picture of Lewis's worlds. His interest is much greater in solutions than in problems. And his method of solution is usually to show what might have been, what can be, and what will be—God's grace as it operates in the past, present, and future. He believed that God had intended man to be His viceroy upon this Earth as the ruler of nature. As God's purposes do not fail, Lewis implies that sometime in the future, either here or elsewhere, this reign will still take place.

In Tor and Tinidril on their garden planet we see the ideal picture of the relationship that might have been between man and the animals. In the tangled jungle around the ruins of Cair Paravel is the illustration of nature today without its leader (although in the feast which Bacchus provides we are reminded that nature has tremendous energy for the benefit of man when he takes his rightful place). And we should not forget that although Narnia is a land of Talking Beasts and other nonhuman creatures, it is always happiest when it is ruled by a son of Adam. Ransom's power over animals in *That Hideous Strength* probably points to the future but also suggests that even in the present man can do wonders if he tries, in ending the strife with the beasts. But the peaceable kingdom which the race will inherit can be seen in *The Great Divorce,* where nature sings its coronation song to transformed man as he rides his stallion into the hills.

But to carry out God's purpose for him both here and hereafter, man must develop certain virtues. Although Lewis's heroes and heroines usually begin with some portion of God-given goodness, they often need the pain and difficult choices they encounter. Suffering can be the seed-bed for Christian growth. And, as Screwtape points out to Wormwood, God's dangerous world develops the fortitude which is the necessary companion of all the other virtues. Not only is the growth of fortitude at the heart of the action in Ransom's first interplanetary adventure, but it is also tested and developed in almost every story which Lewis wrote.

As man is not the master of his fate or the captain of his soul, obedience is demonstrated throughout the fiction. Lewis believed that, although the ultimate allegiance is to God, the hierarchy of authority which God has ordained makes obedience necessary at all levels of creation. The beasts obey Tinidril, the Company at St. Anne's follows the orders of the Director, and the younger royalty of Narnia recognize the authority of High King Peter.

The statement of more than one hero that they are "between the paws of Aslan" demonstrates the sense of Providence that runs through not only the Narnia tales but all the stories. In a universe where the center is everywhere because God is everywhere, luck is not a commodity to be considered. But there are times when Maleldil's voice is not heard, or when Aslan seems to leave his followers to look for the "signs" on their own. It is here that faith is tested as the enemy invites the faithful to seek the creature comforts of Harfang or desert the floating island of God's unknown purposes for the fixed land of one's own plans.

Of the virtue of hope, among several examples is Trufflehunter, whose expectancy never wavers in the dark years of Old Narnia's suppression. And in the dark hours of Narnia's last battle the unicorn shows this Christian virtue as he speaks of the grim Stable Door as the entrance to the delights of Aslan's land. But the supreme exemplar is Reepicheep, whose forward look from the bow of the *Dawn Treader* awaits the fulfillment of his lifelong goal—the utter East and Aslan's country.

And of love there is more to be said than can be covered in this brief summary, even though we have already discussed its vicarious aspect. Jane discovers that love and obedience are inseparable virtues; Digory learns early that love must be chosen before knowledge; and Emeth, the good pagan, finds to his unending wonder that he is "beloved" by the "Glorious One" whom he has sought without knowing his name.

The need-love, the gift-love, the possessive love that ferments to hatred, are spread on the canvas of Glome through the lives of Redival, Psyche, and Orual—the lonely one, the self-giving one, and the devouring one. But the planet of love demonstrates what this world might be if all men loved their fellows with the kind of love which God's grace provides. In fact, the theme that is illuminated from the "Pedestrian" at Much Nadderby to Orual's last broken sentence is that it is the duty and everlasting profit of man to love the highest which he sees.

Such a love will lead him to God, and beyond this life to

the "joy" whose elfin horn has been calling him from the hills of light ever since childhood. The music from another world which Lewis calls "joy" strikes a chord in the human heart and makes a seeker and a sojourner of all who are not imprisoned, like the Dwarfs, within the stable walls of their own self-deception. To each soul it says, "Psyche come!" And when the wandering and the labors have been completed, when the Stable Door has been passed, she will discover to her wonder and delight that she is home at last. With Jewel she will say, "I belong here."

SOURCES OF QUOTATIONS
AND REFERENCES

HAVING ASSUMED that it is unnecessary to document each quotation from the stories under discussion in this study, I will simply list here the editions used.

From Macmillan Publishing Company, Inc.:

Out of the Silent Planet, Macmillan Publishing Co., Inc.

Perelandra, copyright © 1944 by Clive Staples Lewis.

That Hideous Strength, copyright © 1946 by Clive Staples Lewis.

The Screwtape Letters, With Screwtape Proposes a Toast, copyright © 1961 by C. S. Lewis (*Screwtape Proposes a Toast*); copyright © 1959 by Helen Joy Lewis.

The Great Divorce, copyright © 1946 by the Macmillan Company.

The Lion, the Witch and the Wardrobe, copyright 1950 by the Macmillan Company; Collier Books edition, 1970.

Prince Caspian, copyright 1951 by the Macmillan Company; Collier Books edition, 1970.

The Voyage of the "Dawn Treader," copyright 1952 by the Macmillan Company; Collier Books edition, 1970.

The Silver Chair, copyright 1953 by the Macmillan Company; Collier Books edition, 1970.

The Horse and His Boy, copyright 1954 by the Macmillan Company; Collier Books edition, 1970.

The Magician's Nephew, copyright 1955 by the Macmillan Company; Collier Books edition, 1970.

The Last Battle, copyright © 1956 by C. S. Lewis; Collier Books edition, 1970.

From Wm. B. Eerdmans Publishing Company:

Till We Have Faces, copyright © 1956 by C. S. Lewis.

As the reader who is interested in reading further in Lewis might profit from knowing the setting for statements from his other works, I have listed the sources for all those in which the context seemed significant. Scriptural references are all to the Authorized Version.

Chapter 1

1. *Letters of C. S. Lewis*, edited, with a Memoir, by W. H. Lewis (London, 1966), p. 2.
2. *Letters to an American Lady* (Grand Rapids, 1971), p. 29.
3. Roger Lancelyn Green and Walter Hooper, *C. S. Lewis, a Biography* (New York, 1974), p. 300.
4. Green and Hooper, p. 140.
5. *Letters of C. S. L.*, p. 185.
6. Green and Hooper, p. 125.
7. *Letters of C. S. L.*, p. 263.
8. *Letters of C. S. L.*, p. 265.
9. *Surprised by Joy* (London, 1955), p. 129.
10. *S. B. J.*, p. 215.
11. The most complete and up-to-date listing of the writings of Lewis is Walter Hooper's "A Bibliography of the Writings of C. S. Lewis, Revised and Enlarged," in *C. S. Lewis at the Breakfast Table*, edited by James T. Como (New York, 1979), pp. 245–288.
12. *Letters of C. S. L.*, p. 248.
13. "Memoir" in *Letters of C. S. L.*, p. 24.
14. *Mere Christianity* (London, 1952), p. 42.
15. *Transposition and Other Addresses* (London, 1949), p. 42.
16. "The Weight of Glory" can be found in three different volumes: *Transposition and Other Addresses* (American edition titled *The Weight of Glory and other Addresses*), *They Asked for a Paper*, and *Screwtape Proposes a Toast*.
17. P. 224.
18. P. 5.
19. P. 55.
20. *M. C.*, p. 38.
21. *Miracles* (London, 1947), p. 28.
22. *M. C.*, p. 51.
23. *The Problem of Pain* (London, 1940), p. 124.

Chapter 2

1. Quoted by Green and Hooper, p. 165.
2. *Of Other Worlds, Essays and Stories* (London, 1966), pp. 59–73.
3. "Flight."

4. *The Allegory of Love* (London, 1938), pp. 44–48.
5. P. 171.
6. *God in the Dock* (Grand Rapids, 1970), pp. 208–211.
7. *Christian Reflections* (London, 1967), pp. 82–93.
8. P. 76.

Chapter 3

1. Green and Hooper, p. 171.
2. "Tolkien's Magic Ring," *The Tolkien Reader* (New York, 1966), p. ix.
3. *God in the Dock*, pp. 245–249.
4. *Letters of C. S. L.*, p. 195.
5. *Paradise Lost*, Book IX, ll. 906–909 and 997–999.
6. *Poems* (London, 1964), pp. 45–46.
7. *God in the Dock*, pp. 80–88.

Chapter 4

1. 1 Timothy 4:1.
2. *Transposition and Other Addresses*, pp. 55–64.
3. *Transposition and Other Addresses*, pp. 34–44.
4. "Christian Apologetics," *God in the Dock*, pp. 89–103.
5. Quoted in Green and Hooper, p. 178.
6. P. 124.
7. *The Abolition of Man* (London, 1946), p. 21.
8. P. 50.
9. *God in the Dock*, pp. 287–300.
10. P. 39.
11. "Membership," p. 42.

Chapter 5

1. *Transposition and Other Addresses*, p. 56.
2. *Letters of C. S. L.*, p. 188.
3. The "Preface" to the 1961 edition of *The Screwtape Letters*.
4. P. 55.
5. *The Four Loves* (London, 1960), p. 15.

Chapter 6

1. *Selected Literary Essays* (Cambridge, 1969), p. 105.
2. *Of Other Worlds*, p. 15.
3. *Of Other Worlds*, p. 36.

4. *Letters of C. S. L.*, p. 279.
5. *Letters of C. S. L.*, p. 273.
6. *Of Other Worlds*, p. 93.
7. *Of Other Worlds*, pp. 35–38.
8. P. 48.
9. John 21:21–22.

Chapter 7

1. Pp. 133–134.
2. *Selected Literary Essays*, p. 5.
3. Philippians 3:13–14.
4. *Poems*, pp. 43–44.
5. *The World's Last Night and Other Essays* (New York, 1973), pp. 91–92.
6. 1 Corinthians 11:30.
7. *Letters to an American Lady*, p. 21.
8. *Letters of C. S. L.*, p. 169.
9. *The World's Last Night*, p. 29.

Chapter 8

1. Proverbs 23:2.
2. *Letters of C. S. L.*, p. 169.
3. "A Song for St. Cecilia's Day."
4. Book VII, 11. 456–457 and 464–466.
5. *The World's Last Night*, pp. 93–113.
6. P. 61.
7. Romans 2:15.
8. *Letters of C. S. L.*, p. 247.
9. P. 170.

Chapter 9

1. *Till We Have Faces* (London, 1956), p. 1. As this important introductory note is not included in the American editions and as it is referred to several times in this chapter, I include it here in its entirety:

This re-interpretation of an old story has lived in the author's mind, thickening and hardening with the years, ever since he was an undergraduate. That way, he could be said to have worked at it most of his life. Recently, what seemed to be the right form presented itself and themes suddenly interlocked: the straight tale of barbarism, the mind of an ugly woman, dark idolatry and pale enlightenment at war with each other and with vision, and the havoc which a vocation, or even a faith, works on human life.

2. See first note of this chapter.
3. *God in the Dock*, p. 132.
4. *God in the Dock*, p. 102.
5. *Letters of C. S. L.*, p. 181.
6. P. 149.
7. John 14:9.
8. Genesis 28:17.
9. Exodus 20:19.
10. P. 10.
11. *Letters of C. S. L.*, p. 274.
12. John 18:14.
13. Isaiah 53.
14. *Letters of C. S. L.*, p. 289.
15. P. 68.
16. Ecclesiastes, chapters 1 and 2.
17. Romans 7:24–25.
18. *Light on C. S. Lewis,* edited by Jocelyn Gibb (London, 1965), p. 63.
19. *Letters of C. S. L.*, p. 257.
20. Charles Williams and C. S. Lewis, *Arthurian Torso* (London, 1948), p. 123.
21. *Letters of C. S. L.*, p. 271.
22. *Letters of C. S. L.*, p. 269.
23. P. 158.

INDEX